Introducing
Disability Studies

Introducing Disability Studies

Ronald J. Berger

LYNNE
RIENNER
PUBLISHERS

BOULDER
LONDON

BH

Published in the United States of America in 2013 by
Lynne Rienner Publishers, Inc.
1800 30th Street, Boulder, Colorado 80301
www.rienner.com

and in the United Kingdom by
Lynne Rienner Publishers, Inc.
3 Henrietta Street, Covent Garden, London WC2E 8LU

Library of Congress Cataloging-in-Publication Data
Berger, Ronald J.
Introducing disability studies / Ronald J. Berger.
          p. cm.
    Includes bibliographical references and index.
    ISBN 978-1-58826-866-2 (hc : alk. paper)
    ISBN 978-1-58826-891-4 (pb : alk. paper)
    1. Disability studies. 2. Disabilities—Social aspects. 3. Sociology
of disability. 4. People with disabilities. I. Title.
    HV1568.2.B47 2013
    305.9'08—dc23

                                                              2012031434

British Cataloguing in Publication Data
A Cataloguing in Publication record for this book
is available from the British Library.

Printed and bound in the United States of America

        The paper used in this publication meets the requirements
  ∞   of the American National Standard for Permanence of
        Paper for Printed Library Materials Z39.48-1992.

        5 4 3 2 1

5/12/14

For Sarah

Contents

Preface

DISABILITY STUDIES IS A GROWING AND VIBRANT INTERDISCI-plinary field of teaching and scholarship that includes representation from the social sciences, the humanities, and the medical, rehabilitative, and educational professions. Perhaps surprisingly, there is currently a dearth of introductory texts available to use in college courses, and there is a virtual absence of such materials written from an explicitly sociological perspective. This book represents a comprehensive synthesis of what one sociologist thinks is most important to know about disability as a social phenomenon, with a focus on the United States. My aim is to offer students, both undergraduate and graduate, an accessible overview of the field, fleshed out with accounts from the lives of people with disabilities derived from autobiographical, biographical, and ethnographic sources. Through an original distillation of the field, I also aim to make a professional contribution to the advancement of a distinctively sociological approach to the subject matter at hand.

It is arguably true that most of us who have become involved in disability studies either have a disability ourselves or have a family member or close friend who does, and this is the case for me, too. This truism can make an engagement with the subject a rather personal enterprise, replete with passion and emotion, differing opinions, and contentious points of view. One area in which this has become manifest is over disputes about the most appropriate way to talk about "people with disabilities" or "disabled people." This is a matter addressed in Chapter 1, but it is worth noting here as well.

Those who prefer "people with disabilities" believe that such "people first" language allows one to emphasize the person rather than the disability. For the most part, it's fair to say, this is the approach that has gained credence in the United States. At the same time, it is also common, particularly in Great Britain, to use the term "disabled people" to highlight disability as an affirmative identity, not one to be ashamed of, that identifies the common cause of a particular political constituency. In this book, I have chosen not to privilege one designation over the other, understanding that context is everything, and in the context of this book, it does not seem necessary to assert an ideological preference. Above all, because these matters are in dispute, I hope to avoid propagating yet another "politically correct" surveillance or policing system regarding authentic and inauthentic ways of thinking about disability and advocating for disability issues. Whether I have succeeded in this effort is up to readers to judge. But let us at least stipulate from the outset that although we may have disagreements, we are in this fight together!

* * *

I wish to express my gratitude to Andrew Berzanskis, sociology editor at Lynne Rienner Publishers, for his skillful guidance and suggestions in the development of the manuscript; to both Andrew and Lynne Rienner for their support of this project; to the anonymous reviewers for their constructive critiques and suggestions; and to Lesli Brooks Athanasoulis, Sonia Smith, and the rest of the staff at Lynne Rienner Publishers for their fine work bringing the manuscript to publication. I also thank my wife, Ruthy, for her help with proofreading the manuscript and for her enduring love, friendship, and support. Most of all, I dedicate this book to my daughter, Sarah, whose courage and determination know no bounds.

Introducing
Disability Studies

1

Disability in Society

DISABILITY IS A SOCIAL ENIGMA. THROUGHOUT HISTORY people have felt compelled both to stare at the disabled people in their midst and then to turn their heads in discomfort. Franklin Delano Roosevelt is considered by many to be one of the greatest presidents in the history of the United States, but he had to hide his polio-induced paralysis and use of a wheelchair lest the public think him too weak to lead the free world (Fleischer and Zames 2001; Holland 2006). The Hebrew Bible teaches that "thou shalt not curse the deaf nor put a stumbling block before the blind" (*Leviticus*) but also that "if you do not carefully follow His commands and decrees . . . the Lord will afflict you with madness, blindness and confusion of mind" (*Deuteronomy*) (cited in Braddock and Parish 2001:14).

The institution of the "freak show," which reached its heyday in the nineteenth century but lasted in the United States until the 1940s, featured people with disabilities as public spectacle. People with physical disabilities and bodily deformities, as well as tribal non-white "cannibals" and "savages," were displayed for public amusement and entertainment along with sword swallowers, snake charmers, bearded women, and the full-bodied tattooed (Bogdan 1988; see Chapter 3).

The rise of a medical approach to disability, what disability studies calls the "medical model" (see Chapter 2), helped change this state of affairs. People with disabilities were now deemed worthy of medical diagnosis and treatment and viewed more benevolently

1

(Williams 2001). But benevolence may breed pity, and the pitied are still stigmatized as less than full human beings. Thus the Muscular Dystrophy Association's annual telethon, which was hosted by Jerry Lewis for more than five decades, features pitiable "poster children" who help raise money for a preventative cure but does little to improve the lives of those who are already disabled (Haller 2010; Shapiro 1993).[1] Some may wonder why one would even want to live in such a state. In fact, the storyline of Clint Eastwood's 2004 Academy Award–winning *Million Dollar Baby* went so far as to suggest that euthanasia could be the most humane response to quadriplegia (Davis 2005; Haller 2010).

In *Million Dollar Baby*, Maggie Fitzgerald, played by Hilary Swank, is a feisty young woman who wants Frankie Dunn, played by Clint Eastwood, to train her to become a professional boxer. Frankie reluctantly agrees to do so, and as Maggie becomes virtually unbeatable in the ring, he becomes her mentor and friend. When Maggie breaks her neck in a boxing accident (the result of an unscrupulous opponent) and is severely disabled, she does not want to live with quadriplegia and asks Frankie to administer a lethal dose of adrenaline while she is still recovering in the hospital.

Disability scholars and activists were dismayed that so many viewers and reviewers of the film seemed to sympathize with the decision to kill the disabled character, as if her life no longer had meaning.[2] Maggie did not even have the opportunity to receive counseling or physical therapy to adapt to her new condition and consider her options for *living* in the world. "Disability Is Not a Death Sentence" and "Not Dead Yet" read protest signs in Chicago, Illinois, and Berkeley, California (Davis 2005; Haller 2010).

Some nondisabled film columnists, such as liberal writers Maureen Dowd and Frank Rich, were equally dismayed at the protesters' response: What's all the fuss? Isn't this just one artist's view of the situation? Doesn't Eastwood, as a filmmaker, have the right to make any film he wants? People wondered whether the negative reaction to the film might have been fueled by Eastwood's opposition to the **Americans with Disabilities Act*** (ADA), passed in 1990, which

---

*Key terms and laws are indicated in **boldface** the first time they appear in the book.

granted civil rights to people with disabilities in the United States. Appearing before the House Subcommittee on the Constitution in 2000, which was considering a measure to amend the ADA, Eastwood's testimony was received in the context of a lawsuit that had been filed against him by a disabled patron who alleged that his Mission Reach Inn resort in Carmel, California, was inaccessible to disabled guests and was therefore not ADA compliant (Cleigh 2005; Davis 2005; Switzer 2003).[3]

Lennard Davis (2005), among others, wants people to understand that disabled people's opposition to the film was not about Eastwood's anti-ADA politics, or about the storyline of *Million Dollar Baby* alone, but about the entire social and cultural apparatus that invalidates the experience of people with disabilities. According to Davis, the issue is not simply

> that Eastwood is speaking his mind. It's that he's speaking the mind of a country that is largely ignorant of the issues and politics around disability. . . . The history of oppression of disabled people is unknown to most people, and so they see disability as an individual tragedy, worthy of being turned into a movie, and not as political oppression and the struggle to fight that oppression. . . . It's a lot easier to make a movie in which we weep for the personal defeat of a person who loses a leg or two, or cry with joy for the triumph of an individual with disabilities, than it is to change the whole way we as a society envision, think about, and deal with people who are disabled. (p. 2)

And this is why **disability studies**—an interdisciplinary field of inquiry that includes representation from the social sciences, the humanities, and the medical, rehabilitation, and education professions—is vital to an understanding of humankind.[4] It is a way for people with disabilities to stare back at those who have stared at them (Fries 1997), to turn society's gaze back on itself and point out the things that nondisabled people don't seem to notice because, as Davis observes, they "see themselves as living in a mirage of being normal" (2005:3). As a contribution to the advancement of disability studies, this book represents a distillation of the literature, imbued with a sociological sensibility, which aims to illuminate disability as a social phenomenon and help us all to see "how interconnected human beings really are and how very much it diminishes us to assume that any life" is without value (Cleigh 2005:1).

While understanding that disability is a global issue, this book will focus on the United States. Chapter 1 begins our inquiry with a consideration of how disability is spoken about, defined, and understood sociologically; and it introduces the disability rights movement, the movement that is largely responsible for the very existence and disciplinary thrust of disability studies as a particular academic endeavor. Chapter 2 then delineates the diversity of theoretical approaches to the field, beginning with a critique of the medical model and the alternative perspectives, including the social model, that constitute the conceptual core of disability studies. This chapter also examines the question of disability culture and identity, the political economy of disability, the contributions of feminist and queer theory, and disability and symbolic interaction. Next, Chapter 3 offers historical background, tracing the evolving treatment of people with disabilities from preliterate, ancient, and medieval societies through the nineteenth-century and twentieth-century United States.

Chapters 4 and 5 examine disability across the life course, with Chapter 4 focusing on the family and childhood and Chapter 5 on adolescence and adulthood. Chapter 4 considers parental first encounters with childhood disability, the child's perspective on disability, the impact of childhood disability on family life, and the challenges of assessing and receiving special education services for children with disabilities. Chapter 5 looks at relationships with peers, the education system, the world of work, sexual and emotional intimacy, and the receipt of health care and personal assistance.

Chapter 6 takes a phenomenological approach to the subject matter, examining the disability experience from the vantage point of those who live with a physiological-based impairment. Here we consider the ways in which people perceive the world without sight and sound, use sign language, navigate the physical environment with mobility impairments, experience rehabilitation after a spinal cord injury, and participate in disability sports and athletics. Chapter 7 draws on selective examples from classic literature and Hollywood films to examine ways in which disability has been portrayed in popular culture. Finally, Chapter 8 concludes the book by considering a range of issues that inform prospects for the future of disability, including the role of computer technology, the problems of selective abortion and physician-assisted suicide, the place of the medical model in disability studies, and the question of disability and human rights.

Speaking About Disability

Before embarking on such a complex subject as disability, we first need to consider the language we use to talk about it. To begin with, disability studies asks us to become more aware of the words and phrases we may use, sometimes intentionally and sometimes unintentionally, that demean people with disabilities (such as "gimp," "spastic," or "retard"), including metaphors that conflate physical impairment with mental impairment (such as "lame" or "the blind leading the blind") or indifference (such as "turning a blind eye" or "turning a deaf ear"). Or take a word such as "invalid," which is used both to refer to someone with a physical disability and to something that is illegitimate. Nowadays, even the term "handicap" has fallen into disrepute in disability studies. In contrast, disability studies often uses "people first" language, referring to "people with disabilities" to emphasize the person rather than the disability. However, it is also common, particularly in Great Britain, to use the term "disabled people" to highlight disability as an affirmative identity, not one to be ashamed of, that identifies the common cause of a particular political constituency (Gordon and Rosenblum 2001; Kleege 1999; Linton 1998).

To be sure, nondisabled people sometimes find these language issues tiresome and confusing, especially when disabled people appropriate such terms as "gimp" or "crip" in an affirmative way, similar to the way in which gay, lesbian, and transgendered people appropriate the term "queer" as an affirmative identity.[5] Moreover, we now hear people using terms such as "differently abled," "physically challenged," "developmentally challenged," or "children with special needs." Simi Linton, for one, does not find these euphemisms or "nice" terms useful, characterizing them as "well-meaning attempts to inflate the value of people with disabilities [that] convey the boosterism and do-gooder mentality endemic to the paternalistic agencies that control many disabled people's lives" (1998:14). She notes as well that an entire profession called "special education" has been built around the appropriation of a term, "special," which may have been "a deliberate attempt to confer legitimacy on the educational practice and to prop up a discarded group" but nonetheless obscures the reality that society considers "neither the children nor the education" truly desirable (1998:15; see also Connor and Ferri 2007; Wendell 1996).

More generally, the point to be made here is that disability studies is an attempt to reassign meaning(s) to our use of the term "disability" and the ways we speak about it, and in doing so reveal "the complex web of social ideals, institutional structures, and government policies" that impact the lives of people with disabilities (Linton 1998:10). One of our first challenges in this effort is to develop a more systematic working definition, or definitions, of disability. It is to this matter that we now turn.

Defining Disability and the Subject Matter of Disability Studies

To begin with, we need to ask, as does Susan Wendell, "Who defines disability and for what purposes?" (1996:23). Insurance companies or government agencies, for example, may have particular administrative criteria they use to define who is eligible for payments or benefits, and it may be in the interest of these providers "to define disability narrowly" in order to save money (1996:24).[6] Similarly, laws that entitle people with disabilities to services, such as children in schools who need special accommodations, may utilize different criteria. Indeed, anyone who tries to negotiate the administrative-legal system will often find themselves entangled in a maze of competing and contradictory definitions of what it means to be disabled, or disabled "enough," to qualify, whereby they fit "some bureaucracies' definitions of disability and not others" (1996:24; see also Altman 2001; Grönvik 2009).

The field of disability studies, however, is not governed by such administrative-legal criteria; and in this field a discussion of definitional issues typically begins with a distinction between impairment and disability, whereby **impairment** refers to a biological or physiological condition that entails the loss of physical, sensory, or cognitive function, and **disability** refers to an inability to perform a personal or socially necessary task because of that impairment or the societal reaction to it. Although it has been common in the past to also use the term **handicap** to refer to the social disadvantage that accrues to an individual due to an impairment or disability, handicap as a concept is rarely used in scholarly or activist circles these days, largely because it has negative connotations when used to refer to persons with disabilities as inferior or deficient in some way (Miller and Sammons 1999; Wendell 1996; Whyte and Ingstad 1995).[7]

For our purposes, therefore, the distinction between impairment and disability is what is most germane. Thus, for instance, people who use a wheelchair for mobility due to a physical impairment may only be socially disabled if the buildings to which they require access are architecturally inaccessible. Otherwise, there may be nothing about the impairment that would prevent them from participating fully in the educational, occupational, and other institutional activities of society. Or take the case of visual impairment. Nowadays people who wear eyeglasses or contacts don't even think of themselves as having an impairment, because these corrective devices have become commonplace. But if it were not for these technological aids, which are now taken for granted, their visual impairments might also be disabilities.

Moreover, people with disabilities often experience prejudice and discrimination comparable to what is experienced by people of color and other minority groups, and they are therefore socially marginalized and disadvantaged in similar ways (Gordon and Rosenblum 2001; Hahn 1988; Siebers 2008). It remains sadly true that people whose bodies are different from "a society's conception of a 'normal' or acceptable body," even when it causes "little or no functional or physical difficulty for the person who has them, constitute major social disabilities" (Wendell 1996:44). Take the case of facial scarring or disfigurement, "which is a disability of appearance only, a disability constructed totally by stigma and cultural meanings" (1996:44). Lucy Grealy, for example, whose face was disfigured due to surgery for facial bone cancer, recalls with great pain the cruel stares and laughing at her appearance: "I *was* my face, I *was* ugliness," she writes (1997:17). In earlier times, it was even illegal to appear in public if one's physical appearance offended others' sensibilities, as in the case of the so-called **ugly laws**, ordinances that were prevalent in various cities across the United States. The oft-cited Chicago ordinance passed in 1881 (and not repealed until 1973) is a good illustration. It read: "Any person who is diseased, maimed, mutilated, or in any way deformed, so as to be an unsightly or disgusting object, or an improper person to be allowed in or on the streets, highways, thoroughfares, or public places in this city, shall not therein or thereon expose himself to public view, under the

penalty of a fine of $1 [about $20 today] for each offense" (cited in
Schweik 2009:1–2).

More generally, nondisabled people are often uncomfortable,
even fearful, around people with disabilities, as if the disabling condition might be contagious. Robert Murphy thinks that all too many
nondisabled people view people with disabilities as a "fearsome pos-
sibility" (1987:117). They displace their fears that the "impairment
could happen to them" onto the other person. In this way, "the disabled person becomes the Other—a living symbol of failure, frailty,
and [for men] emasculation; a counterpoint to normality; a figure
whose very humanity is questioned" (1987:117). Similarly, in his
book *Stigma: Notes on the Management of Spoiled Identity* (1963),
Erving Goffman argued that disparaging reactions from others serve
to invalidate the disabled person as less than "normal" if not less than
"human" beings. Goffman defined **stigma** as a characteristic of a
person who is "reduced in our minds from a whole and usual person
to a tainted, discounted one" (1963:3). Published the same year as
Howard Becker's *Outsiders: Studies in the Sociology of Deviance*
(1963), Goffman essentially framed the question of disability within
the **labeling theory** school of deviance, which posited that
"**deviance** is not a quality of the act a person commits, but rather a
consequence" of others' reactions (Becker 1963:9). Goffman prof-
fered a general theory of stigma, attributing common devalued statuses to deviants of all types: people with disabilities, gays and lesbians, ex-convicts, mental patients, drug addicts, and alcoholics.[8]

Nancy Miller and Catherine Sammons (1999) observe that it is
natural for people to notice others who look different. Indeed, they
argue, the human brain is hardwired to scan the environment and
notice differences from the routine or "expected average" (p. 7).

> Everybody reacts to differences. In the whole universe of differ-
> ences, some attract us, some surprise or frighten us, and some
> aren't important to us at all. Our reactions to differences are some-
> times complex and confusing. We often want to be open-minded
> and feel comfortable about other people's differences but find that
> some unfamiliar differences make us feel tense and judgmental
> instead. We are caught off guard when someone with an unex-
> pected difference enters the room, and we may feel awkward as we
> try to appear unsurprised. When we see an unsettling difference, it
> can cause anxiety, uncertainty, and even a wish to avoid the other
> person. (pp. 1–2)

Miller and Sammons believe we can all learn to override these reactions through habituation to new experiences and exposure to alternative cultural norms, and in this way expand our "personal comfort zones" about disability and other social differences. Similarly, Spencer Cahill and Robin Eggleston (1995) note that awkward encounters between able-bodied and disabled-bodied persons often stem not from malicious intent but from the uncertainty of what is expected. Should an able-bodied person, for example, offer assistance to someone who uses a wheelchair by opening a door for them or asking them if they need help retrieving something from a shelf in a grocery store? In their study of wheelchair users' public experiences, Cahill and Eggleston found that able-bodied people sometimes feared being rebuked for thinking that the wheelchair user might need help, finding "that they have judged [them] less competent than [they] want to be considered or consider themselves" (1995:693). Cahill and Eggleston also learned about occasions in which a wheelchair user was treated as a "non-person," for instance, when they were with a group at a restaurant and the waiter or waitress asked others what the wheelchair user was ordering, as if they were incapable of speaking for themselves. At the same time, the researchers also learned of many acts of public kindness, where the nondisabled offered wheelchair users much appreciated assistance, which ran counter to the view that people with disabilities are uniformly stigmatized and treated badly (see also Bogdan and Taylor 1989; Makas 1988).

All this is to say that it is important to understand "disability" as a social phenomenon, an experience that cannot be reduced to the nature of the physiological impairment. Rather, it is a product of societal attitudes and the social organization of society. This view is sometimes referred to as a **constructionist**, or **social constructionist**, approach to disability, which understands disability as constructed by or residing in the social environment, in contrast to an **essentialist** view, which understands disability as a condition that resides or is inherent in an individual's particular impairment (Baker 2011; Omansky 2011; Wendell 1996).

To complicate matters further, disability scholars note that impairment itself is a product of social definition, as in the case of medical diagnosis and classification systems that are themselves subject to dispute and change over time (Brown 1995). Take the case of

autism, for example, which is now understood as consisting of a spectrum of conditions that includes people who are considered very "low functioning" and very "high functioning." Autism was discovered separately but nearly simultaneously by Leo Kanner, a US child psychiatrist, and Hans Asperger, an Austrian pediatrician, in 1943 and 1944, respectively. Both Kanner and Asperger chose the term "autism" from the Greek word *autos* (self) to refer to the children's "powerful desire for aloneness" and "anxiously excessive desire for the maintenance of sameness" (Kanner 1943:242, 249). People with autism have difficulty with face-to-face interaction, lacking the ability to empathize with others and appearing emotionally detached. They become attached to routines and can become anxious when these routines are disrupted. They often become focused on specialized, complex topics, which can be associated with a number of strengths, as people with autism can be exceptionally skilled at systematizing information, mathematics, computer programming, music, and art (Cowley 2003; Grandin 2006; Kalb 2005; O'Neil 2008).[9]

Whereas Kanner went on to become a leading figure in child psychiatry, Asperger's clinic was destroyed during the war, and he was virtually ignored outside of Europe until his work was discovered by British psychologist Lorna Wing and translated into English in 1991. It was Wing who popularized Asperger's observation that the condition, now called **Asperger's syndrome** or **Autism Spectrum Disorder**, consisted of a range of conditions that are markedly different from one another (Grandin 2006; O'Neil 2008; Silberman 2001; Singer 1999).

Up until 1980, the term "autism" did not appear as a distinct condition in the *Diagnostic and Statistical Manual* (*DSM*), the official diagnostic guidelines of the American Psychiatric Association. Previously the only mention of it had been as a symptom of childhood schizophrenia, and Asperger's syndrome was not included until 1994 (Straus 2010). Thus, Donna Williams (1992), born in 1963, did not understand her condition as "autism" until she was twenty-five years old. She knew she was not like other children, but did not know why. As a child, she was even thought to be deaf because she avoided eye contact and was emotionally unresponsive to others. Even today, there is some controversy about whether autism, Asperger's syndrome, and a few other disorders should each be characterized as distinct diagnostic conditions, or rather, as constituting a unitary set of conditions that exist along a continuum. Thus, in the 2013 revision of the *DSM*, Asperger's syndrome was placed under the rubric of autism, essentially removing the distinction between them (Baker 2011; Grandin 2006).

Another definitional issue that complicates our subject matter is the distinction between **physical, sensory,** and **cognitive impairments.** In some instances one may find the term "physical impairment" being used to refer to both mobility impairments and sensory impairments such as vision and hearing loss, and in other instances only for mobility and not sensory impairments. As for "cognitive impairment," this term is generally used to refer to a wide range of conditions such as autism, traumatic brain injury, and mental illness. Within this broad category, a distinction is also made between **intellectual disabilities,** the term that is now used to refer to mental retardation and that involves limitations "rooted in sub-average intellectual and adaptive functioning occurring early in life," and **learning disabilities,** a term that refers to limitations involving "the brain's ability to receive, process, analyze, or store information" (Carey 2009:190; see Box 4.3).[10]

Still another issue that complicates our subject matter is the distinction between illness and disability, a distinction some disability scholars and activists insist on making, in part because they want people to know that people with disabilities are often perfectly healthy, requiring no particular medical care.[11] Wendell (1996) thinks that the adamancy by which some have opposed including people with illnesses among the constituency of disabled people may stem from the desire to avoid the additional stigma that is associated with illnesses such as AIDS and cancer. Nevertheless, it remains true that many people with disabilities are also ill, and chronic or life-threatening illnesses, as well as the normal process of aging, can have disabling consequences for individuals (Bury 2000; Zola 1991).[12] Indeed, most anyone who lives long enough can expect to have an experience with disability before they die. Joseph Shapiro adds that fewer than 15 percent of those who are disabled are actually born with their impairment, and therefore anyone at any time, "as a result of a sudden automobile accident, a fall down a flight of stairs," or the acquisition of a serious illness, can join the ranks of people with disabilities (1993:7). One national poll taken in 2004 found that the median age for the onset of disability in the United States was 35.7 years, with 47 percent acquiring their disability after the age of forty (National Organization on Disability/Harris Poll 2004).

FURTHER EXPLORATION

Box 1.1 Counting Disability

Studies that try to count the number of people who have a disability are complicated by the question of how disability is defined, but with this caveat in mind, we can still get an idea of what this number may be. The US Census Bureau, for example, reported that in 2005 about 19 percent of the US population indicated that they had at least some level of disability, with about 12 percent having a severe disability. The census found that nearly 4 percent of people six years of age and older needed assistance with everyday activities such as showering or bathing and getting around inside their homes. While the majority of disabilities were physical in nature, about a third of all those reporting a disability were classified as having difficulty with cognitive, mental, or emotional functioning. Not surprisingly, older Americans reported a higher level of disability than younger Americans, with adults over sixty-four years of age comprising about a third of all those reporting disabilities (Moore 2009).

In addition to census data, a study by the Centers for Disease Control and Prevention (CDCP) reported that in 2005 about 22 percent of US adults had a disability, with about 10 percent indicating they had difficulty walking three city blocks or climbing a flight of stairs. The top ten causes of disability were listed as the following (in order of most common to least common): arthritis or rheumatism, back or spine problem, heart trouble, mental or emotional problem, lung or respiratory problem, diabetes, deafness or hearing problem, stiffness or deformity of limbs/extremities, blindness or vision problem, and stroke (CDCP 2011).

The US Department of Health and Human Services (USDHHS) also collected survey data on adults with disabilities in the United States between 2001 and 2005, operationalizing disability as having difficulty with *basic actions* and *complex activity*. Basic action difficulty was defined in terms of limitations in movement or sensory, emotional, or mental functioning, while complex activity difficulty was defined in terms of limitations in self-care tasks, ability to work, or ability to fully participate in social activities. About 30 percent of Americans reported some kind of basic action difficulty, with the most common related to movement, such as

continues

Box 1.1 continued

walking, bending, reaching overhead, or using their fingers to grasp something. About 13 percent reported noticeable vision or hearing difficulties, and 3 percent reported emotional or cognitive difficulties. Work limitation was the most commonly reported complex activity limitation (12 percent), followed by social limitation (7 percent) and self-care limitation (4 percent). Adults over sixty-five years of age made up about 33 percent of those with basic limitations and 36 percent of those with complex activity limitations (USDHHS 2008).

Internationally, the World Health Organization (2011) reported that in 2010 there were more than one billion disabled people around the globe, about 17 percent of the world's total population. Other international data indicate that disabled people are more likely than nondisabled people to live in poverty, as is true in the United States, although poverty in less developed, nonindustrialized countries is more severe. About 80 percent of the world's disabled population lives in such countries, where just 20 percent of the world's health-care dollars are spent. In many places around the globe, war and armed conflict are major causes of disability. Today, there are millions of disabled refugees and displaced persons in places such as the Middle East, the Balkans, Central Africa, and Southeast Asia; and at least 2,000 people are killed or injured every month by landmines that are buried in more than seventy countries (Albrecht, Seelman, and Bury 2001; Priestley 2001).

Be that as it may, contemporary approaches to disability try to avoid the pejorative connotations of the term and reframe it as a matter of **social difference**. As Miller and Sammons argue:

Everybody's different. Some of us have differences that no one notices, while others are different in very apparent ways. We all look different from others, sometimes by chance, sometimes by choice. Some people move on foot, while others use wheelchairs or other ways of getting around. We communicate in a variety of languages and dialects and also by using hand signs. Our behavior patterns have incredible variety, even within our own families. We all have unique physical strengths and limitations as well as different learning abilities, creative talents, and social skills. (1999:1)

In this way, Christina Papadimitriou (2008b), among others, rejects a conception of disability as undesirable deviance, as a "perversion of the human condition" or unrelenting tragedy that propels people into the depths of despair (Camilleri 1999:849). Rather, disability should be understood as a form of diversity that can be appreciated as a different way of being embodied in the world. Papadimitriou does not view disability and normality as polar opposites but as falling "along a continuum of . . . humanly possible ways" of being (2008b:219), or in Richard Scotch and Kay Schriner's (1997) terms, the natural variation that occurs among human beings. While impairments may never be wished for and are often the source of great suffering (for physical and social reasons), people with disabilities differ quite dramatically in the nature of their conditions, which are not as "wholly disastrous" as people often imagine (Fine and Asch 1988:11). They commonly learn to appreciate and enhance their remaining abilities and to strive for goals and qualities of human worth that are within their grasp (Gill 2001; Potok 2002; Wright 1960). According to Tobin Siebers, "People with disabilities want to be able to . . . live with their disability, to come to know their body, to accept what it can do, and to keep doing what they can for as long as they can. They do not want to feel dominated by people on whom they depend for help, and they want to be able to imagine themselves in a world without feeling ashamed" (2008:69). In almost every case, Siebers adds, people with disabilities have a better chance of enjoying a fulfilling life if they accept their disability as a positive aspect of their identity that provides them with a unique and at times contentious way of being in and viewing the world.

At its core as a scholarly discipline, disability studies rejects approaches to disability that seek to eradicate it. This does not necessarily mean that it opposes rehabilitative interventions that might enhance a person's ability to live the life she or he most wants to live. What it does aim to do is critique "the widespread belief that having an able body and mind determines whether one is a quality human being" (Siebers 2008:4). In doing so, it identifies a source of oppression, **ableism**, which is comparable to racism, sexism, and heterosexism in constituting a system that subjects people to "political, economic, cultural, or social degradation" (Nowell 2006:1179). Ableism assumes that some people (and bodies) are "normal" and superior while other people (and bodies) are "abnormal" and inferior, and it entails institutional discrimination on the basis of this distinction (Linton 1998; Papadimitriou 2001).[13] Siebers calls this the "ideology of ability," which in its simplest form constitutes a preference for able-bodiedness, but in its most radical form "defines the baseline by which humanness is determined, setting the measure of body and mind that gives or denies human status to individual persons" (2008:8). As a dominant or hegemonic ideology, ableism is so taken for granted that it remains unconscious and invisible to most people, even though it constitutes an overarching regime that structures the lives of people with disabilities. Disability studies aims to unmask the ideology of ableism, to deconstruct it, to bring it out in the open for all to see.

The Disability Rights Movement

One cannot begin to approach disability studies without crediting its very existence and conceptual thrust to the contemporary **disability rights movement**.[14] The social movement for disability rights is an international phenomenon, but the movements in the United States and Great Britain are most notable for their contribution to disability studies (Bickenbach 2001; Fleischer and Zames 2001; Shakespeare and Watson 2001). In the United States this movement emerged in the context of other "oppositional movements" of the 1960s, such as the civil rights movement, women's movement, consumer movement, and gay and lesbian movement, which advocated on behalf of previously marginalized and underrepresented political constituencies (Mansbridge and Morris 2001).

We will explore this movement in more detail in Chapter 3, but it is worth noting here that unlike some of the other movements of this era, the disability rights movement does not have a widely known figure with name recognition such as a Martin Luther King Jr., Rosa Parks, Betty Friedan, Gloria Steinem, or Ralph Nader. But Ed Roberts is arguably someone deserving of comparable recognition. Roberts, who was severely disabled from polio—he was a quadriplegic who had some minimal use of his hands—had gained admission to the University of California, Berkeley (UCB), in 1962, the same year that James Meredith became the first African American to attend the University of Mississippi. As a youth, Roberts had had to fight to get his high school "diploma because he had not completed the driver's education and gym requirements. . . . [Then] California's Department of Rehabilitation [CDR] refused to pay for his college education, as it did for other, less disabled students, because

Roberts's [CDR] counselor . . . believed that spending taxpayer money on [him] would be wasted since it was 'infeasible' he could ever work" (Shapiro 1993:44). Roberts took his case to the media, eventually forcing the CDR to relent (Braddock and Parish 2001; Fleischer and Zames 2001; Scotch 2001b).

Roberts's success ushered in opportunities for other students with disabilities at UCB. Influenced by the political radicalism of the day, Roberts and this cohort of activists lobbied for accessibility reforms both on campus and in the larger Berkeley community. They questioned the conventional definition of "independence," which defined it in terms of the tasks a disabled person could perform *without* assistance. Known as the **independent living movement**, activists wanted to define independent living in terms of the quality of life that people with disabilities could achieve *with or without* assistance. They argued that people with disabilities did not simply need custodial care but wanted "to be fully integrated [into] their communities" (Shapiro 1993:52). They also aimed to reverse the power relationship between themselves and the medical, educational, and social service professionals whose services they required. People with disabilities no longer wanted to be treated as clients who were *told* by professionals what to do. Instead, they wanted to be treated as self-advocates and consumers of services who could *decide* what was best for themselves. To achieve these ends, Roberts and his allies established the first **Center for Independent Living** in the United States, which eventually evolved into a nationwide network of consumer-controlled, community-based centers that provide independent living skills training, peer counseling, information and referral, and advocacy for people with disabilities (Fleischer and Zames 2001; Shapiro 1993).

As this type of political activism spread throughout the country, the US Congress eventually responded by passing a landmark piece of federal disability legislation, the **Rehabilitation Act of 1973**, which, among other things, mandated reasonable accommodations in public education and employment, required public institutions to initiate architectural accessibility reforms, and "made it illegal for any federal agency, public university, defense or other federal contractor, or any other institution or activity that received federal funding, to discriminate against anyone solely" for reason of disability (Shapiro 1993:65). Most politicians who had voted for the act, however, had not seriously considered its broader implications and potential costs

FURTHER EXPLORATION

Box 1.2 Judy Heumann: Disability Rights Activist

In addition to Ed Roberts, one of the notable figures in the early disability rights movement is Judy Heumann. Heumann was born in Brooklyn, New York, in 1947, contracting polio when she was eighteen months old. Like Roberts, she became a quadriplegic. One physician advised her parents to put her in an institution, which they did not, and relatives told them that "their misfortune must have been the result of some sin on their part" (Shapiro 1993:56). For three years during elementary school, Heumann was required to receive home instruction because the principal said her presence in a wheelchair was a "fire hazard." But her parents were determined to give their daughter a sound education. They placed her in a school for disabled children, where Heumann soon "realized that the parents of her classmates had low expectations for their children, and that the teachers, when not prodded by pushy parents, respond accordingly" (Shapiro 1993:56). Nevertheless, Heumann graduated high school and was accepted to Long Island University, where she had to fight for "everything from the right to live in a dormitory to getting someone to lift her wheelchair up the steps to the classroom buildings. She organized other disabled students to fight for ramped buildings . . . [and] took part in protests against the Vietnam War" (p. 57).

In 1970, one year after graduating from college with a teaching degree, Heumann was denied a license to teach in New York City's public schools because she could not pass the medical exam. The testing physician questioned whether Heumann could get to the bathroom by herself or help children out of the building in an emergency. A media campaign resulted in her receiving her teaching license. A newspaper headline read, "You Can Be President, Not Teacher, with Polio," and quoted Heumann as saying, "We're not going to let a hypocritical society give us a token education and then bury us" (Shapiro 1993:57). Still, no one would hire her until the principal of the elementary school she had attended offered her a job.

Heumann formed her own disability rights activist group, Disabled in Action. In 1972, she traveled to Washington, DC, to demonstrate at the Lincoln Memorial after President Richard Nixon vetoed a spending bill to fund federal disability programs. In the closing days of the presidential election, she joined with a group of disabled Vietnam veterans to take over Nixon's New York reelection headquarters to demand an on-camera debate with the president himself. The following year, Roberts invited her to come to California to work for the Center for Independent Living that he had just opened (Fleischer and Zames 2001; Scotch 2001b; Shapiro 1993).

of implementation. Thus the Department of Health, Education, and Welfare (HEW) under presidents Gerald Ford and Jimmy Carter tried to stall the development and implementation of enforcement provisions (Braddock and Parish 2001; Fleischer and Zames 2001; Scotch 2001b).

When Joseph Califano, Carter's secretary of HEW, tried to push through regulations that would have allowed "some disabled children to be educated in special schools rather than [in] regular schools adapted for them," disability activists derided the measure as "separate but equal" (Shapiro 1993:68). And when Califano also came out for exceptions to rules requiring wheelchair ramps in schools and hospitals, the activists organized demonstrations around the country, particularly in the ten cities where HEW regional officers were located—Atlanta, Boston, Chicago, Dallas, Denver, Kansas City, New York, Philadelphia, San Francisco, and Seattle, in addition to Washington, DC.

Until this time, the disability rights movement in the United States had been local and disparate; it now became a national and cross-disability movement of diverse groups working together for social change. It was this movement that later culminated in the passage of the ADA, which further expanded the rights of disabled people in both the public and private sectors. Although the implementation of the ADA, like previous progressive legislation for disabled people, has been plagued by controversy over its interpretation and implementation, it marked a seminal point in the legal rights and expansion of opportunities for people with disabilities in the United States (Braddock and Parish 2001; Fleischer and Zames 2001; Scotch 2001b; Switzer 2003).

Joan Tollifson (1997), who is missing her right hand and half of her right arm, describes how exhilarating and empowering it was to be part of this movement. Tollifson writes that while growing up she "used to dream about being in a world where being disabled was no big deal, where no one considered it a tragedy, [where] no one thought you were inspiring or felt sorry for you, [where] no one stared at you" (1997:105). All too many times she experienced complete strangers coming up to her on the street to inquire about her physical appearance and children gasping in horror. People would tell her with tears in their eyes how amazingly well she did things, such as tying her shoes, or that they didn't think of her as disabled— she guesses because they thought that a "real cripple" would have been totally incompetent. Others would "try desperately to pretend that they [didn't] even notice." People would "swallow their curiosity and conceal their discomfort." Adults would tell children who asked her about her arm, "ssshhhhhhh!" (1997:105–106).

Growing up, Tollifson recalls, she intentionally avoided other disabled people, "dis-identifying" with them and refusing to see herself as part of that group. Still, she was in a great deal of emotional pain. While in therapy, she reluctantly joined a group of "marvelous, dynamic" disabled women who shared many of the same experiences she had. She no longer felt isolated and alone and began to realize that her private pain was a social phenomenon, "part of a collective pattern that was much larger than any one of us" (1997:105–106). Indeed, what Tollifson now realized is the essence of what C. Wright Mills (1959) famously called the **sociological imagination**, that personal or private troubles are actually public issues.

In the late 1970s, Tollifson got involved in the disability rights protest movement, participating in a month-long occupation of the San Francisco Federal Building, demanding that the Carter administration sign into law the regulations they had been opposing.

> We created a whole society in microcosm inside that building, with work committees, church services, study groups, wheelchair races, long strategy meetings. People laughed, argued, shared their lives; some even fell in love and later married. In this society, you never had to worry about being discriminated against because of your disability. No one was going to tell you that you couldn't do a particular task because you only had one hand or were in a wheelchair. At last, here was a society where being disabled was no big deal. . . . After a lifetime of isolating myself from other disabled people, it was an awakening to be surrounded by them. . . . Finally identifying myself as a disabled person was an enormous healing. (1997:107)

To be sure, the social category of "people with disabilities" is constituted by a diverse set of conditions and people who "may have little in common except the stigma society imposes on them" (Engel and Munger 2003:14). Moreover, Nick Watson (2002) found that most of the disabled people he interviewed did not consider "disability" a salient part of their identity. They did not dismiss their impairment as irrelevant—it was an undeniable fact of their lives—but neither did they internalize its significance. Although the disability rights movement has aimed to advance an affirmative view of dis-

FURTHER EXPLORATION

Box 1.3 Autism and the Neurodiversity Movement

The concept of neurodiversity, which first appeared in print in an article by Harvey Blume that was published in *The Atlantic* magazine in 1998, originated among self-aware members of autistic communities (Baker 2011; Singer 1999). Nowadays neurodiversity is used to refer to a variety of atypical cognitive styles due to neurological differences, including autism, intellectual disabilities, learning disabilities, attention deficit hyperactivity, epilepsy, posttraumatic stress disorder, bipolar disorder, Tourette's syndrome, and schizophrenia (Antonetta 2005; Baker 2011; Fenton and Krahn 2007). But the impetus for neurodiversity as a *social movement* arguably comes from the community of relatively high-functioning people on the autism/Asperger's spectrum. Within this community, people with conventional styles are referred to as "neurotypicals" or "normies," while people with atypical styles are viewed as part of the normal variation of human beings (Baker 2011; Singer 1999).

Dana Lee Baker notes that autism groups dedicated to neurodiversity evolved to help promote the view of neurological difference as a difference that "can be understood and experienced as much as a source of community and communal identity as can differences more routinely associated" with other forms of diversity such as those based on race, ethnicity, gender, and sexual orientation (2011:20; Fenton and Krahn 2007). Although functioning at the lower end of the autistic spectrum may entail deficits that can include intellectual disabilities and difficulty with speech, functioning at the high end is not viewed as a "disorder" or as a "fundamentally undesirable" element of the human condition and is, in fact, credited with contributing positively to human innovation (Baker 2011:20; Baron-Cohen 2000). Thus evidence from biographical accounts of notable figures in human history, innovators in their respective fields—such as Albert Einstein, Charles Darwin, Wolfgang Amadeus Mozart, Vincent van Gogh, Ludwig Wittgenstein, and Thomas Jefferson—strongly suggests that they meet the criteria now classified under the rubric of autism or Asperger's syndrome (Grandin 2006; O'Neil 2008). Judy Singer (1999) thinks that the development of computer technology and the Internet itself may very well have been, in large part, the product of neurodiversity, and those who at one time were denigrated in popu-

continues

Box 1.3 continued

lar culture as "nerds" or "geeks," such as Bill Gates himself, may have been (are) high-functioning cognitive atypicals. Temple Grandin (2006), who is known for her contributions to animal psychology and the development of humane methods of handling livestock, thinks that many atypical children are being wrongly tracked into special education curriculums in school rather than into programs for the gifted and talented (see Box 6.1). In doing so, both these children and our society are being done a disservice.

ability identity, the people in Watson's study preferred to "negate impairment as an identifier" altogether (2002:524). Siebers, on the other hand, thinks that the notion of disability identity will continue to be useful for advancing the collective interests of disabled people and helping all of us think about "fundamental democratic principles such as inclusiveness and participation" (2006:25). Carol Gill hopes for the day, not when her impairment will be deemed irrelevant, but when disability will provoke "a respectful curiosity about what I have learned from my difference that I could teach society. In such a world, no one would mind being called Disabled. Being unable to do something the way most people do it would not be seen as something bad that needs curing. It would be seen as just a difference" (1994:45). And John Hockenberry wonders, "Why aren't people with disabilities a source of reassurance to the general public that although life is unpredictable and circumstances may be unfavorable, versatility and adaptation are possible; they're built into the coding of human beings" (quoted in Fleischer and Zames 2001:205).

Summary

In this opening chapter of the book, we raised the question of why disability is vital to an understanding of humankind—as a life experience, as a scholarly endeavor, and as a subject for students taking courses in disability studies. We began by considering the language we use to talk about disability, both appropriately and inappropriately. We then raised the thorny issue of defining disability, noting the distinction between administrative-legal definitions and sociological approaches, the latter including a social constructionist view that locates the defining feature of disability as residing in the social environment and that reframes disability as a matter of social difference existing along a continuum of humanly possible ways of being embodied in the world. We also introduced the concept of ableism, the ideology and institutional practice that devalues people with disabilities as inferior and subjects them to discriminatory treatment. Finally, we considered the emergence of the disability rights movement in the United States, which is arguably responsible for the very existence and thrust of disability studies as a distinct academic endeavor. In doing so, we also discussed the independent living movement and the activism that revolved around the federal Rehabilitation Act of 1973, which culminated in the Americans with Disabilities Act of 1990, the landmark civil rights legislation for people with disabilities that we will examine more fully later in the book.

Notes

1. Muscular dystrophy is a group of genetic muscle disorders that weaken the musculoskeletal system and impede movement. The condition is progressive, worsening over time. See Box 8.2 for further discussion of Lewis and the telethon issue.

2. We will discuss the question of physician-assisted suicide in Chapter 8.

3. Eastwood's resort had just undergone a $6.5 million renovation that still left hotel washrooms inaccessible to wheelchair users. The proposed amendment would have required defendants in lawsuits to take corrective actions within 90 days. Eastwood lost the lawsuit and was required to pay the plaintiff's attorney's fees and make his resort accessible.

4. Sharon Snyder (2006) associates the origins of disability studies in the United States with sociologist Irving Zola and the formation of the Society for the Study of Chronic Illness and Disability, later the Society for Disability Studies, in the early 1980s (see also Zola 1982).

5. Robert McRuer (2006, 2010) advances a theoretical perspective he calls "crip theory," which applies insights from feminist and queer theory to disability studies (see Chapter 2).

6. The ADA defines disability as a physical or mental impairment that substantially limits one or more of an individual's major life activities.

7. Two international organizations, the UN and the World Health Organization, were influential in propagating the distinction between impairment, disability, and handicap (Altman 2001; Wendell 1996; Whyte and Ingstad 1995).

8. In this list, Goffman also included women and people of color—indeed, anyone who was not an "unblushing" American male, that is, "a

young, married, white, urban, northern, heterosexual Protestant father of college education, fully employed, of good complexion, weight, and height, and
a recent record of sports" (1963:128).

9. Autism is marked by rapid brain growth between the first 6 to 14
months of life. Researchers now think that this growth process may generate
more sensory neurons than the brain can integrate into a coherent network,
accounting for why people with autism feel anxious around too much stim-
uli and new situations. Autism appears to have a genetic component, but
environmental toxins have been implicated as well (Cowley 2003; Grandin
2006; Kalb 2005; King and Bearman 2011). For further discussion of
autism, see Box 2.1 and Box 4.2.

10. In her history of intellectual disabilities, Allison Carey (2009) traces
the evolution of such terms as "idiot," "moron," and "feeble-minded," and
by the twentieth century, their replacement with "mental retardation," which
at the time was considered less of a pejorative. By the 1970s, the term
"developmental disabilities" came to be seen as less pejorative than mental
retardation and used as an umbrella term for multiple types of disabilities.
Nowadays some school systems also identify a category of "emotional disabilities," which is used interchangeably with emotional disturbances or
behavioral disorders (Virginia Department of Education 2012).

11. Robert Murphy and colleagues (1988) characterize disability as a
condition of social liminality that resides "betwixt and between" the social
states of sickness and health (see also Cahill and Eggleston 1995). The illness versus disability question also involves mental illnesses and includes
conditions such as schizophrenia (Baker 2011).

12. Gary Albrecht (2010) characterizes the "sociology of disability" in
the United States as a subspecialty of medical sociology. He also notes that
US scholars have drawn less from the social constructionist tradition than
their British counterparts. For further discussion of the US and British tra-
ditions in disability studies, see Meekosha (2004), Omansky (2011), and
Shakespeare (2006).

13. Davis (1995) argues that the study of disability necessarily entails the
study of normalcy.

14. Snyder describes disability studies as the "theoretical arm" of the disability rights movement (2006:478).

2

Explaining Disability

IN THIS CHAPTER, WE INTRODUCE AND ILLUSTRATE THE GENeral theoretical perspectives and conceptual models that constitute the core of disability studies as an explanatory or interpretive discipline. **Social theory** can be defined as "a coherent system of logically consistent and interconnected ideas used to condense and organize knowledge" (Neuman 2011:9). In some respects, the perspective of disability studies, as we have discussed in Chapter 1, constitutes a theoretical perspective of sorts because of the ways in which it deconstructs and reconstructs common (mis)perceptions of disability. At the same time, the field can by no means lay claim to a unifying or coherent theoretical approach, as it is constituted by a polyphony if not cacophony of voices (Meekosha 2004; Thomas 2004; Williams 2001). This is to be expected, however, given the interdisciplinary nature of the field and the diversity of phenomena that "disability" comprises.

Disability studies also makes use of the term **model**, in addition to theory, to describe different conceptual approaches to its subject matter. Both models and theories are used to organize and represent information in a way that helps us understand a phenomenon. Mike Oliver (2004) suggests that a model is a framework for translating ideas into practice, while A. Llewellyn and K. Hogan (2000) note that the key element of theory is its link to empirical research, which may confirm or disconfirm the veracity of its propositions. Be that as it may, for our purposes the distinction between a model and theory is relatively inconsequential.[1]

We begin with a critique of the medical model and the alternative perspectives that have been advanced in disability studies: the social model, phenomenology and complex embodiment, and the cultural model. We then examine the question of disability culture and identity, the political economy of disability, and the contributions of feminist and queer theory. While these theories tend to focus on general features of groups, communities, and whole societies, an additional approach focuses on the interpersonal interactions that take place in the local settings of daily life, which is typically framed in terms of a social theory of symbolic interaction.

Beyond the Medical Model

Disability studies characterizes the **medical model** as an essentialist approach that "defines disability as a property of the individual body" rather than the social environment and that is concerned with matters related to the etiology, diagnosis, prevention, and treatment of physical, sensory, and cognitive impairments (Siebers 2008:25). In Michel Foucault's (1979) terms, the medical model is constituted by a set of disciplinary practices aimed at producing passive individuals or "docile bodies" who are expected to adjust to their impairments and comply with the prescribed regimen of rehabilitative treatment administered by medical professionals who occupy a privileged position of authority vis-à-vis patients or clients (French and Swain 2001; Shakespeare 2006; Turner 2001; Wendell 1996).

Additionally, the medical model posits that individuals adjusting to their impairments go through a common sequence of stages that correspond roughly to Elisabeth Kübler-Ross's (1967) well-known schema about stages of grief: denial, anger, bargaining, depression, and (hopefully) acceptance. As Carol Gill describes it:

> According to this framework, the individual's inner experience of disability can be wretched or tranquil, depending on his or her current level of adaptation and its associated emotional state. The individual's relationship to others is similarly mediated by his or her progress through the stages toward adjustment to disability. An individual who reaches emotional resolution and accepts the losses of disability is well positioned for interpersonal success. The person who denies or rails against the losses of disability is less likely to relate well to others. (2001:357–358)

Gill notes, however, that a large body of clinical evidence and empirical research has been unable to validate the expectation that people move through a common or orderly sequence of reactions to disability. This finding would not surprise John Hockenberry (1995), who was paralyzed in a car accident when he was nineteen years old. In his entertaining and enlightening autobiography, Hockenberry describes his experience with the stage of adjustment to disability. To the professionals around him, he writes, "life in a wheelchair . . . began to have meaning by adopting the code of denial, plus depression, plus anger, which equals acceptance. The dignity of human existence was restored according to this code, only after one denied what was happening, got angry, got depressed, and then saw the light" (1995:79). To Hockenberry, however, "trauma did not appear to need any additional meaning, it made sense on its own" (1995:79).

> From the beginning, disability taught that life could be reinvented. In fact, such an outlook was required. . . . Formulae for change and grief and trauma efface the possibility that we each might discover our own way through difficulty, and by doing so reclaim our lives from the oppressive forces that tell us who we are and what we should be. . . . Each person confronts trauma as though it has never before happened. It is this which allows the mind and body to fashion a solution unique and appropriate to the identity of the person. (1995:79, 86)

At the heart of the medical model, critics believe, is an ableist view that depicts people with disabilities as deficient and inherently inferior to nondisabled people, and thus it is they, not society, who are most in need of change. In contrast, the **social model** of disability posits that it is not an individual's impairment or adjustment but the socially imposed barriers—the inaccessible buildings, the limited modes of transportation and communication, the prejudicial attitudes—that construct disability as a subordinate social status and devalued life experience. This model was first articulated by disability activists in Great Britain in the early 1970s, and it substantially influenced the thinking of disability activists and scholars in the United States as well, who view the elimination of such barriers as a matter of legally protected civil rights (Oliver 1990; Shakespeare 2010; Wendell 1996).

Social model proponents were in large part responsible for the critique of the medical model described above. But the social model has been subject to criticism, too. As Bill Hughes and Kevin Paterson suggest, by "focusing on the ways in which disability is socially produced, the social model . . . succeeded in shifting debates about disability from biomedically dominated agendas to discourses about politics and citizenship." In doing so, however, the social model failed to appreciate that impairment itself is an experience that begs for illumination (1997:325). According to Tobin Siebers, whereas "the medical model pays too much attention to embodiment," the social model in its purest form leaves the body out of the picture altogether (2008:25).

To fill this gap in disability studies, some scholars have drawn on the tradition of **phenomenology** to develop what Bryan Turner (2001) describes as a "phenomenology of the body." From a phenomenological perspective, the lived experience of embodied human beings is the starting point for understanding disability. As Christina Papadimitriou observes, "rather than having a body, we *are* our bodies," and our experiences and understandings "are grounded in our active corporeal and intercorporeal involvement in the world" (2008b:219; see also Merleau-Ponty 1962). As such, the distinction between disability and impairment is difficult to maintain; they do not "meet in the body . . . as a dualistic clash of inner and outer phenomena" (Hughes and Paterson 1997:335). Rather, both "inevitably impinge upon each other" and are fully integrated in the embodied whole (Snyder and Mitchell 2006:7).[2]

In this way, a fuller understanding of disability, what Siebers (2008) calls the theory of **complex embodiment**, would not only illuminate the effects of the social environment, including the subjection of disabled bodies to the dictates of medical-rehabilitative practice, but also the pains and pleasures that derive from the body itself. It would acknowledge the chronic pain and secondary health effects that may be associated with physical impairments; that there may be available medical interventions and adaptive technologies that can improve one's quality of life; and that while environmental modifications and services can and should be adapted wherever possible, there are practical disadvantages to impairments that "no amount of environmental change can entirely eliminate" (Shakespeare 2010: 271). Gerben DeJong and Ian Basnett (2001) note, for example, that people with physical impairments may be limited in their ability to engage in the aerobic exercise that is needed to maintain good cardiovascular health and weight control, and they may therefore be more prone to early onset of coronary heart disease or adult diabetes; and people with mental illnesses may require ongoing pharmacologic support and monitoring over the course of their lifetimes (see also Chapter 5).

At the same time, there also is a need to challenge conventional typifications of disabled people as abnormal, inferior, or dependent people who at best should be pitied, treated as objects of charitable good will, or offered ameliorative medical treatment. Rather, disability can be embraced, even celebrated, as a matter of group identity, as other social minorities have done, as part of the broader fabric of human diversity, and as a site of cultural resistance to socially constructed conceptions of normality. This **cultural model** of disability, as some have called it, is illustrated in the phenomenon of Deaf culture, which we will discuss shortly. Simi Linton describes the general features of this model this way:

> The cultural narrative of this community incorporates a fair share of adversity and struggle, but it is also, and significantly, an account of the world negotiated from the vantage point of the atypical. Although the dominant culture describes that atypical experience as deficit and loss, the disabled community's narrative is the creative response to atypical experience, the adaptive maneuvers through a world configured for nondisabled people. The material that binds us is the art of finding one another, identifying and naming disability in a world reluctant to discuss it, and of unearthing historically and culturally significant material that relates to our experience. (1998:5; see also Baker 2011; Snyder and Mitchell 2006)

As such, people with disabilities are also uncomfortable with characterizations of disabled people as attempting to "overcome" their disability, as if there was something that needed overcoming when, in fact, their disability is simply their way of being embodied in the world (Baker 2011; Fries 1997; Linton 1998). It is for this reason as well that disability activists and scholars often decry the media's focus on "human interest" stories of so-called **supercrips**— including disabled athletes as well as supercrip "celebrities" like Helen Keller, Stevie Wonder, and Stephen Hawking—those individuals whose inspirational stories of courage, dedication, and hard work prove that it can be done, that one can defy the odds and accomplish the impossible. The concern is that these stories of success will foster unrealistic expectations about what people with disabilities can achieve, what they *should* be able to achieve, if only they tried hard enough. According to critics, the focus on supercrips works against implementation of social model reforms for people with disabilities (Crow 2000; Hockenberry 1995; Shapiro 1993; Wendell 1996).[3]

At the same time, paradoxically, the "overcoming disability" notion may also suggest that expectations for people with disabilities have been set so low that nondisabled people are amazed when they are able to perform the most mundane tasks—as when Joan Tollifson found people impressed that she could tie her shoes (see Chapter 1)—such as driving a car, getting a college degree, having a job, or even having sex. Hockenberry writes about an episode of *The Oprah Winfrey Show* he watched in which Winfrey interviewed four married couples, each with a disabled partner. "So there's something I wanted to know," Winfrey asked of a wife whose previously able-bodied husband had been disabled in an accident: "[C]an he do it?" When the wife responded, "Yes, he can, Oprah," the audience burst into applause (1995:92).

Disability Culture and Identity

The cultural model of disability, as noted above, views disability as a site of resistance to socially constructed conceptions of normality. In the fashion of other social minorities, people with disabilities have come together to assert an affirmative identity and community of like-minded people. The clearest example of this is **Deaf culture**—the capitalization of Deaf being a symbolic representation that highlights Deaf people as constituting a linguistic minority who use sign language to communicate with one another—and just as other ethnic groups desire to preserve their linguistic and cultural heritages, Deaf people want to do so, too (Aronson 2001; Barnes and Mercer 2001; Lane 1995).

Take the case of Deaf culture on Martha's Vineyard, an island off the coast of Cape Cod, Massachusetts, where deafness was brought as an inherited trait in the early seventeenth century. Inbreeding among the relatively isolated population led to an unusually high proportion of people with inherited deafness. At one time, every resident of Martha's Vineyard spoke sign language, whether they were hearing impaired or not. This culture remained intact for about 200 years, until it was undermined by greater mobility between the island and the mainland (Barnes and Mercer 2001; Groce 1985).

One point of controversy regarding Deaf culture, which is also apparent with other disability constituencies, is the desire for integration or separation vis-à-vis the dominant culture. In a society where most nondisabled people do not use sign language, the desire to propagate and maintain Deaf culture necessitates separate institutions (schools, social clubs, athletic associations, places of worship, and so forth), as well as resistance to technological aids such as cochlear implants that would help deaf people to hear and have a better chance of developing verbal speech.[4] Not all deaf people favor this separatist approach; nor do hearing parents typically favor abandoning strategies for integrating their hearing-impaired children into mainstream society. Moreover, people with hearing impairments differ considerably in the degree of their impairment and in the amenability of their condition to hearing enhancement through technological aids, as well as in the stage of the life course in which they became deaf, hence mitigating their feelings of solidarity and identification with Deaf culture (Barnes and Mercer 2001; Groch 2001; Lane 1995; Tucker 1998).

More generally, beyond Deaf culture per se, the phenomenon of disability culture raises a number of complex issues regarding the tenuous nature of solidarity among people with disabilities. In a survey of disabled people, for example, Rosalyn Darling and D. Alex Heckert (2010) found that people who acquired their disability later in life were *less likely* than those who were born with or acquired their disability earlier in life to identify with the notion of "disability pride" or social model advocacy. Additionally, as noted in Chapter 1, Nick Watson (2002) found that many people with disabilities do not consider disability to be a salient part of their identity. And David Engel and Frank Munger report that the disabled people in their study who were best able to narrate a "forward-looking" account of their life story were those who differentiated "their disability from their sense of self. For these individuals, disability was not the all-pervasive fact of their identity but merely an objective feature of their life experience that had its place among many other features" (2003:46).

Another issue raised by the question of disability culture and identity is the notion of authenticity, that is, who is genuinely "dis-

FURTHER EXPLORATION

Box 2.1 Autism and the Internet

As noted in Chapter 1, people with autism often have difficulty with face-to-face interaction. But on the Internet, freed from the conventional constraints of conversational timing, eye contact, and body language, they may sound "normal" and often eloquent (Singer 1999). In her study, Judy Singer examined communications on the "InLv" e-mail forum for autism, where autistic "members regularly sing the praises of the new medium that allows them to have the communication they desire, while protecting them from the overwhelming sensory overload of human presence" (1999:65). She cites Harvey Blume, one of the first to write about this phenomenon in the *New York Times:* "The impact of the Internet on autistics may one day be compared in magnitude to the spread of sign language among the deaf. . . . In a sense, autistics are constituting themselves as a new immigrant group online, sailing to strange neurological shores on the Internet" (1997, cited in Singer 1999:67).

The themes on these sites downplay the desire for a "cure" and focus instead on self-acceptance and group advocacy. As one Internet user remarked, "On the Internet I found people like me. I learned I wasn't so weird and that I didn't have to pretend to be normal. . . . I could be myself. And it was cool to hear other people's stories" (Bagatell 2010:37). Another person said, "We now have a way to say what we want. It's not possible for others to speak for us all of the time" (Bagatell 2010:37; see also O'Neil 2008).

abled" and who can legitimately claim to represent the entire group. Given the diversity of conditions that constitute disability, for instance, people with more serious impairments may dismiss those with less serious impairments as not "really disabled" (Berger and Feucht 2011; Deal 2003). In one case that received national attention in 2005, Janeal Lee was forced to forfeit her crown and the prizes she received for being selected as the Wisconsin representative to the national Ms. Wheelchair America (MWA) contest (Peters 2005). The national organization, which oversees the individual state contests, ruled that Lee was ineligible because she was not sufficiently disabled. Lee, a high school math teacher, has a progressive form of muscular dystrophy. She uses a wheelchair for mobility and can only stand for about 10 to 15 minutes without tiring. She does walk around her classroom, however, holding onto a chair or desk for stability. When MWA organizers saw a picture in a local newspaper of Lee standing, they declared her insufficiently disabled to compete. According to the organizers, MWA rules required a valid contestant to "utilize a wheelchair for daily mobility."

The use of the term "supercrip" as a derogatory label to describe accomplished people with disabilities is another illustration of hierarchical distinction made by some disabled people. Thus, Mark Deal (2003) reports that young men with muscle-wasting impairments due to muscular dystrophy felt animosity toward those who were able to maximize their upper-body strength to play wheelchair sports. Similarly, in a study of a university wheelchair basketball program known for attracting elite athletes, Ronald Berger (2009b) found a division between disabled students who played basketball and those who did not. Some nonplaying students thought that the athletes were snobbish and elitist, while some athletes felt that students who used power wheelchairs were lazy. Some male wheelchair athletes, too, avoided dating women in wheelchairs because, Berger surmised, the ability to attract able-bodied women bolstered their masculine self-esteem (see also Barounis 2008; Chapter 5).

Thus Ruth Galvin (2003) observes that people with disabilities have created their own divisive identifications that undermine cross-disability or pan-disability consciousness. Lennard Davis (2001) adds that claims regarding authentic or inauthentic disabilities can devolve into "policing action" that turns on itself and reproduces the same hierarchical patterns of inclusion and exclusion that people with disabilities have been fighting against. He thinks that **identity politics**—political arguments and strategies advanced by self-identified social interest groups—is a stage of the disability rights movement whose value may have run its course. Linda Martín Alcoff and Satya Mohanty (2006), on the other hand, think it would be unwise to dismiss the notion of disability identity as no longer meaningful or relevant. As they write, "Identities are . . . social embodied facts about ourselves in the world," about the way in which our social location is "distributed and hierarchically organized" (p. 6). Siebers (2006) concurs, as noted in Chapter 1, believing that disability identity will retain its utility for advancing the collective interests of all people with disabilities. Galvin poses these points of contention as the unresolved paradox of disability culture: "the need to combine versus the imperative to let go" (2003:675).

Disability studies' interface with identity politics, of course, mirrors the more general interface of the social sciences and humanities with identity politics in regard to other groups based on race/ethnicity, gender, and sexual orientation (Gilson and DePoy 2000). While people with disabilities have only lately begun to receive recognition as one of these groups, disability studies itself has been critiqued for neglecting these crosscutting points of inequality that further diversify and fragment the disability community. As Ayesha Vernon notes, people with disabilities come "from diverse backgrounds with a wide range of identities and experiences, and to accept that their only concern is disability is to fall into the same trap as the general population," most of whom see only the disability and not the whole person (1999:385). Similarly, Melvin Juette offers an implicit critique of identity politics and its influence on disability studies when he says that being "a black man with a disability" is only a physical description of his appearance that "does not define" his concept of self (Juette and Berger 2008:155). Rather, Juette views himself as a husband, father, son, brother, uncle, and friend, as well as a successful criminal justice professional and an accomplished Paralympic athlete—"all those things and more. . . . It's unfortunate that people go through life without getting beyond these socially imposed statuses and identities." Although some may view disability as a **master status**—the primary social identifier among multiple possible identities (see Hughes 1945)—people with disabilities do not necessarily see themselves this way.

The Political Economy of Disability

Beth Omansky (2011) argues that disability studies in the United States has emphasized the cultural model, while disability studies in Great Britain has extended the social model through a **materialist** approach, that is, an approach that emphasizes the interface between disability and the economic environment.[5] That characterization may be an oversimplification, given the important work by US scholar Gary Albrecht (1992), but it is arguably true that British scholars have been more likely to highlight the economic context of disability. British scholar Mike Oliver (1990), for instance, notes that the status of people with disabilities is largely defined by their ability or inability to perform productive work, whereby being able-bodied means one is capable of the physical exertions expected in a particular system of labor. Those who cannot work are considered "dependent" and eligible for government aid, while those who can work are not. Oliver also highlights the central feature in the lives of disabled people: their overrepresentation among the ranks of the poor and unemployed. In the United States, the full- or part-time employment rate of disabled adults (18 to 64 years of age) is less than 40 percent of the rate of the general population, and one-third of disabled Americans live in poverty (Stodden and Dowrick 2000; see also Pincus 2011). Moreover, in our culture "the very fact of being employed in itself confers moral citizenship . . . [and] those who do not or cannot work are typically viewed as persons who are not entitled" to the respect due other adult citizens (Engel and Munger 2003:116). Mark Priestley (2001) adds that the economic problems of people with disabilities are especially acute in underdeveloped countries, where economic *survival* is a far more pressing issue than legal *rights* (see also Barnes and Sheldon 2010; Charlton 1998).

Albrecht and his colleague Michael Bury frame the materialist approach to disability through what they call the **political economy** of disability, which makes use of economic concepts like production, distribution, and consumption (Albrecht 1992; Albrecht and Bury 2001). The notion of political economy, derived from eighteenth- and nineteenth-century European analysis, suggests that economic markets should be understood not as fully independent but as interfaced with political forces and governmental policies.

To begin with, Albrecht and Bury note the extent to which disability is produced by industrial processes and government activities that disable people: workplace accidents, environmental hazards, and wars. Historically, they observe, this produced "specific types of disabled people, such as veterans of foreign wars, merchant seamen, and railroad workers, [who] received special benefits due to their historical importance to the nation's political economy" (Albrecht and Bury 2001:588; see also Chapter 3). It is in this context that disability came to be legally and administratively defined, most notably after World War I, when rehabilitation services in the United States, the United Kingdom, and Canada were expanded "to address the needs of veterans and those occupationally disabled in the war effort," with the intent of returning them to work (p. 588). This, in turn, produced various disability stakeholders, both private and public, for-profit and not-for-profit, which defined and responded "to disability through the delivery of health, medical and social services, and activities to prevent disability" (p. 587). Taken as a whole, this constitutes what Albrecht and Bury call the **disability business**, or **disability industry**, which includes medical and health-care professionals; hospitals, assisted care facilities, and home-care agencies; pharmaceutical, technology, and medical supply companies; and insurance companies, advocacy organizations, lawyers, politicians, and consumers. In this way, disability services become commodities that are bought and sold in the marketplace, with some consumption subsidized by the government and some not. Hence a disabled person's access to economic resources has a significant impact on their quality of life.

> Although most disabled people are poor and have little power, those who have good insurance coverage or adequate financial resources are able to access high-quality medical services and purchase the best in assistive technologies, such as high-tech wheelchairs and prosthetics, voice-activated computers and personal assistants, drivers, and exercise therapists. These differences in resources can mark the difference between those who can live independently and those who may have to live in institutions. (p. 588)

In this vein, Hockenberry (1995) writes about an economic hierarchy that existed among his fellow hospital patients based on the degree of insurance coverage they had. The most fully covered individuals were those, like Hockenberry, who were injured in motor vehicle accidents.

> With the pool of all licensed drivers in America paying for it, insurance companies could afford to be generous. Car accident injuries could expect almost complete medical coverage, with wheelchairs provided for the rest of patients' lives in many cases.
>
> People injured in public places such as playgrounds or swimming pools, where liability was a question, came next. They usually benefited from the payout of some insurance policy on the facility where they were injured. They also generally could count on some kind of legal settlement if they sued the facility. The next group were those injured at work, who came under workers' compensation. Coverage here was less than for auto accidents, but

fairly complete nonetheless. Medical bills were paid, but the purchase of wheelchairs was more problematic.

In considerably worse shape were those people with degenerative conditions that came on suddenly. These people often exhausted their insurance in the first weeks of acute care and had little or nothing left for rehab. Such people could count on charity to buy less than state-of-the art wheelchairs and accessories. They were the recipients of a kind of medical rationing. One chair would have to last a long time. It could not be used or abused too much. If it broke down, the Easter Seals donors did not have the resources simply to replace it. . . . The absolutely worst off were the people with the rare degenerative diseases that no one had ever heard of. They had no insurance, no treatment, and the most expensive care. (pp. 34–35)

Thus, given the size and pervasiveness of the disability business in the economy, the distribution of resources that enable people to access goods and services raises ethical issues that "are a barometer for the moral health of a society" (Albrecht and Bury 2001:600).[6]

Insights from Feminist and Queer Theory

The materialist or political economy perspective on disability ignores questions of gender and sexuality as central dimensions of social stratification, and it is to these issues that we now turn. Let us begin with **feminism**, which emerged as a social movement concerned with understanding and alleviating the oppressive conditions that women (and girls) experience as a group. Feminist theory advanced a concept of **gender** (as distinct from biological sex)—the social statuses and symbolic meanings assigned to women and men—and identified societies as **patriarchal** when men are granted more power, prestige, and privilege than women (Jaggar 1983; Oakley 1972).[7] In positing masculinity and femininity as socially constructed, feminist theory advanced a critique of normative concepts of desirable masculine and feminine bodies. As Rosemarie Garland Thomson observes, "One way to think about feminist theory is to say that it investigates how culture saturates the particularities of bodies with meanings and probes the consequences of those meanings" (2010:355). In patriarchal societies that have historically denigrated women as the "frail sex," disabled men have been perceived as feminine and denied their sense of masculine competence, while disabled women have been doubly oppressed, with both genders deemed sexually undesirable or even asexual (Gerschick 2000; Gerschick and Miller 1995; Rainey 2011).[8]

Feminist theory also links disability studies with what Thomson calls the **politics of appearance**, the standardization of desirable bodies that can "be achieved through self-regulation and consumerism," as in the case of cosmetic surgery done to reconstruct the body in the image of an unobtainable yet socially desirable norm (2010:359). Thomson characterizes the interest in cosmetic surgery as a flight from the nonconforming body, which is perceived as unnatural and abnormal, in order to achieve "ostensibly natural looking noses, thighs, breasts, chins, and so on," which are, of course, not natural at all (p. 360). In this way, feminist theory suggests that the denigration of the disabled body participates in a more general social phenomenon that is broader than the issue of disability per se and affects nondisabled people as well.

Additionally, feminist scholars have wrestled with the dilemma of genetic testing and selective abortion and the potential clash between the reproductive rights movement and the disability rights movement (Caeton 2011; Saxton 1998). Whereas feminists want to preserve women's right to choose, some are very uncomfortable with the choice to abort an otherwise wanted fetus because of a genetic disability (Asch and Geller 1996; Hubbard 1990).[9] They worry that the expanded use of genetic screening to identify potential disabilities will put pressure on parents to abort, and that parents who do not will be blamed for imposing a burden on society (Hubbard 1990; Morris 1991; Wendell 1996). Gail Heidi Landsman reports that one woman in her study on motherhood and disability told her that "upon receiving amniocentesis results indicating Down syndrome, her obstetrician automatically scheduled an abortion for her, and that throughout her pregnancy she had to actively justify her decision to bear the child to friends and relatives as well as to medical personnel" (2009:128). Indeed, about 90 percent of pregnant women who learn they are carrying a child with Down syndrome choose abortion (Zuckoff 2002). Susan Wendell (1996) thinks that if potential parents were more enlightened about disability issues, and could expect a greater degree of societal support for raising a disabled child than is often available, more would choose not to abort.

Finally, feminist theory is also concerned with the question of **intersectionalities**, that is, the ways in which different social statuses or "axes of stratification" (Shohat 1998:1)—such as gender, race/ethnicity, class, sexual orientation, and (dis)ability—interpenetrate one another, making assumptions about singular social statuses tenuous (Grabham et al. 2009). Insofar as women have lower social status than men, for example, women with disabilities are doubly oppressed and, on average, have higher rates of unemployment and lower incomes than men with disabilities (Gerschick 2000; Randolph and Andresen 2004). The same is true for disabled people of color (Schriner 2001; Wang 2005). One lesbian recovering from mental illness describes her experience of intersectionality this way:

> I am oppressed as a woman in this society and treated even less favourably as a lesbian woman. But as a "mad" lesbian woman I am treated like the ultimate threat to patriarchal society—a scourge in the community or a contamination. . . . Am I mad because I am lesbian in a heterosexual world? . . . Or am I lesbian because I am mad? . . . These parts of my "being" are so interwoven that I can't separate the strands. (Shakespeare, Gillespie-Sells, and Davies 1996:157)

Another way in which intersectionality is experienced is through differential patterns of domestic abuse and violence. Although children with disabilities, both girls and boys, experience higher rates of physical, emotional, and sexual abuse than nondisabled children, disabled girls experience higher rates than disabled boys (Sobsey 1994; Sobsey, Randall, and Parrila 1997; Sullivan and Knutson 2000). Additionally, disabled women, like nondisabled women, experience more domestic battery (perpetrated by male partners and family members) than disabled and nondisabled men (Sobsey 1994; Thiara, Hague, and Mullender 2011). At the same time, the question of intersectionalities raises issues regarding the reciprocal or mutually constitutive elements of these varied axes of stratification (Lerner 1997; Siebers 2008). In their historical analysis of disability, for example, a matter we will take up in Chapter 3, Sharon Snyder and David Mitchell argue that disability has been "the keystone in the edifice of bodily based inferiority rationales" that have been advanced for other subordinated groups as well (2006:12).

Robert McRuer (2006, 2010) offers yet another example of inter-sectionalities in his effort to inform disability studies with insights from **queer theory**. Queer theory arose following the emergence of the gay and lesbian rights movement, the precursor to the contemporary LGBT movement of lesbian, gay, bisexual, and transgendered people. Just as disability studies raises a critique about the "normal" body, queer studies raises a critique about "normal" sexuality, that is, the assumption that heterosexuality is normal and morally preferable and that other sexualities are abnormal and morally inferior (Butler 1999; Sedgwick 1990; Sherry 2004). Adrienne Rich (1983), for instance, advanced the concept of **compulsory heterosexuality** to highlight the manner in which heterosexuality as a social institution establishes itself as the dominant or hegemonic sexuality, relegating other sexualities to marginal status that are at best tolerated as "alternatives" to the normal but which are still subordinated. As McRuer explains, "it is precisely the introduction of normalcy into the equation that introduces compulsion," because most people want to be normal (2010:384).[10] In this way as well, heterosexuality masquerades as "nonidentity," when, in fact, it is as much an identity as any other.

McRuer's contribution to disability studies lies in his development of **crip theory**, which draws a parallel between compulsory heterosexuality and **compulsory able-bodiedness**, whereby ability masquerades as nonidentity because it is the norm. In doing so, McRuer advances the disability studies critique of ableism, which aims to undermine the assumption that normality and disability are polar opposites and that being nondisabled is good and being disabled is bad (see Chapter 1). He cites the experience of Michael Bérubé (1996), whose son Jamie has Down syndrome with its accompanying intellectual disability (see Box 4.1). Bérubé writes of encounters with people who inquire about Jamie's intelligence. The subtext of these encounters, Bérubé believes, is always the unstated rhetorical question: "In the end, aren't you disappointed to have a retarded child?" (1996:180). It is the assumption, fallacious as it may be, that Bérubé would agree with these inquisitors that most intrigues McRuer, who surmises that this is the same premise that undergirds most nondisabled people's attitudes toward disability more generally: In the end, wouldn't you rather be normal? It is this assumption that leads most pregnant women who learn they are a carrying a child

with Down syndrome to choose abortion, because they cannot anticipate that such children could add joy to their lives and be joyful
about life (Zuckoff 2002). Landsman, a mother of three, with one
child who has multiple disabilities, puts it this way:

> If you had asked me before I gave birth to DJ, my third child,
> would I *choose* to have a child with multiple disabilities, I am sure
> I would have said, "No." But if you had asked me before my *first*
> child was born, would I want to raise a "normal" child who as a
> teenager would be disrespectful, experiment with underage drink-
> ing, have friends I don't particularly like, and not also live up to her
> potential in school, I suppose my answer would also have been no.
> Yet both happened, and both daughters, as well as my athletic and
> academically high-achieving, middle-child son, have enriched my
> life immensely. All evidence now suggests that each of them will
> become a compassionate, caring, and accomplished adult; engaging
> their own particular skills and passions, each will make contribu-
> tions to their communities. Contrary to my earlier certitude, I can
> now find no criteria to determine which child was more appropri-
> ate for me as a parent to bring into the world, or which one's care
> "oppressed" me more as a woman. Some would claim that my feel-
> ings are irrational, the product of an inherently "special" mother's
> love I could—and perhaps should—have been spared; I suggest
> they derive from new knowledge I acquired through the experienc-
> ing of mothering. (2009:216–217)

Just as queer theory resignifies the word "queer" from an epithet
to a positive affirmation, crip theory resignifies the word "crip." In
doing so, it also resignifies the word "severe" as it is used to refer to
those who are "severely disabled." Under the regime of normality,
the severely disabled are regarded as lowest in status, especially
when they are perceived as aesthetically displeasing by conventional
standards (see Deal 2003; Papadimitriou 2001). McRuer offers a different meaning of severe as "a defiant critique, one that thoroughly
and carefully reads a situation" (2010:388). According to this view,
the able-bodied's understanding of severely disabled bodies would be
reversed: the former are deprivileged while the latter are privileged
as "best positioned to call out the inadequacies of compulsory able-
bodiedness" (2010:389). As Siebers suggests:

> While disabled people have little power in the social world, their
> identities possess great theoretical power because they reflect per-
> spectives capable of illuminating the ideological blueprints used to

Box 2.2 Emancipatory Research

Feminist social research and disability studies converge in arguing for a research methodology undertaken on behalf of and to empower research participants. Both aim to give voice to those who have been marginalized by society, making their experiences more visible and accessible to mainstream core groups and helping to facilitate the incorporation of social differences as valued elements of a civil moral community. As a research methodology, both strive for emphatic and intersubjective understanding between scholarly researchers and individuals with whom they collaborate to produce empirical knowledge (Flad, Berger, and Feucht 2011; Frank 2000; Papadimitriou 2001; Reinharz 1992).

In disability studies, especially in Great Britain, this approach is often referred to as **emancipatory research**. According to Mike Oliver, "one cannot 'do' emancipatory research (nor write methodology cookbooks on how to do it), one can only engage as a researcher with those seeking to emancipate themselves" (1997: 25). What this means more precisely is subject to some dispute. While some have defined this approach somewhat narrowly, essentially equating it with participatory research in the context of progressive social action for people with disabilities (Zarb 1992), others suggest that the very act of telling one's story may be empowering in and of itself (Petersen 2011). At the same time, some academics with disabilities believe that nondisabled people are ideologically incapable of conducting emancipatory research, and that they should stay out of disability research altogether (Branfield 1998; Charlton 1998). Rob Kitchin (2000), for one, disagrees, thinking it unwise to leave the field in the hands of a small cadre of academics with disabilities who may have agendas of their own that do not represent the interests of the diverse constituency of disabled people (see also Darling 2000; Duckett 1998). All that is necessary, Kitchin believes, is that researchers approach their topics from a "disabled-friendly" point of view (2000:36).

Be that as it may, emancipatory research participates in a broader trend in qualitative scholarly inquiry, which eschews the idea of the trained "social science voyeur" who stands apart from the experience being observed, remembered, or recorded (Denzin 1998:411). In this tradition, there is an ongoing effort to guard against exploiting informants for the purpose of professional

continues

Box 2.2 continued

aggrandizement and an awareness that a researcher's "primary
obligation is always to the people [they] study," not to their project
or discipline (Denzin 1989:83; Flad, Berger, and Feucht 2011).
Researchers are viewed as engaged in a process of collaboration
with informants who retain some degree of control over the
research agenda, at least with respect to what gets said or not said,
and they are expected to engage in a process of ongoing self-
reflection to clear themselves of personal and professional biases
that may interfere with their ability to hear and empathize with others (Papadimitriou 2001, 2008b; Petersen 2011).

---

construct social reality. Disability identities, because of their lack
of fit, serve as critical frameworks for identifying and questioning
the complicated ideologies on which social injustice and oppression depend. (2008:105)

Disability and Symbolic Interaction

Much of what we have discussed so far in this chapter consists of
broad theoretical critiques of what might be considered the **macrosociological** context of disability, that is, the general features of groups,
communities, and whole societies that structure the disability experience. In this section we consider the **microsociological** context of
disability, that is, the features of social interaction that take place in
the local settings of daily life. These are the circumstances that link
the macrosocial environment to the experience of individuals.

Much social research of this nature takes Erving Goffman's work
on stigma and Howard Becker's work on the labeling of deviance as
points of departure (see Chapter 1). Recall that Goffman defined
stigma as a characteristic of a person who is "reduced in our minds
from a whole and usual person to a tainted, discounted one" (1963:3)
and that Becker defined deviance not as "a quality of the act a person
commits, but a consequence" of others' reactions (1963:9). More
generally, both Goffman's and Becker's conceptual contributions can
be framed in terms of a theory of **symbolic interaction**, which is

most often associated with the foundational work of George Herbert Mead (1934).

The premise of symbolic interaction is that human beings communicate and understand themselves and others through the use of symbols. As we have seen, both disability and normality are imbued with complex and often invisible symbolic representations that structure the nature of interaction between disabled and nondisabled people. Disabled people tend to be viewed and are responded to by nondisabled people in terms of a negative social type—as physical or cognitive deviants—that attributes common symbolic meaning to disparate individuals.

A corollary premise of symbolic interaction is that individuals develop a sense of self through social interaction, with the tendency for individuals to internalize the image that others project onto them, what Charles Cooley called the **looking glass self** (1902). Goffman (1963) was among the first to observe that people with disabilities may try to ward off potential interpersonal devaluation or discreditation, what he called a **spoiled identity**, and preserve an affirmative sense of self through **impression management** strategies such as refusing assistance to demonstrate competency, concealing their disability, or using humor to make others comfortable (see also Goffman 1959).

In one early study, Fred Davis (1961) examined interactions between physically disabled and able-bodied individuals.[11] In the beginning, Davis observed, the relationship was marked by strain and inhibition, leaving the disabled person with "good reason to believe that he [was] . . . being denied the status of social normalcy" (p. 122).[12] To alleviate this strain, the disabled person used various "ice-breaking" tactics such as displaying wit and charm, expressing particular attention to or agreement with topics of interest to the nondisabled person, and leveraging the "normalization potential" of being seen with an attractive companion who was not disabled (p. 128). If the relationship was to proceed further, the disabled person had to assist the nondisabled person with learning how to respond to potentially discrediting encounters that would disrupt the process of normalization, such as inaccessible buildings that would make it difficult to socialize in particular environments or the intrusion from others who offered unwanted assistance.

In his study of blind people's interactions with social service professionals, Robert Scott (1969) found blind people presenting themselves as dependent and compliant in order to meet professionals' expectations of them and make it easier to receive needed services. While some clients internalized this role, others only masqueraded as compliant in order to avoid being seen as bitter or ungrateful. Gelya Frank (1988), on the other hand, found people with congenital limb deficiencies refusing to pine for normality and instead openly displaying themselves without prostheses to forge a more empowering autonomous identity (see also Frank 2000).

Robert Bogdan and Steven Taylor (1989) examined the ways in which nondisabled people in caring and accepting relationships with severely disabled people—including those with profound intellectual disabilities and who drooled, could not speak, or were prone to soiling themselves—helped construct a view of them as valued human beings. These included establishing the disabled person's individuality by emphasizing that he or she had particular likes and dislikes such as tastes in food, music, or preference for particular recreational activities. The nondisabled person also helped the disabled person select clothes and maintain an attractive grooming style to manage a "normal" appearance.

Diane Taub, Elaine Blinde, and Kimberly Greer (1999) studied a group of physically disabled male college students who, according to the researchers, participate in disabled sports in order to demonstrate competency and preserve a sense of masculinity. In his study of wheelchair athletes, however, Berger (2009b) argued that athletes are not necessarily compensating for presumed inadequacies, but are engaged in affirmative "oppositional identity" work that scrambles the categories of ability and disability in ways that have the potential to alter public perceptions of athleticism and (dis)ability (see Chapter 6).[13]

Hilde Zitzelsberger (2005) interviewed women with physical disabilities who described their feelings about being *visible* to others in terms of their disabilities, but *invisible* in terms of their other attributes. One informant explained that she felt visible as a woman who "walked down the street with crutches," but invisible "as a woman that could have a relationship, as a woman that could be a friend to someone, as a woman that could be seen in a workplace, as a woman that could be a mother one day" (p. 394). Another woman talked about others' surprise when they learned she was married and had children. "I think I break that stereotype," she said. "And they're really surprised and they'll say . . . 'Oh, how do you manage?' . . . Or they'll say, 'That's great.' Well, you wouldn't go up to somebody and say, 'That's great you have children.'" And another woman with a facial difference described her strategy for presenting herself in a way that made it easier for others to accept her:

> I need to know that they see what I want them to see. . . . The projection that I put out is that I love myself, I love the way I look. . . . My body language, which is friendly, upbeat, energetic, a little in your face, a little pushy. But you know, what kind of makes people not see the other stuff, is my smile, my eyes, eye contact, how I touch people, . . . the way I move my body . . . in a way . . . that says I want to include you. (p. 396)

Nancy Herman (1993) studied the experiences of ex–psychiatric patients attempting to reintegrate themselves into the community after a period of hospitalization. One strategy they used was selective disclosure and concealment, trying to determine who was trustworthy and who was not. One man said he had learned through "trial and error," noting that when he was first released from the hospital he was naïve and assumed he could be honest with others; that approach, he said, turned out to be a mistake, and since then he "pretty much dummied up" (p. 308). But one woman had a more successful disclosure experience when she told her uncle, who was very supportive and helped her put her "mind at rest, to realize that having a mental illness isn't so bad" (p. 312). Others even engaged in preventive disclosure. As one man said, "I figured out that, for me, it is best to inform people right off the bat about my mental illness. . . . Because you don't waste a lot of time developing relationships and then are rejected later" (p. 313). Still others tried to attenuate potential rejection by explaining that mental illness is no different from a physical illness. One woman said she tells others it's simply a "biochemical imbalance—something that millions of people get" (p. 314); and one man said he tells them "the problem isn't anything [he] did—it's a biological one" (p. 313).[14]

In their research on wheelchair users in public places, Spencer Cahill and Robin Eggleston (1994, 1995) found that disabled people used humor to defuse potentially embarrassing and discreditable situations such as difficulty moving through crowded or narrow passageways, knocking merchandise off shelves, or rolling into standing strangers. They did this by openly laughing about themselves or, in one case, jokingly requesting a big round of applause for making a successful maneuver. Wheelchair users also learned to manage their emotions by withholding expressions of anger when they felt slighted or insulted. They were not always successful or desirous of doing this, however, and when they expressed their feelings they did not necessarily elicit apologies or embarrassment, but sometimes reciprocal anger. At the same time, the researchers found that nondisabled people sometimes feared being rebuked for offering assistance that was unwanted. All told, Cahill and Eggleston suggest that interactional situations entail much potential for misunderstanding, and that awkward encounters often stem not from malicious intent but from uncertainty about what is expected.

Michael Lenney and Howard Sercombe also examined reactions to disabled people in public places, focusing on the phenomenon of staring. As we noted in Chapter 1, it is natural to notice people who look different, but nondisabled people often feel a "conflict between the 'desire to stare' and the 'desire not to stare'" (2002:8). In their study, Lenney and Sercombe observed Elton, a young man with a severe form of cerebral palsy who is not verbal and communicates using his head, facial expressions, and deep guttural sounds, in a public café and bar.[15] They found that nondisabled people "were conscious about not wanting to be seen to be staring at Elton," and those who did not stare thought that it would be rude and an invasion of his privacy to do so (p. 12). But Elton did not want to be ignored either, and some people were genuinely curious about getting to know him. There is a subtle distinction, the researchers note, between "interacting and being impolite, and interacting and being polite" (p. 12). Elton "does not like people staring if it feels hostile. Yet if they are smiling and staring that is okay (or perhaps if they are smiling, that doesn't count as staring)," especially if the person staring is an attractive female (p. 13). Through the use of a communication book made up of several hundred words, Lenney and Sercombe translated (with Elton's approval) his "voice" on this matter:

> I see myself as being no different to other people . . . [but] I am at times concerned about my image. I am concerned that people look at me and think I cannot understand them. People need to understand that there is nothing to fear by talking to me, so long as I have my wrist restraint on. My restraint helps me contain my arms as they are prone to flail out when I spasm. . . . I like looking at

beautiful women . . . [and it] is okay for beautiful women to stare at me. I do not like it when people pretend to like me. I also get upset when people I like do not come over and talk to me. (p. 11)

To some extent, the nature of the interactions described in this study are generic, that is, they could be observed among any group of people, disabled or nondisabled. As Lenney and Sercombe observe:

Choosing to interact or not to interact requires a complex level of communication, both visually and verbally. This complexity requires mindful maneuvering. In some cases, when interacting or not, people choose to mask their intentions and motivations for their behavior. Therefore, at an individual level, it is recommended that people attempt to observe what motivates them to avoid or associate with people who are different. At a social level, it is recommended people carefully attempt to interact with people who are assumed to be different, with the aim of defusing constructed stereotypes. (p. 17)

Summary

In this chapter we reviewed different theories and models that form the conceptual core of disability studies. We began by considering the medical model and the alternative perspectives that have attempted to dislodge medical-rehabilitative approaches as the preeminent elements of the field. These latter perspectives include the social model, which focuses on the socially imposed barriers that construct disability as a subordinate social status and devalued life experience; phenomenology and the theory of complex embodiment, which focus on the embodied experience of disability as the combined effect of "inner" and "outer" phenomena; and the cultural model, which focuses on disability as a matter of group identity, comparable to the identities of other social minorities, that is embraced as a valued form of human diversity and a site of cultural resistance to socially constructed concepts of normality.

Next, we explored the cultural model more fully, focusing on Deaf culture and the nature of disability identity more generally. We also considered controversies within the disability community about authentic vs. inauthentic disability identities that are indicative of the tenuous nature of the solidarity that exists among diverse constituencies of disabled people.

Taking a different turn, we examined the political economy of disability, noting the economic context of disability and the constellation of private business and government-administered programs that constitute the disability industry. We also looked at the contributions of feminist and queer theory. Feminist theory raises issues about the politics of appearance that sets the standards for what is deemed a desirable body and that reveals controversies over the practice of genetic testing and selective abortion; it also draws attention to the differences among people with disabilities that are related to axes of social stratification based on gender, race/ethnicity, class, and sexual orientation. Queer theory draws attention to the ways in which a social practice such as heterosexuality establishes itself as compulsory, that is, as normal and morally preferable to other sexualities that are deemed abnormal and morally inferior; crip theory, in turn, adopts this notion to reveal the phenomena of compulsory able-bodiedness that constructs disability as an inferior mode of being in the world.

Whereas much of this chapter focused on the macrosociological context of disability, the general features of collective life that structure the disability experience, the last section focused on the microsociological context, the features of social interaction in the local settings of daily life. Here we looked at various strategies used by people with disabilities to ward off potential discreditation and assert an affirmative sense of self in interactions with others.

Notes

1. For further consideration of models of disability that are outside the focus of this book, see Altman (2001).

2. We will take up this perspective more explicitly in Chapter 6.

3. For a more balanced and nuanced view of the "supercrip" phenomenon, see Berger (2009b).

4. The cochlear is the portion of the inner ear that translates sound waves into hearing. A cochlear implant is an electronic device that is surgically implanted in the inner ear and activated by a device worn outside the ear. Unlike a hearing aid, it does not make sound louder or clearer. Instead, it bypasses the impaired parts of the ear and directly stimulates the auditory nerve that sends signals to the brain.

5. See Chapter 1, note 12.

6. For discussions of the international context of the disability business, see Albrecht and Bury (2001), Barnes and Sheldon (2010), and Charlton (1998).

7. Judith Butler (1999) questions the conventional distinction between sex and gender, arguing that both are socially constructed.

8. One study found that housewives, the elderly, and disabled people were judged by respondents as being equally incompetent and pitiable, but also warm (Fiske et al. 2001).

9. We will discuss this issue more fully in Chapter 8.

10. This is especially true in the United States, where being "normal probably outranks all other social aspirations" (Warner 1999:53).

11. Davis uses what is now considered rather archaic language when he talks about the relationship between the "handicapped" and "normals."

12. One nondisabled person was surprised to meet an attractive woman using a wheelchair. "How strange that someone so pretty should be in a wheelchair," he said (Davis 1961:124).

13. See Schwalbe and Mason-Schrock (1996) for a general discussion of oppositional identity work.

14. Other strategies used by Herman's informants included making jokes about other mental patients to disidentify with them, avoiding associations with other ex-patients, selectively educating others about mental illness, demonstrating competencies in everyday tasks, and getting involved in political activism around mental illness issues.

15. For more on cerebral palsy, see Chapter 4, especially note 1.

3

History and Law

DISABILITY IS A UNIVERSAL PHENOMENON, ALBEIT ONE THAT is subject to historical and cultural variations, that has been prevalent throughout the history of human societies, from small-scale, preliterate communities to complex nations such as the United States. In this chapter, we trace the evolving treatment of people with disabilities through preliterate, ancient, and medieval societies; the uneven march of progress initiated by the Enlightenment era; and the nineteenth- and twentieth-century United States, including the emergence of the rehabilitation movement and the political and legal history of the Americans with Disabilities Act.

Preliterate, Ancient, and Medieval Societies

Historically, attitudes toward people with disabilities have been shrouded in insidious mythologies, often of a religious or quasi-religious nature (Braddock and Parish 2001; Winzer 1997). This view is revealed in anthropological evidence from preliterate societies, which according to Jessica Scheer and Nora Groce's review, has found tribes justifying infanticide with the belief that a disabled child represented an evil spirit, "perhaps the offspring of a human mother and a supernatural being," or by the belief that a disabled child was a divine punishment for parental misconduct (1988:28).[1] Scheer and Groce report, for example, that the African Dogu believed that women who copulated with a bush spirit gave birth to disabled children, while the African Bantu believed that "mothers who engaged in incestuous sexual unions with kinsmen" gave birth to disabled children (p. 28). The African Neur, on the other hand, believed that a disabled child represented "a hippopotamus that had been mistakenly born to human parents" and should therefore be returned to its proper place "by throwing it into the river" (p. 28).

In her study of the Punan Bah of the Central Borneo region of Malaysia, Ida Nicolaisen (1995) found that the body of a newborn child was considered to be little more than a physical shell, not yet human. The child only became human when an ancestor spirit took possession of the body, and a severe physical deformity was attributed to the bodily presence of a nonhuman spirit. At the same time, the Punan Bah did not consider people who were blind, deaf, or who limped to be nonhuman. Nicolaisen also found that the Punan Bah believed that the father was to blame for his child's impairment, except in the case of blindness, which they blamed on the mother, believing that if she allowed "her husband or any other man to have intercourse with her during pregnancy," the eyes of her child would be damaged by the "man's sword" (p. 42).

In her study of the Maasai, a nomadic pastoral tribe of Kenya, Aud Talle (1995) found that the people made a distinction between those who were physically impaired and those who were mentally impaired, referring to the former as *olmaima* (crippled) and the latter as *olmadai* (fool). According to the Maasai, the defining feature of disability was the practical incompetence of being unable to help oneself, necessitating the reliance on others for daily tasks. Talle also found that the Massai did not blame the *olmaima* or *olmadai* for their condition, and they even thought there was *engolan* (divine power) in the "sick thing." They also believed that to ridicule another person's impairment was to tempt fate, for "if you incite it, it may reappear," and they therefore avoided any direct mention of the subject, either good or bad (p. 60).

Elsewhere there is evidence of role adaptation for people with disabilities in small-scale societies. Scheer and Groce (1988) report that the blind of the African Kanuri specialized in rope making, and the blind of the African Besongye worked as musicians. The blind of San Pedro Yolox in Mexico practiced beggary to contribute to their local kinship clan. They also weaved twine nets, sorted coffee beans and ears of maize, and pulled garden weeds, and at times they were expected to interpret dreams, thereby giving advice to others in their group. And the large albino population of Cuna Indians on the Panamanian San Blas Islands adapted to their sensitivity to direct sunlight by working as night fishermen.

Turning to ancient Greece and Rome, before the biblical time of Christ, the birth of babies with obvious physical deformities was blamed on parental misconduct that had displeased the gods.[2] Although infanticide was not uniformly practiced, in the Greek city-state of Sparta an infant born with an obvious physical deformity was required by law to be killed in order to mollify angered gods. On the other hand, infants with hearing and visual impairments and intellectual disabilities were not generally viewed as deformed, especially when the impairment did not become manifest until later in life. Moreover, public assistance was available in parts of the Greek and Roman empires for individuals whose impairments precluded them from working, especially for those who sustained injuries on the battlefield (Braddock and Parish 2001; Garland 1995; Winzer 1997).[3]

In Rome, a father retained the right to reject a child at birth if he chose to do so, and he was empowered by law to kill, exile, or sell his unwanted children into slavery (de Mause 1981; Winzer 1997). For children who were allowed to live, girls were sometimes forced into prostitution and boys were trained as beggars or sold as rowers. Children with intellectual disabilities, who were called *Moriones*, were sold for use as household amusements. Anticipating the "freak shows" of the modern era, a specialty market was even established for buyers of dwarfs, giants, hunchbacks, people without arms or legs, and so forth (Stainton 2008; Winzer 1997).

In Chapter 1, we noted that the Hebrew Bible preached paradoxical attitudes toward people with disabilities—do not curse the deaf or put stumbling blocks before the blind, but beware that God might inflict madness or blindness on you should you disobey his commandments. Following the life and death of Christ, however, the New Testament stories of Jesus's healing of the sick and disabled were interpreted by Christians to mean that such people exist to reveal the power of God. In the book of John, for example, Jesus is asked whether a man's blindness had been caused by his sinfulness or the sinfulness of his parents. Jesus replied that it was neither but rather a mechanism for God's work to be revealed in him (Braddock and Parish 2001). Later, under the doctrines of grace and divine plan developed by the influential theologian Augustine (354–430 CE), people with disabilities gained broader acceptance, not as equally

valued human beings, but as inferior beings worthy of "charity ultimately undertaken for the salvation of the giver, rather than the welfare of the recipient" (Stainton 2008:485).[4]

During the medieval days of Europe, also called the Middle
Ages, which lasted from the fifth to fifteenth centuries, various types
of conditions such as mental illness, epilepsy, and deafness were
often attributed to demonic possession, and persons exhibiting such
traits were subject to imprisonment, torture, and execution (Braddock
and Parish 2001; Winzer 1997).[5] Later, Martin Luther (1483–1546),
founder of the Lutheran religion, would describe children with intellectual disabilities as *massa carnis*, a mass of flesh with no soul who
were "filled with Satan," the father of idiots (quoted in Barr 1913:26;
Kanner 1964; Winzer 1997).[6]

At the same time, as David Braddock and Susan Parish (2001)
observe, there were emerging institutional supports for disabled people, such as monastically inspired hospices for the blind and mentally
ill, which reflected a more compassionate attitude, albeit one that
kept the disabled cloistered and segregated from the general society.
Importantly, Braddock and Parish note the expansion of **leprosariums**, institutions used to quarantine people with leprosy during the
twelfth century, many of which were the work of charitable religious
orders. This approach to leprosy represented the first time that "segregated facilities were systematically used in Europe to address the
issues presented by people with disabilities," and the separation of
"lepers was a harbinger of the perceived merits of segregation and
confinement of other disabled people" (2001:20). Thus, when leprosy
in Europe virtually disappeared by the sixteenth century, many of the
leprosariums were converted to "madhouses" for people with mental
illnesses and, in some cases, for people with intellectual disabilities
as well (see also Alexander and Selesnick 1964).[7]

During the Middle Ages, the relationship between poverty and
disability also became more salient. The existence of poverty was
considered "part of the natural order, and the poor were perceived as
offering opportunities for wealthier citizens to do 'good works' by
providing alms" (Braddock and Parish 2001:19). At that time, begging by people with disabilities was not stigmatized or criminalized,
as it later was, and there were even "guilds and brotherhoods of blind
beggars [who] organized to address issues of competition" among
them (2001:20). By the sixteenth century, however, begging fell into

disrepute as institutionalization of those who were unable to provide for themselves emerged as an alternative when other familial and community supports were unavailable. Rarely were these places called "asylums," a term that was first used in the late eighteenth century to describe "a hospital for lunatics" (Winzer 1997:99).

The Uneven March of Progress

The **Enlightenment**, or Age of Reason, was a seventeenth-century philosophical movement that sought to replace a supernatural understanding of the world based on superstition and faith with a more scientific view based on evidence and reason (Braddock and Parish 2001). This movement laid the groundwork for a medical approach to disability that attempts to ascertain scientific causes and implement appropriate treatments or remedies. Pre-Enlightenment physicians had already made primitive efforts to administer medical treatments (Braddock and Parish 2001; Winzer 1997). For instance, physicians bore holes in the heads of the mentally ill in order to release the stones or black bile that they thought were causing the illness, and one treatment of deafness had consisted of frying earthworms with goose grease and dropping the solution into the ears. An influential medical treatise of the late seventeenth century, Karl Paullini's *Flagellum Saltus* (From Sickness Arises Health), advised "the usefulness of voluntary beatings in many diseases of the head; Beatings in melancholia; in frenzy; in paralysis; in epilepsy; in facial expression of feeble-minded; in hardness of hearing; in toothache; in dumbness; in hysterical crying; in nymphomania" (quoted in Bromberg 1975:53). As bizarre and unscientific as these methods seem today, they were the rudimentary beginnings of a medical model of disability, which, in the contemporary era, has led to remarkable progress in our understanding of the etiology, diagnosis, and treatment of physiological-based impairments.

The Enlightenment also encouraged a more humanistic view of people with disabilities as educable and worthy of educating. European and Turkish monks are credited with first undertaking the education of deaf people, which began in Spain as early as the sixteenth century. Initially this education involved training in sign language or **manualism**. Over time, proponents of manualism often clashed with proponents of **oralism**, which entailed the belief that verbal articulation was necessary for deaf people to be educated and achieve social acceptance (Braddock and Parish 2001).

In the United States, by the nineteenth century, specialized residential schools for deaf and blind students staffed by a growing cadre of professional disability educators expanded rapidly. The first school for the deaf, the American Asylum for the Deaf and Dumb, was established in Hartford, Connecticut, in 1817. The cofounders of the school, Thomas Hopkins Gallaudet, a hearing US minister, and Laurent Clerc, a deaf teacher from France, were proponents of manualism (Baynton 2010; Edwards 2001). Clerc, who did not speak, first achieved notoriety while accompanying Gallaudet on a fundraising and promotional tour for the new school. Addressing audiences in sign, ably translated by Gallaudet, Clerc made for "a powerful symbol of manualism" (Edwards 2001:60). According to one observer of the day:

> This person never heard a sound or uttered a word, being deaf and dumb from his birth. Yet he is so quick and intelligent, that he has become acquainted with both the French and English tongues, which he writes with grammatical accuracy. . . . In him we have an example of the ability of a person, himself deaf and dumb, to give the necessary instruction to others laboring under similar disabilities. (cited in Edwards 2001:60)

Historians of the manualism versus oralism debate note that manualists were very much motivated by an evangelical drive to bring Christianity to the hearing impaired. Left on their own, Collins Stone wrote in 1848, "the light of divine truth" would never light their paths (cited in Baynton 2010:38). Some even believed that deaf people had been blessed by God to learn sign language and thus endowed with a special gift that "rescued them from silent ignorance" and brought them closer to their creator (Edwards 2001:59). As Douglas Baynton observes, "Deaf people were thought to have a great moral advantage in that they have been left relatively unscathed by a corrupt world. . . . [Deafness] is a positive good if temporary and discovered by the right people but an evil if neglected and left uncultivated" (2010:39).

Under the tutelage of Gallaudet, the French Sign Language used by Clerc became the basis of **American Sign Language** (ASL), which Gallaudet described as the "visual language of natural signs, manifested by the countenance, and the attitudes, movements, and gestures of the body" (cited in Edwards 2001:65). Thus, within residential schools for the deaf that practiced manualism, where deaf people used sign language on a daily basis, ASL developed as an evolving language with its own syntax, abbreviations, and facial and gestural expressions (Edwards 2001).[8] But in the period after the Civil War, oralists began to express concern that the segregation of deaf youths in special schools was producing a population of outsiders who were in danger of becoming isolated from the broader national community. These reformers believed that "homogeneity of language and culture" was essential to building a stable social order that was otherwise being undermined by "unchecked immigration and expanding, multiethnic cities" (Baynton 2010:36). Believing in the inherent superiority of oral communication, they thought that deaf people could never fully become Americans unless they learned oral speech. Otherwise, they would forever remain foreigners in our midst.

To be sure, oralists realized that some people would not be able to develop the ability to speak, but at least they should master lip reading so they could "follow the conversation of hearing people well enough to participate in society" (Edwards 2001:70). In response to such claims, manualists asserted that they also "strove to bring deaf people into communion" with the wider society, and they thus advocated the learning of written English. Nevertheless, oralists of the day insisted that oral speech was essential to the development of the human personality, and as Alexander Graham Bell asserted, to "ask the value of speech is like asking the value of life" (cited in Edwards 2001:72).[9]

During the time when these issues were being debated, residential schools for the blind also expanded, an effort that was aided by the popularization of Braille, a system of raised dots that enabled blind people to read that was developed by Louis Braille, a blind man from France, in 1829 (Braddock and Parish 2001). Most noteworthy among the schools that opened in the United States, because of its later connection with Helen Keller, was the Massachusetts Asylum for the Blind, later named the Perkins Institution and Massachusetts School for the Blind, which was founded in 1832 under the leadership of Dr. Samuel Gridley Howe (1801–1876). Howe, a medical doctor, had no prior experience in the education of blind children. He decided to tour Europe to learn about their methods, but came away believing that they focused too much on arts and crafts and did little to teach them academics and educate their intellect. His success in teaching Laura Dewey Bridgman, who was both deaf and blind—due to scarlet fever she contracted at the age of two—brought him considerable notoriety. Biographer Dorothy Hermann describes Howe's pedagogy this way:

> Howe began Laura's education by handing her ordinary objects such as a key or a spoon, with their names pasted on them in raised letters. Next she was permitted to feel the work in raised letters on a separate piece of paper. Some weeks elapsed, and Laura still did not realize the point. Then, suddenly, she realized that it had a purpose. The word *spoon* in raised type meant a spoon, and if she wanted a spoon, she could use the sign instead of the spoon to indicate what she wanted. Next Howe and her teachers taught her the manual finger alphabet of the deaf [not the Braille system], which had first been used in France in the early part of the eighteenth century. (1998:16)

Across the Atlantic Ocean, English novelist Charles Dickens was intrigued enough to come to the United States to meet Bridgman. Of Bridgman, Dickens wrote:

> [B]lind, deaf, and dumb, . . . a fair young creature with every human faculty, and hope, and power of goodness and affection, enclosed within her delicate frame, and but one outward sense—the sense of touch. . . . Her face was radiant with intelligence and pleasure. Her hair, braided by her own hands, was bound about a head, whose intellectual capacity and development were beautifully expressed in its graceful outline, and its broad open brow; her dress, arranged herself, was a pattern of neatness and simplicity; the work she had knitted lay beside her; her writing-book on the desk she leaned from. (cited in Hermann 1998:17)

This was the type of notoriety that would bring Perkins to the attention of Helen Keller's parents and make Helen the Perkins school's most famous student. (See Box 3.1.)

Despite the apparent march of progress in efforts to educate people with disabilities, many of the residential facilities evolved from well-intentioned training schools into mere custodial institutions. All too often, people with disabilities were segregated along with orphans, the elderly, the infirmed, and the poor into places that were

FURTHER EXPLORATION

Box 3.1 Helen Keller and Annie Sullivan

The remarkable life of Helen Keller (1880–1968), as is well known, was integrally tied to the life of Annie Sullivan (1866–1936), her teacher and lifetime companion. Annie's mother died when she was eight years old, after which she and her younger brother, Jimmy, were abandoned by their father. Annie and Jimmy were subsequently sent to live in a state-run infirmary in Tewksbury, Massachusetts, where poor abandoned children were warehoused and allowed to freely mingle with older patients who had highly contagious diseases. Jimmy contracted tuberculosis and died (Hermann 1998).

Before arriving at the infirmary, when she was five years old, Annie had contracted a contagious disease of the eye that left her visually impaired (though not completely blind). When she was fourteen years old she was transferred to the Perkins school, where she learned to spell and read Braille and eventually became a teacher herself (Hermann 1998).

Building on the methods developed by Samuel Gridley Howe to teach Laura Bridgman, Annie helped Helen, who had become deaf and blind due to scarlet fever when she was nineteen months old, develop her language and communication skills and hone her intellect. Helen's accomplishments soon outpaced Bridgman's, and she became a national celebrity, earning a college degree at Radcliffe, writing several books, and appearing in a motion picture about her life (Hermann 1998).

During their lifetimes, Helen and Annie were often aided by wealthy philanthropists who provided them with much-needed financial assistance. But this support was not always enough, and they had to earn a living by touring the country, where Helen displayed herself (with Annie's assistance) like a vaudeville entertainer, impressing audiences with her wit and intelligence. She also devoted herself to the cause of people with disabilities, particularly the blind. But her support for women's suffrage, birth control, and governmental assistance to the unemployed, and especially her advocacy of socialism, made her a controversial figure (Hermann 1998; Nielsen 2004). Of these activities, Keller wrote, "So long as I confine my activities to social service and the blind, they compliment me extravagantly, calling me the 'archpriestess of the sightless,' and 'modern miracle,' but when it comes to a discussion of a burning social or political issue, especially if I happen to be, as I so often am, on the unpopular side, the tone changes" (quoted in Crow 2000:854).

caretaking facilities at best and prison-like warehouses at worst (Baynton 2010; Braddock and Parish 2001; Hermann 1998).

Specialized institutions for the mentally ill also played a role in this history. Typically called asylums in their day, the first mental hospital in the United States was established in Virginia in 1773, but the expansion of these facilities did not accelerate until the 1840s, in part due to the activism of social reformer Dorothea Dix, who sought to improve the treatment of people with mental illness. Although the physician-superintendents of the early institutions believed that mental illness was curable and that patients could eventually be returned to their communities, the facilities soon became severely over-crowded and the commitment to treatment was abandoned "in favor of custodial arrangements designed to protect society from the per-ceived threat posed by people with mental illness" (Braddock and Parish 2001:34; Rothman 1990; Scull 1991).

The superintendents of these asylums were also "among the first in the United States to call for separate provisions for people with intellectual disabilities," and in 1846 Howe was appointed by the Massachusetts legislature to head an inquiry into the prevalence of intellectual disabilities in the nation (Braddock and Parish 2001:36). A few years later, Hervey Wilbur opened the first US institution that was specifically designed for this population in Syracuse, New York. Initially intended to provide training and education that would pre-pare individuals with intellectual disabilities for their return to com-munity life, like the institutions for the mentally ill, these places devolved into facilities offering "lifelong protective custodial care" (p. 37).

Moreover, societal views about disabilities were influenced by the pervasive racism of the time. In the US Census of 1840, for example, free blacks were inaccurately reported to have an incidence of mental illness that was eleven times higher than slaves' and six times higher than whites', statistics that were used to justify slavery (Gilman 1985). As Vice President John Calvin, the most vocal advo-cate for the slave-holding states, wrote:

> The census and other authentic documents show that, in all instances in which the States have changed the former relation between the two races, the condition of the African, instead of being improved, has become worse. They have been invariably sunk into vice and pauperism, accompanied by the bodily and men-

tal inflictions incident thereto—deafness, blindness, insanity, and idiocy—to a degree without example; while, in other States, which have retained the ancient relation between them, they have improved greatly in every respect—in number, comfort, intelligence, and morals. (cited in Gilman 1985:137)

It was in this context that a notable regressive element in the history of disability emerged with the **eugenics movement** in the late nineteenth and early twentieth centuries. Eugenics, which means "well born" or "good genes," was a social philosophy that advocated public intervention to regulate the genetic composition of the population by encouraging the breeding of parents thought to possess "good genes" and by discouraging the breeding of parents thought to possess "bad genes." One of the initial targets of eugenics policies in the United States was European immigrants, who, just prior to World War I, were forced by the US government to take intelligence (IQ) tests upon arrival at ports of entry. Some of these immigrants were denied admission because of their alleged intellectual disabilities and forced to return to their country of origin. Some physicians sympathetic to eugenics refused to administer life-saving treatments to infants born with disabilities or birth defects, hence facilitating their deaths. Involuntary sterilization of institutionalized residents with cognitive disabilities also was commonplace in some states, a practice that was upheld in the US Supreme Court decision of *Buck v. Bell* in 1927. Some 65,000 people were sterilized in a practice that was all too common through midcentury, and in some cases even later (Braddock and Parish 2001; Davis 1995, 2002; Snyder and Mitchell 2006).[10]

The eugenics movement targeting people with disabilities reached its most radical form in Nazi Germany, when tens of thousands were sterilized and a quarter million gassed with the full cooperation of the medical establishment. The Nazis cited the American practice of sterilization as a justification: "What we racial hygienists promote is not all new or unheard of. In a cultured nation of the first order, in the United States of America, that which we strive toward was introduced and tested long ago" (cited in Rubenstein and Roth 1987:141; see also Berger 2012).

Another regressive development in the history of disability was the so-called **freak show**, which reached its heyday in Europe in the nineteenth century and lasted in the United States until the 1940s.

Freak shows featured a cast of characters who were displayed for public amusement: people with physical disabilities, deformities, and other oddities—such as those without arms and/or legs, midgets and giants, Siamese twins and bearded ladies, as well as so-called tribal nonwhite "cannibals" and "savages," sword swallowers, snake charmers, and the full-bodied tattooed. The "exhibits were extremely popular at circuses, fairs, and exhibitions," and some even took the form of museums (Braddock and Parish 2001:37). The "attractions" at these shows were often sold to entertainment entrepreneurs "who maintained the right to display them for the duration of their lives" (p. 38). Freak show entrepreneurs often fabricated exotic tales of "wild and far-flung origins of the people who were exhibited" (p. 38). As a social institution, the freak show helped reinforce onlookers' sense of their own normality and superiority and helped construct disability as the ultimate form of deviance (Bogdan 1988; Davis 2002; Thomson 1997).

Rehabilitation and Reform

Regressive practices such as eugenics and the freak show notwithstanding, gradual progress for people with disabilities in the United States continued with the **Progressive movement** of the late nineteenth and early twentieth centuries. Advocates of progressivism believed that individuals, businesses, and government all had a responsibility to work together to ameliorate the impact of inequalities and injustices that were associated with the early stages of industrialization and urbanization. It was in this context that reforms such as public health programs, food and workplace safety regulations, workers' compensation, child labor laws, and expanded assistance to disabled war veterans took hold (Hickel 2001; Scotch 2001b). It was also the era in which the ideology of rehabilitation for people with disabilities gained momentum. Proponents of rehabilitation, however, were often of two minds. **Medical rehabilitationists**, precursors of the medical model, believed that individuals needed to be changed, while **social rehabilitationists**, precursors of the social model, believed that society needed to be changed (Byrom 2001).

According to Brad Byrom (2001), the reformers who led the early rehabilitation movement were initially focused on the problem of the mobility impaired, mainly amputees and paraplegics, people whom they referred to as **cripples**. The meaning of this term at that time was not simply a description of a common physical condition but of a state of economic dependency. In their critique of economic dependency and desire to overcome it, the rehabilitationists were forerunners of the independent living movement that emerged several decades later (see Chapter 1). They believed that it was the duty of every *male* citizen to work. As Byrom observes:

> Through work, men contributed to the well-being of the nation, set an example for younger children, and symbolized the most prized aspect of the American character—independence. Without work, men became parasites feeding off the labor of others. . . . To rehabilitationists, dependent cripples symbolized the antithesis of American citizenship, challenging America's identity as the land of opportunity. Such a situation necessitated reform. (2001:135)

The rehabilitation of crippled children, a sympathetic constituency, was the primary target of this movement, and the institution of the **hospital-school** was the mechanism of reform. Between 1890 and 1924, some seventy facilities were opened. Most of the hospital-schools were set up for boys, but girls were also included. Although it was men of that era, not women, who were expected to work, disabled women were believed to be unfit for marriages; therefore, they needed to find work too (Byrom 2001).

The precedent for the hospital-school was the New York Hospital for the Ruptured and Crippled (NYHRC), founded in 1863, the first institution to address the problem of the crippled child. Under the leadership of Dr. James Knight, who served as its first superintendent, the residents of NYHRC were treated with "orthotic devices to correct or brace disabled limbs, a dietary regime and physical exercise, as well as moral instruction, academic education, and vocational training to bring his pupil-patients into conformity with nondisabled norms" (Byrom 2001:136). Knight was a critic of the unproven and risky surgical procedures that were practiced in his day. But by the end of the nineteenth century, advances in medical technology such as anesthesia and x-rays gave orthopedic surgeons, once called "sawbones," newfound respect, especially after World War I, when a number of US doctors, including notable hospital-school orthopedists, visited the battlefields of Europe where they developed "innovative methods of repairing injured muscles, bones, and tendons" (p. 149).

More generally, World War I was a key turning point for positioning disabled war veterans as a sympathetic constituency for the receipt of benefits, and positioning physicians as the gatekeepers of those benefits. The **War Risk Insurance Act**, passed by the federal government in 1914 and amended in 1917, paralleled Progressive-era reforms in the area of worker's compensation.[11] Within the first five years after the end of the war, some 930,000 World War I veterans applied for these benefits. At that time, amputations and blindness were thought to be the most common war injuries, but nearly half of all compensation claims involved cases of tuberculosis, heart ailments, and war neurosis, what would later be called post-traumatic stress.[12] In contrast, fewer than 5,000 were amputees and fewer than 200 were blind. Physicians working for the Veterans Bureau, founded in 1922, were charged with determining whether existing ailments were in fact due to military service, and of all cases adjudicated by June 1924, about half were rejected. Of all claims adjudicated between June 1925 and June 1926, nearly three-quarters were rejected. Moreover, physicians were especially likely to disallow claims by black veterans, whom they considered congenitally predisposed to tuberculosis and lacking standards of personal hygiene, despite the absence of clinical studies demonstrating this assumption (Hickel 2001).

In addition to the War Risk Insurance Act, Congress passed legislation between 1917 and 1920 funding vocational training and rehabilitation programs aimed at helping disabled veterans become more employable. And in 1920 the **Disabled American Veterans of the World War** was formed as an advocacy organization that counseled veterans and helped them negotiate the government bureaucracy that controlled access to resources. Although the early disabled veterans movement often sought to disassociate itself from civilians who had disabilities, the **Paralyzed Veterans of America**, established in 1946, acknowledged the affinity between the two groups. They also recognized the disparity in the way disabled veterans and civilians were treated, noting that civilians lacked the services that veterans received, and they protested the racial bias in veterans programs, noting that "a spinal cord knows no bias" (cited in Fleischer and Zames 2001:173).

Additionally, by midcentury a host of other civilian organizations had emerged to represent the interests of various constituencies of disabled people (Braddock and Parish 2001; Fleischer and Zames

Table 3.1 Notable Disability Advocacy Groups, 1880–1950

Group	Year Founded
National Association for the Deaf	1880
Disabled American Veterans of the World War	1920
American Foundation of the Blind	1921
National Easter Seal Society	1922
March of Dimes	1937
National Federation for Infantile Paralysis	1937
National Federation of the Blind	1940
Paralyzed Veterans of America	1946
United Cerebral Palsy Association	1949
Association of Retarded Citizens	1950

2001; Scotch 2001a, 2001b; see Table 3.1). Parents of children with intellectual disabilities, for example, developed advocacy organizations to improve the treatment of their children both within institutions and within the community (Carey 2009). In 1946, the **National Mental Health Act**, which created the National Institute of Mental Health (NIMH), was also enacted, and by the late 1950s every state in the union "had at least some community-based mental health services stimulated in part by the NIMH" (Braddock and Parish 2001:44). Along with special education reformers, they sought to change the criteria for evaluating citizenship and moral worthiness, as well as the justification for receiving services, from a person's potential for economic productivity and independence to a person's potential for personal growth.

The Contribution of Franklin Delano Roosevelt

Franklin Delano Roosevelt (1882–1945), as noted in Chapter 1, is considered by many to be one of the greatest presidents in the history of the United States, but he had to hide his polio-induced paralysis and use of a wheelchair lest the public think him too weak to be a national and world leader. During his public appearances, Roosevelt "worked hard to master the use of leg braces that would lock in place when he was lifted to a standing position and allow him, with great effort and with some support from another person at his arm, to swing each leg forward as if he were walking" (Holland 2006:520). In private, however, he relied on a wheelchair for mobility.

Roosevelt came from a wealthy family and attended Ivy League schools. Prior to contracting polio at the age of thirty-nine, he served as undersecretary of the US Navy under President Woodrow Wilson, was a vice-presidential candidate on the Democratic ticket that lost the election in 1920, and was elected governor of New York in 1928. At the onset of his paralysis, Roosevelt sought a cure for his condition.[13] He learned about another man with a disability, Lewis Joseph, who claimed to have experienced "improvement in the functioning of his legs after spending a summer in the mineral waters of . . . [a] spa in Warm Springs, Georgia" (Holland 2006:517). During his first visit to the spa in 1924, Roosevelt found that the warm mineral water— which kept a constant temperature throughout the year and had a higher density that increased buoyancy—helped him to "exercise and perform muscle stretches for longer periods of time than had been typical for him" before (p. 517).

While Roosevelt gradually gave up hope for a cure, he came to believe that Warm Springs could provide those living with paralysis a supportive environment in which to enhance their health and quality of life. Using two-thirds of his personal wealth, Roosevelt purchased the Warm Springs property and pursued "his vision for a new rehabilitation community" (Holland 2006:517). The first brochure of the **Warm Springs Hydrotherapeutic Center**, which carried Roosevelt's signature, read:

> It is not the desire or intention to make the Hydrotherapeutic Center at Warm Springs a hospital or sanitarium, but a place where these patients can live as far as possible normal lives, and at the same time receive the best treatment known to science at the present time.
>
> To these special methods of treatment must be added the psychological effect of the group treatment, the stimulus caused by a number of people pursuing the same end, and each spurring the other on to more and better effort.
>
> In spite of the strides of medical science and the generous gifts to preventive medicine, comparatively little has been accomplished toward the restoration to active and useful citizenship of the more than 300,000 people in America who are partly or wholly crippled.
>
> I think most cripples, children or adult, are worth taking an interest in. Economically, this work is sound; humanly, it is right. Incidentally it is reaching out into a field which no other agency is

now adequately reaching. We need pioneers. (cited in Holland 2006:518)

In making these claims, Roosevelt was establishing Warm Springs as another precursor to the independent living movement. At a time when public transportation and buildings were inaccessible to wheelchairs, Warm Springs created an accessibly designed environment. In 1931, a newspaper article in the *Macon Telegraph* reported:

> At Warm Springs everything is [accessible]. Ramps give convenience to the hotel, not a step or a threshold may be seen in any of the cottages. . . . "Architects make things hard when they design public buildings, theoretically for the use of all the people," a woman at Warm Springs declared. "Look at the post offices, courthouses, railroad stations, churches and the Federal edifices in Washington! All of them with smooth slippery staircases up to their doors. The approach to the library of Columbia University in New York City is a solid mass of railless steps. To save me I can't get into the New York post office on Eighth Avenue—neither can the great majority of Polio cases in Manhattan. Beauty of design in entrances seems to sacrifice ease of access." (cited in Holland 2006:518)

In this way, Roosevelt brought a special sensitivity to the problems faced by people with disabilities and other people in need. And as president during the Great Depression, his program of social reform included the **Social Security Act** (SSA) of 1935, which provided benefits for the unemployed, elderly, widows, and destitute children, as well as assistance to the blind and children with disabilities. In the 1940s, this program was expanded to include aid to seriously disabled people who were homebound as well as disabled adults requiring vocational rehabilitation services. In 1956, the SSA was amended to create a federal cash-benefit program, **Social Security Disability Insurance**, for workers who acquired a long-term disability. And in 1972, the Supplemental Security Income program was added, which provides a federal cash-benefit for individuals with disabilities who have very low incomes, regardless of their working history. These individuals also qualify for Medicaid, which was established in 1965, the federal-state program for low-income individuals and families (Braddock and Parish 2001; Scotch 2001a, 2001b; Switzer 2003).

68

Box 3.2 Beyond Institutionalization: The Rise of Deinstitutionalization

Institutionalization of people with mental illness and intellectual disabilities continued unabated through the first half of the twentieth century. In addition to overcrowding, the residents in these facilities were subjected to a good deal of physical and emotional abuse, and what often passed for "treatment" resembled something more "like a hospital for the care of sick animals" than a place for rehabilitation or education (Switzky et al. 1988:28). Electroshock therapies for people with mental illness became commonplace in the 1930s and for several decades thereafter. Psychosurgery lobotomizing patients was practiced, though not as extensively, through the 1950s. And between 1946 and 1973, illegal research on people with intellectual disabilities—testing foods laced with radioactivity and exposure to the hepatitis B virus—was conducted at facilities in Massachusetts and New York (Braddock and Parish 2001; Carey 2009; Moreno 1999; Rothman and Rothman 1984).

By the 1950s, several factors led to the abatement of these practices in the treatment of mentally ill people: public exposés of the deplorable conditions in these institutions, the introduction of antipsychotic drugs, and growing support for community-based treatment that accompanied the creation of the NIMH (Braddock and Parish 2001). In 1960, the election of President John Kennedy reinforced these trends and "ushered in the modern era of intellectual disability services in the United States" (Braddock and Parish 2001:46). Kennedy, whose sister Rose had been lobotomized and institutionalized because of her intellectual disability when she was in her twenties (Leamer 1994), called for "an intensive search for solutions to the problems of the mentally retarded" (quoted in Braddock and Parish 2001:46). He created the President's Panel on Mental Retardation, which recommended "substantial downsizing of institutional facilities and an expansion of community services. . . . Kennedy also signed into law the **Community Mental Health Centers Act** of 1963, which stimulated the development of such centers across the country" (p. 46).

Hence, the era of **deinstitutionalization**—the policy of moving people from institutional confinement to the community and the closing of all or part of these facilities—was ushered in. As such, the number of institutionalized people with mental illness, which peaked at more than 558,000 in 1955, and the number of

continues

Box 3.2 continued

institutionalized people with intellectual disabilities, which peaked at more than 194,000 in 1967, began to decline (Braddock and Parish 2001; Torrey 1997). This deinstitutionalization movement was not without problems, however, and the promise of community treatment was not always forthcoming. Overall, those with intellectual disabilities have fared better than those with mental illness in receiving the community services and support programs they need. The latter group, on the other hand, suffers from significant problems of undertreatment and homelessness. Currently, there are about 2.2 million people with serious mental illnesses living in the community who do not receive any psychiatric care, a population that comprises an estimated one-third to one-half of all homeless adults. Often their aberrant behavior leads them into contact with law enforcement authorities and subsequent incarceration in the criminal justice system, where about 7 percent of people in US jails and 16 percent in US prisons have been diagnosed with mental illnesses (Arons 2000; Braddock and Parish 2001; Lamb and Bachrach 2001; Torrey 1997).

The Politics of the ADA

In Chapter 1, we reviewed some of the history of the contemporary disability rights movement, noting the role of Ed Roberts and the Berkeley, California, independent living movement. We also discussed the Rehabilitation Act of 1973 and the subsequent controversy over its funding and provisions that spawned a national and cross-disability movement of diverse groups working together for social change that eventually led to the passage of the Americans with Disabilities Act in 1990.[14]

In addition to the Rehabilitation Act, there was other federal legislation passed before 1990 that established a precedent for the ADA (see Table 3.2). We will forgo a review of each of these acts and focus instead on the politics surrounding the ADA's passage, which entails a fascinating piece of disability history. The first version of the ADA was proposed in 1988 by a group of Ronald Reagan Republicans, whom the president had appointed to the little-known

Table 3.2 Notable Federal Disability Legislation, 1968–1988

Legislation	Year Passed
Architectural Barriers Act	1968
Urban Mass Transportation Assistance Act	1970
Rehabilitation Act	1973
Education of All Handicapped Children Act	1975
Developmental Disabilities Assistance and Bill of Rights Act	1975
Civil Rights of Institutionalized Persons Act	1980
Telephone Communications for the Disabled Act	1982
Voting Accessibility for the Elderly and Handicapped Act	1986
Air Carrier Access Act	1986
Protection and Advocacy for Mentally Ill Individuals Act	1986
Fair Housing Amendments Act	1988
Hearing Aid Compatibility Act	1988
Telecommunications Accessibility Enhancement Act	1988

Sources: Jaeger (2012:40); Switzer (2003:93).

National Council on the Handicapped (NCH), which had been established in 1978 as an advisory board in the US Department of Education. The sweeping civil rights bill was drafted by attorney Robert Burgdorf Jr., who had lived most of his life hiding paralysis in his upper right arm (from polio) and who had been denied employment because of it. Another NCH member was Justin Dart Jr., a paraplegic wheelchair user (also from polio) who had experienced discrimination as well (Fleischer and Zames 2001; Shapiro 1993; Switzer 2003).

The Burgdorf-Dart version of the ADA was introduced in Congress during the closing days of 1988 to almost universal disregard. Reagan apparently did not even know of the bill's existence, and the media ignored it. After George H. W. Bush assumed the presidency in 1989, disability activist Patrisha Wright led the charge to reintroduce the bill. Wright was an orthopedic surgeon who had developed a degenerative eye disease that left her with double vision. She eventually landed a job in a California nursing home and became involved in the independent living movement for people with intellectual disabilities and cerebral palsy (Shapiro 1993; Switzer 2003).

Working with Democratic senators Tom Harkin of Iowa and Edward Kennedy of Massachusetts, Wright rewrote the ADA to make it more politically acceptable. The original version had required all public and commercial buildings (not just federal buildings or federal contractors) and every transportation system, restaurant, theater, and so forth, to be made accessible within two years. Even a small retail business on a second floor would have had to be accessible. The modified bill stipulated that only new buildings, or old ones undergoing major renovation, would have to be accessible. Also dropped from the original bill was a provision that would have allowed people with disabilities to sue for punitive damages if they faced discrimination from a business. In addition, the new version stipulated that modifications were to be made only if they were easily achieved and at reasonable expense. A small business might be required to spend a few hundred dollars, a larger one several thousand, depending on the resources of each. The law did not set a dollar figure, however. It would rely on common sense and eventually the courts, if necessary, to determine a business's obligations (Shapiro 1993; Switzer 2003).

Many businesses, particularly small ones, complained that the law was too vague and potentially costly, but others had by now come to view people with disabilities as a new source of labor and customers. Moreover, they did not want to look like bigots fighting a civil rights bill that appeared to have bipartisan support. Importantly, influential political figures on both sides of the aisle had personal experiences with disability. Senator Harkin, for example, had a brother who was deaf, and Senator Kennedy had a sister who was intellectually disabled. Republican senator Lowell Weicker of Connecticut had a son with Down syndrome, Republican senator Orin Hatch of Utah had a brother-in-law with polio who slept in an iron lung at night, and Senate Republican leader Bob Dole of Kansas had a paralyzed right arm, the result of a World War II injury. President G. H. W. Bush himself had a three-year-old daughter who had died from leukemia, and a son (Neil) with a serious learning disability. His youngest son (Marvin) had had his colon removed and wore a plastic ostomy bag; he also was the spokesperson for the Crohn's and Colitis Foundation of America. And Bush's favorite uncle, once a surgeon, had contracted polio at the height of his professional career (Shapiro 1993).

Still, President Bush appeared to be oddly cast to become the disability rights president. In 1982, as vice president, he had seemed one of its staunchest opponents. The Reagan-Bush administration advocated governmental deregulation, and Bush's first task as vice president was to head the newly created Task Force for Regulatory Relief. At first, he actually aimed to dismantle some of the regulations aiding people with disabilities that had been passed in the 1970s, but disabled people and their parents across the country rallied to protect their hard-fought gains. Vice President Bush realized that this constituency could cause problems for the administration, so he agreed to meet with its representatives. In particular, he met with Evan Kemp, a man with muscular dystrophy who used a power wheelchair, who was director of the Ralph Nader–funded Disability Rights Center.[15] Kemp convinced Bush with a conservative argument: People with disabilities wanted independence; they wanted to get out of the welfare system and into jobs. They were seeking personal responsibility and empowerment, not government entitlements. Kemp's arguments helped convert Bush to the disability rights cause. At the Republican National Convention in 1988, candidate Bush became the first presidential nominee to acknowledge people with disabilities as a political constituency that deserved representation, and he spoke about this issue on the campaign trail (Shapiro 1993).

Some 180 national disability organizations representing people with a variety of impairments endorsed the ADA. The sole holdout was the National Federation of the Blind, which rejected any special help that might lead sighted people to conclude that blind people are inferior. The bill was passed by an overwhelming majority in the Senate and House and was signed into law by President Bush (Shapiro 1993).

The Legal Aftermath of the ADA

The provisions of the ADA impact both the public and private sectors. To begin with, it requires all government entities, regardless of size, to provide people with disabilities with

> an equal opportunity to benefit from all of their programs, services, and activities. This includes public meetings, recreational services, transportation, health care, voting, and other programs. To ensure equal opportunity, [they] must follow specific architectural standards in the construction of new buildings or when altering or remodeling older ones. If a building or service cannot be provided in an accessible form, the activity must be relocated. . . . Exemptions are possible only if there is a demonstration that the modifi-

cation would fundamentally alter the nature of the service, program, or activity being provided or that it would result in undue financial or administrative burdens. (Switzer 2003:113)

Similar provisions apply to all public accommodations and services—including restaurants, hotels, retail stores, movie theaters, sports stadiums, private schools, and day-care centers—offered by private entities. Additionally, private employers of more than fifteen people must also provide "reasonable accommodations" to otherwise qualified individuals, unless those accommodations would prove an "undue hardship" (Fleischer and Zames 2001; Scotch 2001b; Switzer 2003).

As was the case with previous disability legislation, however, the ADA has been plagued by controversies regarding its interpretation and application, especially because of its use of such ambiguous phrases as "reasonable accommodations" and "undue hardship." Numerous cases have been adjudicated by the Department of Justice, with most being resolved through settlement agreements. By July 1998, some 500 cases had reached the appellate court level. Some of these court cases have been decided in ways that implement the ADA, while others have not (Colker 2005; Mezey 2005; Switzer 2003) (see Table 3.3).[16]

Among the cases reaching the US Supreme Court that affirmed the ADA were ***Bragdon v. Abbott*** (1998) and ***Olmstead v. L.C. and E.W.*** (1999). In *Bragdon*, the court held that a woman with AIDS (acquired immunodeficiency syndrome) who had been denied treatment by a dentist was protected by the ADA. And in *Olmstead* it ruled in favor of two women with mental disabilities who had been voluntarily admitted to a state hospital and confined to the psychi-

Table 3.3 Notable US Supreme Court Cases, 1998–2004

Cases	Affirmed ADA (+)/Narrowed ADA (−)
Bragdon v. Abbott (1998)	+
Olmstead v. L.C. and E.W. (1999)	+
Sutton v. United Airlines (1999)	−
Garrett v. Alabama (2001)	−
Toyota Motor Mfg. v. Williams (2002)	−
Tennessee v. Lane (2004)	+ / −

atric unit but then denied a request to be treated in a community-based program. The court said that the ADA's provision regarding the right to be treated in "the most integrated setting appropriate to the needs of qualified individuals with disabilities" was applicable in this case, though it noted that this right was provisional and needed to be balanced against the cost to the state (Colker 2005:130; Mezey 2005; Switzer 2003).

Among the cases that have restricted the applicability of the ADA was *Sutton v. United Airlines* (1999). In this case, twin sisters with visual impairments that were correctable with eyewear had "applied to be pilots and claimed discrimination when they were not hired" (Switzer 2003:140). The court ruled against them, arguing that "individuals whose conditions do not substantially limit any life activity and/or are easily correctable are not disabled according to the ADA" (Fleischer and Zames 2001:103; see also Bagenstos 2009).

In the 2001 case of *Garrett v. Alabama*, the court ruled against a nurse, Patricia Garrett, who was demoted from her job as director of obstetric/gynecology neonatal services at the University of Alabama hospital after undergoing surgery, radiation, and chemotherapy for breast cancer. Garrett had taken a four-month leave of absence under the Family and Medical Leave Act, and upon returning to work the university demoted her to a lower-paying position as a nurse manager. The court ruled against Garrett's claim that she was entitled to monetary damages. Chief Justice William Rehnquist, writing for the majority in a five-to-four decision, argued that the constitution does not require states to make "special accommodations for the disabled, so long as their actions towards such individuals are rational" (cited in Colker 2005:134). While the justices in the minority questioned whether the university's decision was in fact rational, Rehnquist argued (incorrectly) that there was a dearth of evidence documenting that the public sector (as opposed to the private sector) had a history of irrational discrimination against people with disabilities (Colker 2005; Switzer 2003).

The following year, in *Toyota Motor Mfg. v. Williams* (2002), the court ruled that the ADA did not apply to carpal tunnel syndrome (CTS). In that case, Ella Williams, an automobile assembly-line worker with CTS, claimed that the repetitive motion associated with use of pneumatic tools had caused her painful muscle injuries. Toyota temporarily reassigned her to work as a vehicle paint inspector, which mitigated the CTS, but when she was then asked to perform other manual tasks, the pain returned. Toyota, however, did not allow her to be reassigned to the inspection position (Bagenstos 2009; Colker 2005).

Later, in the 2004 case of *Tennessee v. Lane*, the court simultaneously ruled in favor of a disabled plaintiff *and* opened the door to narrowing application of the ADA. In September 1996, the plaintiff, George Lane, had been compelled to appear at the Polk County courthouse to respond to criminal charges that had been filed against him. Lane, who uses a wheelchair for mobility and cannot walk or climb stairs, was forced to crawl up a flight of stairs to attend the proceedings on the second floor because the courthouse did not have an elevator. In October, Lane was summoned to appear again, but this time he insisted on an accessible courtroom. The Polk County court refused to make this accommodation, but offered to have court employees carry Lane upstairs. Lane rejected this offer, saying it would be unsafe, upon which he was arrested for failure to appear before the judge. Lane, in turn, sued for violation of the ADA (Colker 2005).

In another five-to-four decision, the court ruled in favor of Lane, but the wording of the decision left some disability rights advocates concerned. Writing for the majority, Justice John Paul Stevens stated that "this case is not [about] whether Congress can validly subject the States to private suits for money damages for failing to provide reasonable access to hockey rinks, or even to voting booths, but whether Congress had the power . . . to enforce the constitutional right of access to the courts" (cited in Colker 2005:142). Thus Ruth Colker concludes:

> The *Lane* decision probably has few implications for other ADA . . . cases other than cases involving voting rights. In a footnote, it mentions evidence about the inaccessibility of voting to some individuals with disabilities. And its phrase, "even to voting booths," suggests that voting, like access to courthouses, is a fundamental right that is properly protected. . . . What else is protected, however, is unclear. Other important state services include higher education, health care, and incarceration. It is not clear that individuals with disabilities who have arguably faced discrimination in those areas could bring a claim for monetary damages against the state. It is not clear that the *Olmstead* decision, itself, withstands the *Lane* decision. (2005:142)

Moreover, the narrowness of the *Lane* decision is highlighted by the fact that the four judges in the minority were not even willing to concede that the ADA mandates accessibility accommodations to courthouses. As Justice Rehnquist wrote, "A violation of due process occurs only when a person is actually denied the constitutional right to access a given judicial proceeding. We have never held that a person has a *constitutional* right to make his way into a courtroom without any external assistance" (cited in Colker 2005:142). Overall, Colker describes the court's rulings regarding the ADA as operating like a pendulum that sometimes swings to disabled plaintiffs and sometimes to defendants, leaving the future of disability law very much in doubt.[17]

Summary

In this chapter we traced the treatment of people with disabilities from preliterate, ancient, and medieval societies through nineteenth-century and twentieth-century America. Historically, attitudes toward people with disabilities were shrouded in mythologies that, with some exceptions, subjected the disabled to mistreatment, exploitation, physical punishment, and death. Progress over the centuries, on the other hand, was reflected in a more benign approach that positioned disabled people as the objects of charitable goodwill and worthy of humane treatment in residential settings. This progress, however, has been attenuated by regressive practices such as eugenics, the freak show, and the mistreatment of disabled people in institutions of custodial care.

By the nineteenth century, specialized residential schools for deaf and blind students had formed based on the belief that youths with disabilities were educable and worthy of educating, although professional educators clashed over proper methods of instruction. By the twentieth century, the view that people with physical disabilities should receive rehabilitation services gained momentum. One well-intentioned reform was the growth of hospital-schools for so-called crippled children. War veterans, too, were a sympathetic constituency that encouraged the expansion of publicly funded programs for people with disabilities. And Franklin Delano Roosevelt played a role in the uneven march of progress through his sponsorship of the

Warm Springs Hydrotherapeutic Center and support of social reforms that benefited people with disabilities.

The remainder of the chapter focused on the political climate and constellation of interests that led to the passage of the Americans with Disabilities Act in 1990. We also looked at the key US Supreme Court decisions that have affected the interpretation and application of the ADA, some of which ruled in favor and some against disabled plaintiffs, leaving the future of disability law in doubt.

Notes

1. Evidence from primates (chimpanzees and rhesus monkeys) finds disabled members being taken care of by family and other members of the group (Braddock and Parish 2001; Goodall 1971; Scheer and Groce 1988).

2. The Egyptians appear to have been the first to be concerned with studying causes and cures for disabilities, and there is evidence that blind people were trained by priests in music, art, and massage (Winzer 1997). For a discussion of disability myths in Hindu mythology, see Singh and Ghai (2009).

3. Classical Greek thought equated reason with human value, with Aristotle believing that for daily living sight was the most important human sense, while hearing was the most important for the intellect (Stainton 2008; Winzer 1997).

4. Adopting the Aristotelian logic of hearing as central to intelligence (see note 3), Augustine believed that people who were born deaf could not be practicing Christians because they were incapable of literally hearing the word of God (Winzer 1997).

5. This was also a period in which heretics were burned at the stake for witchcraft (Braddock and Parish 2001; Winzer 1997).

6. John Calvin (1509–1564), another leader of the Protestant Reformation, also held such views (Braddock and Parish 2001; Winzer 1997).

7. See Chapter 1, note 10.

8. Nowadays, many schools for the deaf use a manually coded English called signed English, with some requiring students to think linguistically in English before they can think linguistically in ASL. Edwards believes that manualist educators of the nineteenth century "would be appalled both at this educational approach and at what they would perceive as unqualified teachers in deaf classrooms" (2001:77). For further discussion of this issue, see Benderly (1990), Cohen (1994b), and Chapter 6.

9. The influential educational reformer Horace Mann was also a leading proponent of oralism (Edwards 2001).

10. In the state of North Carolina, the practice of forced sterilization was not terminated until 1974. In January 2012, the state estimated that from

1,500 to 2,000 victims were still alive. One victim, Elaine Riddick, was sterilized when she was fourteen years old. Poor and black, a daughter of alcoholic parents, Riddick became "pregnant after being raped by a man from her neighborhood" (Zucchino 2012:B1). Social workers referred her to the state's Eugenics Board, which concluded that she was "feebleminded" and doomed to "promiscuity." Her illiterate grandmother marked an X on a consent form, and just hours after Riddick gave birth to her son, the doctors cut and cauterized her fallopian tubes, unbeknownst to her. "They butchered me like a hog," Riddick recalled years later. "I was just a girl who was raped, and then the state raped me all over again" (p. B1).

11. These reforms built upon the military pension system that had been established during the Civil War as a way to recruit Union soldiers, reassuring "enlisted men that their wives would receive payment if they were killed, or soldiers would receive a lifetime of financial support if injured" (Johnson 2011:1; Linker 2011).

12. The term "post-traumatic stress disorder" was not coined until the mid-1970s.

13. Jonas Salk developed the first successful preventative polio vaccine in 1955, effectively eliminating polio as a major cause of disability.

14. In 1988, another notable protest of that era took place at Gallaudet University, a school for the deaf and hearing impaired. The protest revolved around the complaint that the university had never had a deaf president ever since its founding in 1864. The action resulted in the appointment of I. King Jordan (Fleischer and Zames 2001).

15. Kemp, the first "Jerry's kid" from Jerry Lewis's muscular dystrophy telethon (see Chapter 1), was appointed by President George H. W. Bush to head the federal Equal Employment Opportunity Commission in 1989.

16. It is not my intention to review all of the cases here, of which there are many, but only to mention a few notable ones that have reached the US Supreme Court. For further discussions, see Bagenstos (2009), Colker (2005), Mezey (2005), and Switzer (2003).

17. In response to decisions that narrowed the scope of the ADA, the US Congress sought to clarify its original intent by passing the ADA Amendments Act of 2008. While defining disability as a physical or cognitive impairment that "substantially limits" a major life activity, it said that mitigating measures such as assistive devices, auxiliary aids, and medical therapies and supplies (other than corrective eyewear) have no bearing on whether a disability qualifies under the law (Bagenstos 2009; Baker 2011).

More recently, in *Hosanna-Tabor Evangelical Lutheran Church and School v. Equal Employment Opportunity Commission* (2011), the Supreme Court ruled that a Lutheran school teacher suffering from narcolepsy who was fired from her job was not entitled to sue her former employer for discrimination under the ADA. Cheryl Perich taught mostly secular subjects, but she also taught about 45 minutes of religious instruction a day. She was considered a "called" teacher and deemed a "minister" by her church. In ruling against her, the court sought to protect the church's "ministerial exception" to the ADA.

4

The Family
and Childhood

THE LIFE COURSE MAY BE DEFINED AS AN AGE-GRADED
sequence of socially defined roles and events that individuals enact
over time (Elder, Johnson, and Crosnoe 2004). In examining disability across the life course, it makes sense to begin with the family,
which Laura Marshak, Milton Seligman, and Fran Prezant describe
as "the primary and the most powerful system in which a person ever
belongs" (1999:2). In this chapter, we will consider contemporary
childhood disability in the context of parental and familial relationships and controversies about special education services, and in the
next chapter we will consider issues pertaining to contemporary adolescence and adulthood.

Before embarking on this inquiry, we should note that individuals and families differ considerably in how they respond to a family
member who is born with a disability or becomes disabled later in
life. This response is not only related to the nature of the impairment,
but also to the family's economic resources and prior beliefs about
disability. Moreover, as Sara Ryan and Katherine Runswick-Cole
suggest, it is unwise to view "families with disabled children as a
discrete phenomenon," because these families "are so variable that
they probably have as much in common with mainstream families as
with each other" (2008:202). Thus generalizations about the family's
experience of childhood disability should be made with caution.

We should also remind ourselves that disability entails a wide
range of physical, sensory, and cognitive impairments, each with
possible manifestations that range from mild to severe, and many

children have multiple disabilities. In a study of mothers of children with disabilities, Gail Heidi Landsman (2009) found that more than 40 percent of the mothers had children with multiple disabilities or significant developmental delays in more than one area. Lest one think that these experiences are entirely uncommon, about 10 percent of all children have some form of disability or chronic illness in their early years (Naseef 2001), and about 4 percent of families report living with a child between the ages of five and fifteen who has at least one disability (Wang 2005). Moreover, with the advent of infant intensive care units and aggressive medical interventions that have increased the survival rates of premature infants who are more vulnerable to conditions such as cerebral palsy—a nondegenerative condition caused by damage to the brain before, during, or shortly after birth[1]—the prevalence of children with disabilities has been steadily increasing (Landsman 2009; Lorenz et al. 1998).[2]

It is important to understand that this state of affairs did not come about because of advances in the medical field alone, but also because of changes in societal attitudes toward infants with disabilities. In particular, two well-publicized cases in the early 1980s marked a turning point in this change. In the first, in 1982, the parents of an Indiana boy born with Down syndrome and an esophageal blockage decided to forgo treatment of the blockage upon the advice of their physician. He died six days later. The following year, the parents of a New York girl born with spina bifida and hydrocephalus declined surgery for their daughter after their physician told "them that without treatment, she would die more quickly" (Asch 2001:303).[3] The girl did not die, but she did live with severe physical and cognitive impairments (*New York Times* 1992). Adrienne Asch describes the rationales given at the time for withholding medical intervention in such cases:

> [the reduction of] the physical suffering and pain of the potential treatments as well as the impairments themselves; the conviction that technology was being used to sustain children who would have short, painful, and miserable lives regardless of what was done for them; the anguish for parents who had to watch a child die slowly after enduring fruitless medical procedures; disappointment for parents who would not have the healthy child they expected and desired and might instead have to raise one who would always have disabling conditions; and belief that the millions of dollars spent for such treatments were better spent in other ways. (2001:303–304)

The aforementioned cases, known as Baby Doe and Baby Jane Doe, respectively, raised a legal and political uproar, including outcry from the disability rights community, who believed that the denial of beneficial treatment to infants with disabilities represented a discriminatory view held by medical professionals that a disabled life was not worth living. Indeed, research shows that medical professionals significantly underestimate the quality of life of disabled people compared to the assessments of disabled people themselves (Gerhart et al. 1994; Gill 2000; Longmore 2003; see also Chapter 8). With the backing of pro-life activists as well, the administration of President Ronald Reagan pushed for the passage of the **Child Abuse Amendments of 1984**, also known as the **Baby Doe Amendments**, which called for the medical treatment "of newborns unless the infant was likely to die regardless of such intervention" (Asch 2001:304). In a subsequent US Supreme Court decision in 1986, the law was deemed unconstitutional, with the court ruling that the federal government did not have the right to overrule parents and require medical treatment for infants born with serious birth defects (*New York Times* 1992). Nevertheless, it is fair to say that the attention given to this issue did have an impact on societal attitudes. While most cases of this nature do not involve infants with clearly identifiable conditions such as Down syndrome or spina bifida—but rather premature and low-birth-weight infants who, if treated successfully, become part of the disabled population—newborns in the United States today are generally the beneficiaries of all "medically indicated treatments" (Asch 2001:305).

Parental First Encounters with Childhood Disability

We will begin with a consideration of how prospective parents become aware that their child may have a disability, which sometimes happens before birth because nowadays it is common for women who become pregnant to undergo prenatal testing—the two most common being a blood test known as maternal alpha-fetoprotein and ultrasound imaging—in an effort to determine whether the fetus is "normal" (Landsman 2009). If a problem is detected, the often unstated assumption is that this information will be used to make a decision about continuing or terminating the pregnancy. It is also a means for parents "to reassure themselves and others that they are doing everything possible to eliminate the risk of maternally induced poor fetal outcomes" (Marshak, Seligman, and Prezant 1999:44; see also Browner and Press 1995).

Among women who are in their mid-thirties or older, who have a greater likelihood than younger women of giving birth to a child with Down syndrome, it is also common to undergo amniocentesis to determine whether the fetus has a chromosomal abnormality that is indicative of this condition (see Box 4.1). Down syndrome occurs in about one out of every 800 live births, and although three-quarters of children with Down syndrome are born to women *under* thirty-five—because most babies are born to younger mothers—the odds of an older woman having a baby with this condition are proportionately higher than a younger woman's (Zuckoff 2002).

As we noted in Chapter 2, about 90 percent of pregnant women who learn they are carrying a child with Down syndrome choose abortion (Zuckoff 2002), and many other mothers who have given birth to a child with a disability admit that they might have aborted the fetus if they had known of the impairment beforehand (Landsman 2009). According to Landsman, in spite of the concerns of disability rights advocates about the use of selective abortion to prevent the birth of disabled people (see Chapters 2 and 8), "the wider society has largely accepted the process under the morally less ambiguous rubric of preventing birth defects. . . . Most pregnant women . . . have come to assume that it is possible to have what is defined as a perfectly 'normal' child," and they have internalized "the culturally constructed assumption that disability is a socially devalued birth outcome" (2009:3, 41, 44).

In most cases, parents do not discover there is something awry with their baby until after birth. At that time parents may sense that something is wrong, even when they are not told so explicitly by the medical staff, who may nonetheless give off unintentional clues (Marshak, Seligman, and Prezant 1999). As one mother recalled, "I remember . . . [t]he doctor did not say anything at all when the baby was born. Then he said, 'It's a boy,' and the way he hesitated. I immediately said, 'Is he all right?' And he said, 'He has ten fingers and ten toes,' so in the back of my mind I knew there was something wrong" (Darling 1979:129).

In her study of dwarfism, Betty Adelson (2005) provides accounts of mothers' initial after-birth experiences. In one instance:

FURTHER EXPLORATION

Box 4.1 Down Syndrome

The discovery of Down syndrome is attributable to the British doctor John Langdon Down (1828–1896). While working as a medical superintendent for the Earlswood Asylum for Idiots, Down developed an interest in the classification of people with intellectual disabilities, a term that was not used in his day (see Chapter 1, note 10). At the time, in the mid-nineteenth century, professionals assumed a three-tier classification for cognitive impairments: *idiocy* (the most severe), *imbecility,* and *feeble-minded*ness (the least severe). Down thought this scheme was oversimplified and did not adequately account for the differences among patients under his supervision (Wright 2004; Zuckoff 2002).

Down further classified idiots and imbeciles under his care according to three types: Ethiopian, Malay, and Mongolian, giving varying physical descriptions of each. It was the Mongolian type that became the first clinical description of people now characterized as having Down syndrome: "The face is flat and broad, and destitute of prominence. . . . The tongue is long, thick and is much roughened. The nose is small. The skin has a slight dirty-yellowish tinge, and is deficient in elasticity, giving the appearance of being too large for the body" (Zuckoff 2002:33).

In the 1930s, scientists started to suspect that Down syndrome had something to do with abnormal chromosomes, a hypothesis that was definitively proven in 1959. The normal individual has a genetic makeup of twenty-three chromosomal pairs, or forty-six chromosomes, with each pair contributed by the mother and father. In Down syndrome there is an extra forty-seventh chromosome, most often contributed by the mother. As the cells of the fertilized egg replicate, the chromosomal abnormality repeats itself. In 90 percent of the cases, the condition results in a miscarriage. In the other 10 percent a person is born with Down syndrome. Scientists are still uncertain as to why the extra chromosome causes the condition.

People with Down syndrome are characterized by cognitive impairments, although the degree of disability may vary considerably. Most have IQs between 40 and 70, with 100 being the average for the nondisabled population. A smaller percentage is either below or above the 40–70 range. About 40 percent of children with

continues

Box 4.1 continued

Down syndrome also have heart defects, and nearly all have loose joints and low muscle tone. Thyroid and digestive tract disorders, leukemia, and Alzheimer-like symptoms also occur more often than among the general population. As recently as the late 1960s, the average life span for people with Down syndrome was just two years. Today the average life span for Caucasians with Down syndrome has reached fifty years; but for African Americans it is only twenty-five years. The racial differential is attributable to differences in "socioeconomic status, education, community support, [and] medical or surgical treatment of serious complications" (Zuckoff 2002:36).

a mother had to wait 12 hours before her son was finally brought to her. All day, the nurses had avoided her, even neglecting her bedpan. Her request for information about exactly what might be wrong . . . were met with "I'll go see"—but the nurses never returned. Only after her husband phoned her physician that night did a pediatrician appear. (p. 159)

Another mother described how she felt this way:

The obstetrician came in first and he was very awkward and didn't say very much. He said, "She's going to be short, but it's going to be all right." He didn't tell us she was going to be a dwarf. . . . The pediatrician came in a bit later. He said he had never seen a dwarf child. He was very blunt and businesslike. He said, "Your child is a dwarf, and the condition is called achondroplasia [a hereditary condition]. She's never going to be any taller than four feet, and there will be these kinds of problems. But she'll probably be all right." Still, he was doing his homework. By the second morning he came in with a medical book—a textbook. He turned to a page and said, "This is what she's going to look like." There was a picture of a nude, female adult dwarf with only the face and eyes blackened out. I noticed the webbed fingers and the sway back. Frankly, it was shocking to look at it. (p. 159)

At times, the medical staff will withhold information because they are uncertain about what is going on and it is prudent to remain cautious until more information can be gathered. And unlike Down syndrome, it is rare for conditions such as cerebral palsy, muscular dystrophy, and autism to be determinable at birth (Hedderly, Baird, and McConachie 2003; Landsman 2009). In the case of learning disabilities, these difficulties may not manifest themselves until the child enters elementary school. Even then it may take some time to be noticed and diagnosed, because some learning disabilities may not be revealed until the child enters higher grades where more advanced reading, writing, and mathematics skills are required (Kirk 2002; Marshak, Seligman, and Prezant 1999). In his study based on interviews with parents of children with disabilities, Colin Ong-Dean (2006) found that, overall, the median age of diagnosis was five years, while the median age of diagnosis for learning disabilities was seven and a half years.

In the case of Nathaniel McDermott, who was born with a genetic condition called Apert syndrome, his condition was visible at birth (McDermott 2000). First noted by the French physician Eugene Apert in 1906, Apert syndrome is characterized by certain malformations of the skull, hands, and feet, which include the fusion of the bone plates in the skull as well as webbed appendages. Nathaniel's mother Jeanne describes her initial reaction to the discovery that her son was born with a bodily difference.

> When the doctor nervously placed the minute-old baby in my arms, Ted [her husband] circled us in a tightening embrace. Deep shock brought an exaggerated calm in the moment that I touched the baby's hands. They looked like mittens! A tiny thumb was separate but pearly skin joined the other fingers together, making little pink cups.
>
> That's no big deal, I thought with a flash of intuition. Ted gently stroked the baby's tall bulging head, felt the bumpy ridge about his eyes that made him look as if he had worn a tight hat whose band had left its mark. . . . "He's not the baby I imagined," I sighed. (pp. 8, 18)

Landsman notes that "[c]ontrary to the traditional response of congratulations on the birth of a baby, the mother of a child with disabilities is often treated as if she has no baby to celebrate" (2009:57). As one mother told her, "I remember people stopping by, and I wanted so badly for somebody to say congratulations. Instead, I'm in this room by myself. People sent some flowers, but nobody knew what to say or to do, and it was the most horrible feeling, because . . . like it is a tragedy" (p. 49). Another mother recalled, "When she was born and people heard there was something wrong, like the congratulations disappears. You don't get any of that. It's like you didn't have a baby" (p. 57). And another said, "It's like nobody wanted to see pictures of her. . . . Nobody like oohed and aahed" (p. 59).

In her memoir, Emily Rapp (2007) describes her mother's recollection of the nurse's reaction in the hospital after she gave birth to Emily. Emily was born with one leg visibly shorter than the other, a consequence of a congenital bone-and-tissue disorder that would eventually require amputation of her left leg just above her knee. "The nurse gave mom a look she would get used to. Later, I would also come to know it well: A look of pity, sadness, with kindness. . . . 'We just don't know what God is going to do,' said the nurse. . . . 'We just don't know His plan'" (p. 11).

Furthermore, many mothers "report that others—be they strangers, friends, or extended family members—often openly question the value of their disabled children and in turn extend that devaluation to question the wisdom of investing time and energy in their nurturance" (Landsman 2009:75). One of the mothers interviewed by Landsman was told, "Well, now you need to decide if you're going to sink your whole life into Ryan, or if you're going to have more kids and create a normal family environment" (p. 75).

Upon first realizing that her child has a disability, many mothers respond by blaming themselves. Women of a religious bent may think it is a punishment from God. Rapp's mother repeatedly exclaimed, "Oh God, it's my fault." Her mother had memorized a biblical passage about the sins of the fathers (and by inference the mothers) being "visited upon their sons and, in this case, their daughters" (2007:10; see also Darling 1979; Marshak, Seligman, and Prezant 1999). On the other hand, some women will be told by others that God has chosen them to be mothers because they are somehow special, an observation that some mothers appreciate and others resent. As one woman told Landsman, "I was talking to my cousin and she says 'You know, Mary, only certain people are blessed with certain kinds of kids and certain people can deal with it and certain people can't, but my own belief is He chose you because He knew you could do it.' And that made me kind of happy to hear . . . a relative of mine saying that" (2009:78).

Another mother was told, "God never gives babies to parents who don't have extra love to take care of them, sick babies to parents that can't take care of them, and I think . . . it does take a special person to have a baby with problems and be there for them and love them and help them" (p. 81). Some mothers, on the other hand, did not appreciate these kinds of remarks.

> [T]hat's a crock of bull. They say, well, you know you have to—God—because you have patience or whatever. You have no choice. This is it. You know either you give them up, send them away to a home or you deal with it. It's not in between. I choose to deal with it. (p. 79)

> I've heard that a lot. . . . I don't think that we are special parents, any specialer than any other parent. . . . I think you just handle what is given to you. You know, it's either that or crumble. (p. 80)

> You know that whole idea of . . . this only happens to special people . . . I find it annoying when people say that. I think it certainly *makes* you different. . . . We're not special parents, we're average normal people who had this . . . happen to us. And we're doing the best we can, and maybe in the end we might turn out to be special parents, but we're just normal people struggling with . . . making the best out of the situation we've got. (p. 82)

Research finds that "parental adjustment to childhood disability may be related to whether a child was planned for or desired" (Marshak, Seligman, and Prezant 1999:55). Parents who had planned for the child, as opposed to those who did not, seem to experience a greater sense of injustice when their child is born with a disability (Siegal 1996). Additionally, younger couples seem better able to adjust to their new situation than "older couples because their life style preferences are not as fixed, because they can decide to have more children, and because . . . [they have more] physical energy" (Marshak, Seligman, and Prezant 1999:55). Mothers who give birth to newborns with serious disabilities, however, are more likely to undergo tubal sterilization in the ensuing months than are mothers who give birth to newborns with mild disabilities or no disabilities, either because they don't have the time and resources to take care of another child (disabled or nondisabled) or because they are concerned about giving birth to another child with a disability (Park, Hogan, and Goldscheider 2003).

Be that as it may, the mothers in Landsman's study felt that "their ability to obtain good medical care and their responsible behaviors before and during pregnancy should have protected them from bad birth outcomes; but they also felt that a healthy baby was their moral due, the just consequence of having made the right choices" (2009:37). As one said: "You know, I never realized that that could happen. . . . And that, why me? . . . why my kid? I never smoked. I never drank. . . . I never did anything wrong. I had a doctor from when I was four weeks on. You think there's no way" (p. 30). Another said:

> It tears at you that you worked so hard, and you ate well, and you exercised, and you did everything possible that you could do to make sure you had a healthy baby. . . . And there's hundreds of babies that their parents eat junk food and smoke cigarettes and do drugs. These babies don't seem to be born with birth defects. The anger that you feel when you work so hard, and you still end up with a baby's that got a problem. (pp. 30–31)

Still other women blamed the medical personnel for mismanaging "their child's birth or subsequent health care," portraying them "as having undermined all the hard work they had personally done to ensure the healthy development of the fetus" (pp. 39–40).

In general, fathers tend to be more stoic, less emotional than mothers when hearing the news that their child has a disability, a reaction that is consistent with traditional gender role socialization. They may think that men in the family are supposed to be able to "fix" things and feel impotent to do so. Whereas mothers are more concerned with their ability to cope with childcare responsibilities, fathers are more anxious about the prospects of their child—especially their sons—adopting socially acceptable behaviors, participating in sports, and enjoying occupational success (Lamb and Meyer 1991; Marshak, Seligman, and Prezant 1999; Meyer 1995; Naseef 2001).

Overall, parents feel a range of emotions, including guilt, denial, anger, and grief, the latter precipitating "a mourning period much like the death of a family member" (Marshak, Seligman, and Prezant 1999:32; Meyer 1995; Naseef 2001). Most expectant parents have a lot of hopes and dreams for their children, and some of these will need to be let go. Over the long term, however, parental sorrow is more likely "to be periodic rather than continuous, with the level of intensity" varying according to the child's accomplishment, or nonaccomplishment, of various developmental goals and transitional life experiences, as well as the coping styles of individual parents (Marshak, Seligman, and Prezant 1999:48; see also Graungaard, Andersen, and Skov 2011; Ytterhus, Wendelborg, and Lundeby 2008).

Measuring Up to the Norm

In contemporary society, parents', teachers', and physicians' perceptions of children and their expectations regarding their performance are filtered through a medical model that defines disability as a property of the child, concerning itself with the diagnosis and treatment of impairments that signal a deviation from the norm (see Chapter 2). Lennard Davis (1995) traces the emergence of the notion of the "average" or "norm" to the mid-nineteenth century, which he contrasts with the notion of the "ideal." Offering the example of the nude Venus, Davis argues that historically the concept of the ideal body was an imaginative and unobtainable form, linked to the divine and never to be found in the real world. As Landsman explains, "in a culture with an ideal form of a body, *all* individual members of the population are below the ideal [and] there can be no demand that people have bodies that conform to the ideal" (2009:71).

Davis credits the French statistician Adolph Quetelet (1796–1874) with formulating the concept of the average human as "the average of all human attributes in a given country," which paradoxically became "a kind of ideal, a position devoutly to be wished" (1995:26–27). Nowadays this is ascertained through pediatric examinations and standardized tests that are used to evaluate a child's achievement of developmental milestones that measure whether he or she is atypically below an acceptable deviation from the norm in the areas of physical, cognitive, and/or social development. Infants and toddlers, for example, "are expected to be able to turn over, crawl, walk, [and] utter words" within certain windows of time (Leiter 2007:1631).

Physicians realize that every child develops at his or her own pace, so when children seem to be lagging behind, they will in most instances adopt a "wait and see" approach, not wanting to jump to conclusions or err in such a serious matter (Naseef 2001). While some parents will resist a diagnosis of disability, hoping that a developmental delay, for instance, is not a sign of mental retardation, others want answers as soon as possible so they can become eligible for needed services and get on with a protocol of rehabilitative treatment (Hogan 2012; Landsman 2009; Leiter 2007; Naseef 2001). As one mother explains, "I feel that doctors still tend to keep quiet until it gets to a point where it's too obvious . . . and [they finally] say, 'yes it is cerebral palsy.' . . . I'd rather know up front if I've got an instinct there's something wrong" (Garth and Aroni 2003:569). Moreover, parental anxiety can be "heightened when doctors use medical jargon instead of down-to-earth language to explain their concerns and uncertainties" (Naseef 2001:227). Some parents may also "engage in 'doctor shopping,' which may make them susceptible to 'quack' treatments, although some shopping may be necessary to reach a professional who can make a definitive diagnosis" and recommend the best available treatment (Marshak, Seligman, and Prezant 1999:49). Almost all of the parents in Ong-Dean's (2009) study engaged in some degree of "lay re-skilling" to educate themselves about their child's condition (see Lupton 1997), with about half reading twenty or more articles and two or more books, as well as attending two or more support meetings held by specific disability groups.

In all fairness to physicians, the complexity of many developmental problems requires an evaluation by a multidisciplinary team of specialists, and access to these medical resources may be out of the reach of families who lack adequate health insurance. Moreover, parents often ask doctors to make predictions they cannot make, such as "When will she walk?" "Will his learning catch up with other kids?" "Will she grow out of it?" (Landsman 2009:64). On the other hand, many parents report hearing an overly negative prognosis that turned out to be wrong (Hogan 2012; Naseef 2001).

In 1975, the US Congress passed the **Education for All Handicapped Children Act**, reauthorized and amended in the **Individuals with Disabilities Education Act** in 1990, guaranteeing a free public education to children with disabilities, along with appropriate accommodations and special education services (Fleischer and Zames 2001; Marshak, Seligman, and Prezant 1999). In an amendment passed in 1986, it also created the **Early Intervention Program**, which provides services to children under the age of three who have been identified as having a developmental disability. Currently, a child is deemed eligible for this program when she or he "(i) is experiencing developmental delays, as measured by appropriate diagnostic instru-

FURTHER EXPLORATION

Box 4.2 Is the Prevalence of Autism Increasing?

In Chapter 1, we noted that it was not until the 1990s that the notion of autism as consisting of a spectrum of conditions became popularized. Since then there has been a rise in reported cases, but the reasons for this rise are unclear (King and Bearman 2011). Autism appears to have a genetic component, but environmental toxins are implicated as well. In the 2000s, a movement of parents with autistic children came to believe, based on research that later proved to be unsound, if not fraudulent, that the presence of mercury in childhood vaccinations was causing an epidemic of autism (Langan 2011; Offit 2008). This movement gained a lot of attention through the efforts of Jenny McCarthy, "an actress and author of popular books about pregnancy and childbirth," who published a book entitled *Louder Than Words: A Mother's Journey into Healing Autism* in 2007 (Langan 2011:198).

Also implicated in the rise of autism prevalence is the greater tendency on the part of medical professionals to diagnose children's presenting symptoms as autism, leading to what some researchers describe as a **diagnostic substitution effect** (Bishop et al. 2008; Coo et al. 2008; King and Bearman 2009, 2011; Shattuck 2006). Thus, a few studies have found that increased rates of autism have been "accompanied by concurrent declines in the prevalence of mental retardation and other developmental disabilities" (King and Bearman 2011:324). In a study of California, for example, Marissa King and Peter Bearman (2009) found that nearly a quarter of the increase in identified autism cases was attributable to these effects. Research also has found that "community resources—including screening resources, service availability, educational spending levels, the number of school-based health centers, and the number of pediatricians in the community—have been tied" to the prevalence of autism diagnoses (King and Bearman 2011:324; see also Barbaresi et al. 2005; Mandell and Palmer 2005; Palmer et al. 2005).

ments and procedures in one or more areas of cognitive development, physical development, communication development, and adaptive development; or (ii) has a diagnosed physical or mental condition that has a high probability of resulting in developmental delay" (cited in Leiter 2007:1634).

Some parents, intuitively aware that their child needs help, desire eligibility for early childhood services, while others are reluctant to have their child labeled as developmentally delayed or disabled (Leiter 2007; Ryan and Runswick-Cole 2008). As their child gets older and is eligible to attend public school, children who have not yet been labeled face being "outed" by teachers and other school officials. At this point, parents may have mixed feelings about whether their child would be better off or worse off by receiving special education services. Though they may think that their child needs help, they also worry that a label would lower teachers' expectations and put them at risk of being made fun of by their school peers (Connor and Ferri 2007; Marshak, Seligman, and Prezant 1999). On the other hand, parents of children who are bright but have various learning disabilities and/or attention deficit/hyperactivity issues may find school officials reluctant to recommend their child for services. As one parent said:

> All the teachers in the preschool . . . described her as a "free spirit" rather than as a child with significant problems. Only one student teacher even mentioned that we might anticipate difficulty in the first grade. . . . Rather than plant negative expectations from the outset, we decided that maybe we should take a wait and see approach. After all, only one teacher out of many even noticed any difficulties at all. Maybe she would blend in, maybe the summer [would be] a time of maturation. . . . But . . . [w]ithin the first three months of first grade, our daughter was behind in everything, couldn't attend to a task, and came home with a daily note in red across the top of her reading worksheets which said "Will not listen!" When we agreed that she definitely needed school-based assistance, the school evaluators said she scored too high on some tests to have a justifiable problem. (Marshak, Seligman, and Prezant 1999:68)

Other parents note that they had worked hard with their child at home to help prepare them to meet normative expectations at school, only to find that they still came up short. As one parent said:

> You spend years teaching your child how to throw and catch a ball. She finally gets it right and you are ecstatic. It is one of those moments of joy and satisfaction that your child can learn and progress with attention and practice. Suddenly your joy is tempered by the realization that while you have spent years mastering the simple task of throwing and catching, your child's peers have worked on batting, basketball, soccer. . . . (Marshak, Seligman, and Prezant 1999:71)

FURTHER EXPLORATION

Box 4.3 Learning Disabilities

The term "learning disability," which first gained credence in the early 1960s, is used as an umbrella category that refers to a variety of conditions that affect "people's ability to either interpret what they see and hear or to link information with different parts of the brain" (National Institute of Mental Health [NIMH] 1993:4). These limitations can show up "as specific difficulties with spoken and written language, coordination, self-control, or attention" that impede a person's ability in the areas of reading, writing, and mathematics, as well as difficulties with fine motor skills (such as those needed for cutting and writing) and gross motor skills (such as those needed for coordinated movement) (1993:4). Learning problems related to attention deficit, hyperactivity, and autism may co-occur with learning disabilities but are not the same as them; neither are learning disabilities the same as intellectual disabilities. There appears to be a genetic factor in some learning disabilities, since they tend to run in families. However, prenatal exposure to toxins, including a mother's use of alcohol and drugs, as well as environmental toxins such as lead are also implicated (Engel and Munger 2003; Heward 2008; NIMH 1993). Currently, 4.3 percent of all public school students, and nearly half of all students who qualify for special education services, are diagnosed with at least one specific type of learning disability, making it the largest single type of disability among children in the United States (Danforth 2009; Dillon 2007; National Center for Education Statistics 2011).

The Child's Perspective

Thus far we have focused on the parents' perspective on childhood disability. But what about the perspective of the children themselves? Here, for the most part, we have to rely on adults' retrospective reflections of their childhood, since research with children with disabilities is sparse (Garth and Aroni 2003). In one of the few studies based on interviews with children, Clare Connors and Kirsten Stalker (2007) asked seven- to fifteen-year-olds to talk about various aspects of their experience. When asked about the main source of information about their impairments, the youths uniformly said it was their parents, who gave them one of three types of explanations: "the child was 'special,' [the] impairment was part of God's plan for the family, or there had been an accident or illness around the time of birth" (p. 24). Overall, however, there was little discussion in the family about their impairments; a number of youths said they had never talked about it, and in some cases there seemed to be a pattern of avoidance about the subject.

Connors and Stalker also found that most of the children had undergone "multiple hospital admissions, operations and regular outpatient appointments" but at the same time had acquired "a practical, pragmatic attitude" toward their circumstance, with none viewing it as a "tragedy" and some saying it was not a "big deal" (2007:24–25). On the other hand, the children did experience cruelty from other children, with almost half being the victims of bullying. One boy said he was "made fun of" at school nearly every day (p. 28).

Frequent hospitalizations and medical procedures are also a topic in retrospective accounts of childhoods. Earlier, for example, we introduced Emily Rapp, who was born in 1974 with a congenital bone-and-tissue disorder that eventually required amputation of her left leg just above her knee. The procedures were done progressively, beginning with her foot a few months before she was four years old. By the time she was eight, she had had dozens of operations.[4] Of her first operation, Rapp recalls:

> I never fully understood the gravity of what was going on or what was at stake. . . . Nothing at that age seems permanent; a person believes that everything can be fixed. What I knew was that Mom slept in a cot she made up in the morning before the nurses came around; people were nice to me; the baby with cancer whose room was next to mine had wispy, angel-like hair. I liked worrying about her. Cancer was far worse than anything I had or ever would have. I was told it could kill you. (2007:27)

Emily does remember feeling phantom pain, which results from the brain continuing to send false messages to the limbs that have been removed, and when the pain came, Emily's mother "would rub the 'ghost' of [her] foot for hours" (p. 27). For years she also had a horrible, recurring nightmare of "a trash bin for amputated limbs—a huge, green-sided metal bin big enough to fit several people inside. Nurses and doctors I had never met had the job of dumping the newly severed parts. . . . Inside were piles of bare, amputated feet, hands, entire legs and arms, all floating in blood" (p. 28). Emily also recalls the discomfort of having to wear a cast, how hot it was during the summer and how it smelled. And then there were the exercises and physical therapy, and how to explain to the other kids who asked, "What happened to your leg?" (p. 31).

> For a few weeks, my stump, when it was briefly free of the Ace bandage, was a red and shriveled thing, like a mutilated, blood-soaked baseball bat. The skin smelled rank, and the bones inside felt like noodles. . . . These were my first real memories of my body. They were already memories of a body that would be no more, that was on its way out, disappearing. . . . I thought of myself as linked to . . . the stump I'd been given, the way I could move the muscles on the bottom and the side; . . . the way I could bend it like a length of flexible tubing and fold it across my right leg in order to sit cross-legged on the floor. That was my body. At this young age, I simply accepted the body as it was, while also feeling anxious to be more mobile, to really *move.* (p. 37)

Like Emily Rapp, Diane DeVries (born 1950) was born with a limb abnormality, but in her case she was without lower limbs entirely and with only "above-elbow upper extremity stumps of about equal length" (Frank 1988:98). When she was five years old, Diane was fitted with prosthetic devices, and later she started using "a three-wheel scooter propelled by crutches held with her artificial arms."

> At about 12, [Diane] started to use an electric wheelchair, which to her appeared more normal . . . than the tripod-like scooter; at the same time, she rejected the artificial arms, which she now describes as having made her look like "a little Frankie" (Franken-stein monster). During those years, Diane underwent numerous surgeries to blunt the growth of bone spurs in her upper extremity stumps. It was Diane's dream to learn to use functional artificial legs, but this was judged to be clinically impossible. For a period of time in high school, she wore a pair of nonfunctional cosmetic legs. . . . Unaided by prostheses, Diane is able to write with a pen held between stump and cheek, to feed herself with an adapted fork on an arm band, to pick up a glass, to use a push-button phone, to open a door by the door knob, and to operate the lever on her electric wheelchair. (pp. 98–99)

Diane's current view about prostheses is that they are purely cosmetic, that she has as much or more functionality without them. They can at times be painful to wear, too, as the rubbing of the stump

against skin can cause sores. Of her childhood, Diane recalls sub-
scribing to her father's naturalistic explanation for her limb deficiencies: "It was just something that happened" (Frank 1988:103). When
asked how old she was when she first realized she was different from
other people, she says, "It never hit me one day. . . . I realized that
right away." When asked if she had been aware that people outside
her family were staring at her, she says, "I always knew it. It was
always there because my body was different." When asked how she
felt about it, Diane says, "Certain things could happen during the day
to make me sad or mad, 'cause I could go . . . weeks without it both-
ering me at all, because nothing happened. But something *could*
[always] happen" (p. 103).[5]

Like Diane DeVries, Matt Glowacki (born 1973) came to the
conclusion that wearing a prosthetic device was not suitable for him.
Matt was born with normal arms, but without legs; as an adult, his
lower limbs extend just 13 to 14 inches below his pelvis. At the time
of his birth, Matt's parents have told him, the doctors were unsure if
he would even live, because they were concerned about other complications that might develop. In recounting his story, Matt glosses
over his parents' reactions and focuses instead on practical matters
related to the accessibility of his family's home. They had just built a
new tri-level house and thought about selling it, but they decided that
Matt would just have to learn how to get up and down the stairs on
his own. "I kind of did a shoulder roll up and down the stairs," he
recalls, aided by draw handles that his father installed on the side of
the stairs that Matt used to pull himself along (Berger 2009b:64).

When Matt was a toddler, at a time when other kids his age were
walking, he crawled around on the floor. Then his parents bought
him a Tonka truck that he laid on and pushed with his hands. After
that, he moved on to a skateboard. He also tried artificial legs for a
while, but they felt unnatural and he did not like them. Nonetheless,
Matt wore the prostheses on and off for about nine years. By the
ninth grade, however, he started incorporating a wheelchair into his
repertoire of assistive devices (Berger 2009b).

Matt says that the conventional thinking during his youth was
that amputees or other people without limbs should wear prostheses
so they could look like everyone else. In fact, the doctors told Matt
that in order to grow up "normal," he needed to be as tall as the other
kids. Matt thinks that prostheses might be more suitable for amputees

who have their knees intact. In that case, one could probably walk as well with artificial legs as without them. But because Matt's legs are too short, they do not serve as effective levers that allow him to manipulate the prostheses. If he used them, he would have to walk with crutches, which would be much slower than the wheelchair he uses today. Matt looks at prostheses like a toupee, something you wear for appearance, but that has no functionality for people like him (Berger 2009b).

Like many other children with disabilities, Amy Bleile (born 1977) underwent repeated surgeries during her childhood. Born four months premature, barely viable at a little over two pounds, "Everyone thought I was going to die," she recalls being told by her mother (Berger 2009b:77). After a while, Amy's mother realized that her daughter was not reaching the developmental milestones expected of children her age, and she suspected that something was wrong. The doctors tried to assure her that Amy's delays were due to her premature birth. At the age of two, however, she was diagnosed with cerebral palsy.

During the first few years of her life, Amy was enrolled in an in-patient hospital preschool where she periodically stayed six weeks at a time—without her parents, which the staff said would be distracting—to receive physical and occupational therapy. As one would hope, Amy's mother was a loving parent who advocated on her daughter's behalf, but Amy's father was another matter altogether. He was an alcoholic and an emotionally abusive man who never accepted the reality of Amy's impairment. He simply thought that Amy was lazy and all that she needed was a healthy dose of tough love. Amy's parents eventually divorced, and Amy, her younger brother and sister, and her mother were often in dire financial straits. Nonetheless, Amy found her early school experiences fairly easy to bear—it was not until high school that things got bad for her (see Chapter 5)—but she did have to be bused to an accessible school, which was not the same school as her siblings attended. There were also many hospitalizations during the school year, which disrupted her education (Berger 2009b).

Thus far we have been talking about youths who have a **congenital disability**, which refers to a condition that develops before, during, or shortly after birth. In contrast, Jeremy Lade has an **acquired disability**, one that occurs later in life, in his case a result of an automobile accident he was in when he was eight years old. On a family trip in the summer of 1989, the Lade family was hit by a truck that veered in front of their car. Jeremy was wearing a seatbelt, but it was resting too high on his torso; later the Lades learned that this was due to a design defect. Jeremy bolted forward as the vehicles collided, bending at his navel and shattering one of the vertebrae in his back. A piece of the vertebrae cut through his spinal cord, and he was instantly paralyzed. "I couldn't feel my legs," Jeremy recalls, "I knew it right away" (Berger 2009b:84).

Jeremy's brother, who was a couple inches taller and thus avoided the same fate, broke his back. But after months of wearing a back brace and undergoing rehabilitation, he made a full recovery. His mother broke her wrist, which required casting, and her face was cut badly; and his father incurred only a minor cut on his forehead. As he looks back on that day, Jeremy says, "It was kind of funny because all the ambulance people were worried about my eye," which was cut and bleeding and required two stitches. They kept shouting, "We got to take care of his eye! We got to take care of his eye!" (Berger 2009b:84).

After Jeremy was taken to the hospital, the doctors performed exploratory surgery to make sure there was no internal bleeding, which there was not. The next ten to twelve days were a blur. "I didn't really know what was going on," he says. "People were coming and going. It took a while for everything to sink in" (Berger 2009b:84). Jeremy recalls that his mother was "pretty tore up about it. My dad too. . . . But they were pretty strong in front of me, which made me strong too." Eventually, Jeremy came to view his predicament as "an obstacle that I just had to overcome." When things got hard, he would think, "I can beat this" (p. 84).

Jeremy initially spent only about three weeks in the hospital, undergoing physical therapy and learning how to use a wheelchair— "some old folding chair," not the sporting kind he uses today (Berger 2009b:85). His parents also had to make modifications to their home so that it was wheelchair accessible. At considerable expense for a family of modest means, the Lades installed a wheelchair ramp and widened the front door to make room for his chair.

Up until that time, Jeremy had never seen anyone in his small town in northern Wisconsin using a wheelchair, and it was "a struggle every day," he says, to learn how to use one to get around (Berger 2009b:85). His father taught him to "jump" up and down curbs, because there were no curb cuts, which was "a painful process [with] many a bump on the back of [his] head." His mother tried to coddle him a bit, but his father would have none of that, realizing that Jeremy needed to learn how to do things on his own. Since the elementary school he had been attending was inaccessible to wheelchairs, Jeremy also had to switch schools and make new friends, a difficult process for any youth of that age. But Jeremy thinks the experience made him more outgoing than he otherwise would have been if he "had just hung out with the same group of friends [he had known] since Kindergarten" (p. 85).[6]

Impact on Family Life

Up until the first half of the twentieth century, parents were routinely encouraged to institutionalize their disabled children, and those who decided to take care of them at home were often told that to do so would deprive them of vital therapeutic and educational services. But in the 1960s and 1970s, as a corollary of the emerging independent living movement, a coalition of disabled adults, parents, and professionals began working to increase access to community services that would enable families to better care for disabled children at home (Calton 2010; Landsman 2009; Leiter 2004). Commenting on "the fact that alternatives to raising a disabled child at home are chosen by other women," none of the mothers in Landsman's study "sought information about such options; all were raising their child . . . at home and planned to continue to do so" (2009:7). Robert Naseef observes that nowadays the pendulum has even swung the other way, as parents "are routinely expected to care for a child . . . regardless of the severity of the situation . . . [or] how it affects each family member" (2001:247). Still, many children with disabilities are put up for adoption, and about 12 percent of all adopted children ages five to fifteen in the United States have at least one disability, including about 20 percent of children with Down syndrome, who are typically relinquished by their birth parents almost immediately after diagnosis. Many of these children first live in foster families before they are adopted, with some foster parents adopting multiple disabled children during the course of their lifetimes (Glidden 2006).

Much of the family literature on raising a child with a disability focuses on the ongoing stress of family life, especially the demands

on time and financial resources (Calton 2010; Naseef 2001; Neff 2010). As Marshak and colleagues observe, the "chronicity of care" involved in raising a child with a disability constitutes a central element that distinguishes these families from those confronting more acute crises (1999:25).

> For some families, the care is necessary 24 hours a day, 7 days a week, for many years. The stress can be relentless, draining the family physically and psychologically. Add to this the financial worries that may exist, and the family has the potential for being at risk. The degree to which the family has problems may depend on how it conceptualizes its life circumstance, how supportive family members are of one another, the availability of social support outside the family, and the existence of financial concerns or other family problems. (p. 25)

In one of the most definitive studies to date, Dennis Hogan (2012) culled data from more than a half dozen US national surveys and interviews with two dozen mothers of children with disabilities. He found that parents of children with disabilities had a higher likelihood of getting a divorce than other parents, much of this due to the stress of financial insecurity and the difficulties of balancing caregiving and employment. Mothers were less likely than fathers to be involved in paid employment, and single mothers were especially struggling to make ends meet and provide the care that their children needed. Hogan also found that about a third of the children with disabilities were living in single-parent households, and about a third of the families raising children with disabilities were living in poverty. Other research indicates that the poverty rate among families living with childhood disability was highest for African Americans, followed by Hispanics and Native Americans, and then Pacific Islanders and Asian Americans. The lowest rate was for Caucasians (Wang 2005).

These burdens notwithstanding, many families exhibit remarkable adaptability and resilience. Much of their ability to respond in this way, as we have suggested, depends on whether or not the parents are embedded in a system of supportive relationships. In this regard, the other children in the family are key factors. They may need to help out more with caretaking than would otherwise be the case. There are risks in doing so, however, as they may feel angry and resentful (and feel guilty for feeling this way) for having to put their lives "on hold" while the family gathers its resources to take care of a disabled child. They may have difficulty talking about their feelings with their parents, a topic that makes them feel even more uncomfortable than sex. If the lines of communication are left open, however, these issues can be resolved. Sometimes having a child with a disability in the home can also bring the family closer together, and in the long run siblings may turn out to be more caring people than those who live their lives in a more self-centered manner (Grossman 1972; Marshak, Seligman, and Prezant 1999; Meyer 1995; Naseef 2001).

The support of grandparents, especially their ability to provide childcare, can also be important. On the one hand, grandparents can be a source of stress if they are not accepting of the child. On the other hand, some grandparents may be even more receptive "because they are one step removed" and are not involved in the childrearing on a constant basis (Marshak, Seligman, and Prezant 1999:65).

The support of other relatives and friends is important for a successful family experience with childhood disability, too. Eric Barber was born in 1970 with a rather severe case of scoliosis, an abnormal curvature of the spine. When he was three years old, life-threatening complications necessitated surgery that left him paralyzed and in need of a wheelchair for mobility. When he was a child, however, he did not have much trouble accepting his condition; to him, it was just the way things were. He attributes this attitude to the way he was treated by his family, including his extended family of relatives.[7] Eric regularly played with a dozen or so of his cousins, who never coddled him. He credits them with starting, in his words, "my love affair with sports, because they included me in everything they did" (Berger 2009b:52).[8] Eric wrestled with them in his wheelchair, pitched or played the outfield when they played baseball, and ran pass patterns or played quarterback when they played football. He even got *tackled* in his chair! "I don't know if they really thought of me as disabled," he wonders, "if it crossed their minds or if they thought they were doing something noble. . . . [But] they treated me as a player like everyone else . . . not as their cousin with a disability" (p. 52).

In addition to a family support system, or in the absence of one, parents often find that they need to become advocates for their children to access the resources they need, especially in their schools, even to the point of getting involved in political activism (Darling

1988; Naseef 2001; Ryan and Runswick-Cole 2008). This advocacy extends to playing an intermediary role in everyday interactions. In his research with mothers of children with autism, for example, Bill Rocque (2010) heard stories from mothers who felt they needed to explain their child's unusual behavior to others. One mother told him of an incident in which she had to explain to a receptionist at a doctor's office, who was looking visibly uncomfortable, that her son's crying quite loudly was not evidence of a "spoiled child" but of autism. A couple of the mothers also told him of proactively approaching new neighbors to assuage their discomfort: "I might say that 'this is Trevor; he has autism. And what that might mean is that you might find him in the back of your pickup cab, or on the top of your car.' I just try to make it kind of light hearted . . . to anticipate what somebody might be uncomfortable about, and help them get over that" (p. 494). Another mother said:

> I went over and I introduced myself, and I brought Taylor with me. . . . When Taylor left I said, "by the way, he is a very high-functioning autistic, so there are some little strange things you might see him do, just so you're aware." I don't say much more than that, because they won't quite understand. I just give a brief little explanation so that whatever he does they're not going to be like "what's wrong with that kid?" (p. 492)

Such efforts at mediation notwithstanding, some parents find themselves increasingly isolated from their neighbors and even their old friends. Remarks from the following parents interviewed in other studies are indicative of this experience:

> I noticed a change in our friends, or maybe I just started noticing the kinds of things they were saying about kids with problems and didn't like what I was hearing. I just stopped seeing them. When it became apparent that people didn't understand our son's behavior, it just became easier to stay at home. (Marshak, Seligman, and Prezant 1999:83)

> With most people, [it's] "don't bring Lisa around. If you have to I understand but we prefer you don't." . . . Friends . . . basically don't want anything to do with you. They just don't want to be bothered. . . . "It's not my kid. It's your kid. It's your problem. . . . Thank God it's not me." (Green et al. 2011:145)

> All the [friends] I had before [Brandon] was born are gone. My best friend, Molly, won't call me anymore. She says I have no time

for her. They don't understand . . . why I have to take him with me, and they can't deal with the things that he does, or how he looks. (Hogan 2012:50)

Regardless of the challenges facing parents of children with disabilities, many families find that caring for a disabled child is a life-affirming experience that brings unexpected rewards. In Donald Meyer's anthology *Uncommon Fathers: Reflections on Raising a Child with a Disability* (1995), some of the fathers describe having a disabled child as an opportunity for personal growth, not the least of which is a greater awareness about disability issues, about the issues we have been discussing in this book. As one father said:

> I've realized personal growth by trying to transcend my own selfish interests. . . . I have been indelibly sensitized to the misfortunate in our society. I have developed far greater compassion. This is part of a life-long journey—I would not have come this way if Andy hadn't come into my life. And the seeds of a good man are already sown in the soul of Andy's brother. . . .
>
> I am humbled by the dignity and strength with which other families bear the weight of their disability—some burdened with inconceivably dreadful situations. . . . [Y]et each day these families sacrifice and struggle to create a fulfilling and dignified life for these children and their siblings. These are incredibly gritty, courageous struggles, and there are many unsung heroes. (pp. 23–24)

Another father described his feelings this way: "Jessica has taught me what true love is. . . . The joy of loving is its own reward. . . . Life is a precious gift to be cherished and nurtured the best you know how. . . . Jessica taught me that life doesn't *have* quality, life *is* quality" (p. 203).

In her study of mothers of children with disabilities, Landsman (2009) heard similar stories of personal transformation and descriptions of children as giving parents the gift of caring, the most precious of which, the mothers said, was the gift of unconditional love. As one mother explained:

> Years ago . . . I had asked the Lord to teach me unconditional love, and I think I wanted him to diffuse it into my brain—not have to go through any fiery experience and to burn it into me—but I just wanted to know what it was like to love people without putting expectations on them of performance and other things, and it really wasn't until six months later that we found out about Ryan . . . so this situation is invaluable in that way. . . . I learned about my own

conditional love . . . and there never would have been a spotlight on it if it hadn't been for Ryan. (p. 150)

Another mother put it this way:

I remember saying—praying one time, you know, in a little personal moment, it's like "Geez, I really wish I knew what unconditional love was." I have these relationships and I love them, *if* they're good, *if* they love me, *if* they give me cards, *if* they—it's like, I want to know what that real unconditional love is. It's like, hello! Be careful what you ask for because you might just get it. (pp. 150–151)

The Dilemmas of Special Education

Prior to the passage of the Education for All Handicapped Children Act (EAHCA) in 1975, four million children in the United States did not receive special education (SE) services, and another one million "received no schooling whatsoever" (Connor and Ferri 2007:63). With the passage of the EAHCA, however, children with disabilities were not only entitled to a free public education accompanied by appropriate accommodations and services, but also to be placed in the "least restrictive" educational environment. What that term meant, however, remained subject to dispute, and for years disabled children continued to be isolated in segregated settings—in residential programs, separate schools, and segregated classes in regular public schools, often in a basement or separate trailer facility (Marshak, Seligman, and Prezant 1999). It took a series of lawsuits and appellate court decisions between 1979 and 1994 to enforce the least restrictive mandate, requiring schools to provide any necessary supplemental aids, including assistive technology and teacher aides, to integrate children with disabilities in regular classrooms (Fleischer and Zames 2001). However, in *Hartmann v. Loudown County Board of Education* (1997), an important federal appellate court case involving an autistic youth, the court ruled that "mainstreaming was not required when (a) a student with a disability would not receive benefit from such a placement, (b) marginal benefits would be significantly outweighed by benefits that could be obtained in a separate setting and (c) the student is an ongoing disruptive force" in the classroom (Connor and Ferri 2007:68).[9]

The process of qualifying for SE services entails an evaluation by a team of school officials, including a teacher, and depending on the nature of the disability, a school psychologist, physical therapist, and/or speech pathologist. Assessments "may include formal tests, observations, and family history," as well as evaluations of "sensory and motor functioning, intellectual ability, academic achievement, communication skills, and social and emotional status" (Marshak, Seligman, and Prezant 1999:199). Reports from outside professionals, including medical doctors, may also be included in the evaluation.

As noted earlier, some parents want their children to qualify for services, while others are concerned about the adverse effects of labeling their child as a person with special needs. The ambivalence that some feel about this dilemma is further complicated by the documented racial disparities in official labeling, with African Americans three times more likely than Caucasians to be labeled mentally retarded, two times more likely to be labeled emotionally disturbed, and nearly one and a half times more likely to be labeled learning disabled (Parrish 2002).[10] Students from lower-class backgrounds are also more likely to be diagnosed with learning disabilities than students from higher-class backgrounds, and boys are more likely to be diagnosed than girls (Carrier 1986; Coutinho and Oswald 2005; Shifrer, Muller, and Callahan 2010).[11]

The reasons for these disparities are not completely understood, however. In their research on learning disabilities, for example, Dara Shifrer, Chandra Muller, and Rebecca Callahan (2010) found that socioeconomic status explains the disparities by race, but it is not clear whether this association is due to discrimination or actual disabilities that are a consequence of environmental factors affecting childhood development—such as fewer familial resources, poorer nutrition and health, and underfunded schools—that put the poor and racial minorities at risk (see also Shonkoff and Phillips 2000). Somewhat ironically, when the learning disability construct first gained credence in the 1960s, it was higher-status parents who were most interested in receiving the diagnosis for their children so they could receive SE services while not being considered mentally retarded (Carrier 1986). But over time, as the diagnosis was institutionalized, the hitherto mentioned disparities emerged (Ong-Dean 2006).[12]

The statistical disparities notwithstanding, if a child is deemed eligible for SE, an **Individualized Educational Plan** (IEP) is written that includes a "description of the child's present levels of performance," the "annual goals and short-term objectives for the children to target during the coming year, . . . the services and specialized instruction to be provided . . . and how they will be provided," the amount of time the child will spend in a regular classroom setting, and the criteria and methods that will be used to evaluate progress (Marshak, Seligman, and Prezant 1999:119). By law, parents have a right to participate in the meetings that are held to discuss the IEP, and national surveys indicate that 86 to 93 percent of parents of disabled children had attended a meeting in the current or preceding year (Special Education Elementary Longitudinal Study 2005).[13] Families with household incomes of $25,000 or less reported somewhat lower attendance than those with higher incomes, and African American and Hispanic families reported somewhat lower attendance than Caucasian families, but these differences were not large.

When parents and school officials are on the same page, IEP meetings tend to be uneventful, but if there is a difference of opinion, they can be quite tense. Often parents feel intimidated and are reluctant to challenge the authority of the school staff, even when they think their child has been incorrectly diagnosed or is receiving the wrong programming, and they often feel like token participants, given the opportunity to speak but feeling "that their opinions are irrelevant next to the opaque technical reports of school professionals" (Ong-Dean 2009:28). While educators welcome parental support and involvement, they expect parents "to trust their judgments and assessments" (Lareau and Horvat 1999:42). Not surprisingly, parents of professional and relatively privileged backgrounds are generally more successful in negotiating the system and getting what they need for their children, but even these parents can find the process quite frustrating (Hogan 2012; Leiter 2012).

Nevertheless, advocates of SE believe that with proper diagnosis and assistance children with disabilities can develop alternative learning strategies that will help them keep up with their peers and be successful in school and later in their occupational careers (Kemp, Smith, and Segal 2012; Kirk 2002; NIMH 1993). Whether this is best accomplished in separate or inclusive settings, however, has provoked considerable disagreement (Connor and Ferri 2007).[14] Critics believe that SE in segregated settings lowers expectations for students and contributes to the long-term exclusion of people with disabilities from mainstream society. According to Len Barton and Felicity Armstrong, "The existence of segregated provisions, catering for 'special' pupils taught by 'special' teachers supported by 'special' courses in teacher training, has all contributed to the legitimation of values, attitudes, and practices that are inimical to the realization of an inclusive society and educational system" (2001:707; see also Lipsky and Gartner 1997). Writing specifically of learning disabilities, Scot Danforth summarizes the views of SE critics:

> Over the past three decades, the American public schools have misused the category of learning disability as a jargon-heavy, seemingly authoritative way of blaming individual students for the instructional and organizational shortcomings of the public schools. Rather than serving as a pathway to helpful treatment and support, the learning disability diagnosis has become a stigmatized ticket to an isolated classroom or school where the educational recipe consists of low academic expectations, an overrepresentation of students of color and those from low-income families, and decreased chances of high school graduation. (2009:15)

In a study based on "letters to the editor" published in newspapers, David Connor and Beth Ferri (2007) sampled a range of public opinion on the benefits and advantages of inclusion versus separation in SE. One mother of a boy who has autism explained her support for inclusion this way: "We want Mark to be a member of society. . . . Mark has gained many skills in the last three years [after being put in a regular classroom], skills that would be lost if he is put in a class with four other autistic children, as school officials recommended" (Connor and Ferri 2007:68). Another mother said that her son "may not be as intellectually capable as others in his grade, but he has greatly improved his self-esteem and his desire to go to school" after being put in a regular classroom (p. 66). Still another mother said that she once believed her son had a limited future, but with inclusion he had become "a self-sufficient young man who is not going to need a group home or supported work environment" (p. 66). And an art teacher noted an added benefit of inclusion: "My own children . . . [are] much more aware of handicapped people as just kids; they're not as fearful. I think that as adults we're accustomed to backing off. . . . This is a big advantage for everyone" (p. 66).

At the same time, mainstream teachers often feel woefully unprepared to teach children with special needs, and some parents fear that policies of inclusion will siphon off needed funds from the students who are in most need of SE and lead to the "dismantling of all that is good about existing services for children with disabilities" (Connor and Ferri 2007:64). As one woman said, "It is absurd to plan inclusion of students with significant disabilities in overcrowded classrooms where the teacher has received no more than a crash course in special education" (p. 72). One teacher who was cynical of inclusion added, "Many of us see this as sharing the air in a building, but not really having anything to do with the educational value for special education children. This is not an education plan but a space plan" (p. 72). Additionally, some opponents of inclusion believe that such policies are motivated more by a desire to control costs than by humanitarian considerations.[15]

Connor and Ferri also found that some parents were concerned about the ability of their children to keep up in mainstream class-rooms. As one parent said, inclusion "tosses the disabled child into an environment in which the child cannot possibly develop, and in fact, may regress, while simultaneously depriving the remainder of the class of critical classroom instruction" (2007:67). Similarly, a parent interviewed by Marshak and colleagues said:

> In order to keep up with the mainstream classes, the child's home-work workload sometimes exceeded five hours a day. Five hours of sheer torture. This was after spending a full day in school and com-ing home feeling frustrated, defeated, and exhausted. Other kids played outside, did things with friends, joined clubs, or relaxed while our child worked from the time she came home until we made her go to bed. The only break was for dinner. (Marshak, Seligman, and Prezant 1999:74)

Moreover, many people in the deaf and blind communities believe that separate education in specialized or residential schools is supe-rior to mainstreaming.[16] Leah Hager Cohen, for instance, thinks that deaf students benefit from an environment in which "all the students can converse with each other, all the information is presented visually, teachers sign and Deaf adults serve as role models" (1994a:11A). "To many Deaf people," she adds, inclusion "is at best maddeningly naïve; at worst, chauvinistic. The history of Deaf people is one of mandated assimilation: we can make you more like hearing people, we can make you more normal" (p. 11A; see Chapter 3).

Likewise, Beth Omansky (2011), who is legally blind—which she describes as residing in the "borderland" between being totally blind and partially sighted[17]—is also an advocate of separate education for blind students. As she writes:

> My parents wanted me to be as "normal" as possible, and so they decided to keep me in the regular public school system. They believed this would serve my overall development better than attending school with other blind children only. . . . However noble their hopes for me were (and I have no doubt they deeply wanted the best for me), an accessible education wherein I could learn blindness skills was traded off for the appearance of normality. (2011:76)

Omansky regrets that borderland blind people like herself are pushed to remain on the sighted side of the border. Consequently, they are encouraged to use the residual vision they have rather than learning how to read Braille, and this impedes development of reading skills and causes children to fall behind their sighted classmates. More generally, as Thomas Hehir (2002) observes, an ableist perspective that devalues disability and assumes "it is preferable for disabled students to do things in the same manner as nondisabled kids" pervades the educational system, including SE.

Connor and Ferri conclude that while many parents believe that their children's needs would not be met without SE services, the "paradox of special education is that it is both a service and a disservice" (2007:74). Margret Winzer (2000) thinks that the best strategy is to offer students a full range of services that avoids a "one size fits all" approach. Whether that entails "the child receiving educational services in the general classroom; moving out of the classroom for short periods of time to get remedial help; or working in a resource room, self-contained classroom, or even a separate setting must be determined individually" in terms of which educational environment will best help the child succeed and prepare him or her to become an active and productive citizen in society (p. 20).

Summary

This chapter began our two-chapter coverage of disability across the life course by focusing on childhood disability in the context of parental and familial relationships. First, we examined the initial responses and experiences of parents upon learning that their child has a disability. In addition to dealing with their own emotional issues, parents also were confronted with awkward and dispiriting reactions of others. We then considered the parental challenges and frustrations involved in assessing and receiving services for children who do not meet normative developmental milestones. We also examined the child's perspective on disability, primarily through retrospective accounts of past childhoods, offering examples of children with both congenital and acquired disabilities; and we looked at the impact of childhood disability on family life—the burdens, adaptations, and life-affirming experiences—including the practical and emotional impact on parents, siblings, and other relatives. Finally, we considered the dilemmas of special education services and the policy of including children with disabilities into mainstream classrooms.

Notes

1. Although cerebral palsy is a common diagnostic term, it glosses over a wide range of impairments. Some people with cerebral palsy are only affected in their lower body, some in their upper body, and some in both their upper and lower body. Some have intellectual disabilities and some do not. Some are able to speak and some cannot (Berger and Feucht 2011).

2. A 2004 national survey found that in 1986 20 percent of people with disabilities had acquired their disability before the age of nineteen, whereas in 2004 30 percent had acquired their disability before that age (National Organization on Disability/Harris Poll 2004).

3. Spina bifida entails an incomplete closure of the spinal column that occurs during the first month of pregnancy. Hydrocephalus entails an excess of cerebrospinal fluid in the cranial cavity. Like other disabilities, the degree of physical or cognitive impairment associated with these conditions may vary in severity.

4. When Rapp was six years old, she gained some notoriety as a "poster child" for the March of Dimes. We will discuss her story further in Chapter 5.

5. See Frank (2000) for a more complete account of DeVries's life.

6. Lade eventually became a world-class Paralympic wheelchair basketball player.

7. Preethy Samuel, Karen Hobden, and Barbara LeRoy (2011) found that racial/ethnic minority families were less likely than white families to seek out extrafamilial sources of community support. Rather, minority families, like Barber's African American clan, tended to rely on extended kinship networks of support. Samuel and colleagues also speculate that "minor-

ity families may be more resilient to disability related discrimination . . . because of exposure to discrimination in a race-related context" (pp. 72–73).

8. Like Lade, Barber became a world-class Paralympic wheelchair basketball player. When he was sixteen years old, he also had the opportunity to play Michael Jordan in a game of wheelchair basketball for a reality TV program called *NBC Sports Fantasy*. For an African American youth growing up in the city of Chicago who idolized Jordan, this was an especially momentous experience for Barber, who won the game, with Jordan trying his best, by a score of 20 to 14. For an account of the game, see Berger (2009b).

9. Margret Winzer and Kaz Mazurek describe the general state of affairs in US classrooms at the dawn of the twenty-first century in this way: "Although the most significant movement toward general classrooms has occurred in the disability categories that include students with the milder disabilities—learning disabilities, speech and language impairments, orthopedic impairments, and other health problems—in all other categories there is a trend toward moving students into less restrictive settings" (2000:xii).

10. While some studies in the 1970s and 1980s indicated that misdiagnosed Hispanic students were overrepresented among students officially labeled as mentally retarded, these disparities have abated over the years (Ong-Dean 2009). Still, minority students for whom English is a second language remain at risk of misdiagnosis (Artiles et al. 2005; Shifrer, Muller, and Callahan 2010).

11. Kristen Anderson (1997) suggests that the relatively "good" behavior of girls may allow them to slip "under the radar" of school officials.

12. See Carrier (1986) and Danforth (2009) for historical accounts of the development of the learning disability construct.

13. Students are also allowed to attend these meetings, though they are more likely to do so as they get older.

14. For a discussion of educational policy in comparative perspective, see Barton and Armstrong (2001).

15. Proponents of inclusion counter that part of teachers' and school officials' resistance to inclusion may stem from their concern that children with disabilities will lower average student scores on achievement tests that are used to evaluate teacher and school performance (Connor and Ferri 2007).

16. Specialized residential schools are available for youths with a range of disabilities. A study by the Joseph Rowntree Foundation found that residential schools were not a preferred option for a majority of parents, but they sought them out after negative experiences with nonresidential local schools. Although homesickness was common, some disabled youths said they liked the opportunity to become more independent and make friends with other youths like themselves (Abbott, Morris, and Ward 2001).

17. See Chapter 6 for a definition and further consideration of legal blindness.

5

Adolescence and Adulthood

HAVING THUS FAR DISCUSSED CHILDHOOD DISABILITY IN THE context of parental and familial relationships and controversies about special education services, this chapter continues our examination of disability across the life course, moving now to adolescence and adulthood. In doing so we will consider issues related to relationships with peers, the education system, the world of work, sexual and emotional intimacy, and health care and the receipt of paid personal assistive care.

The Trials and Tribulations of Adolescence

Adolescence as a distinct stage in the life course emerged in the late nineteenth century with the rise of industrialization and urbanization (Eisenstadt 1956; England 1967). With the concomitant emergence of compulsory education laws, school-age youths began to spend the greater part of their days segregated from adults in educational institutions. In contemporary society this segregation increases the frequency and intensity of interaction among peers who look to one another for social approval and personal validation (Berger 2009a; Schwartz and Merten 1967).

As is well known, adolescence is a tumultuous stage of the life course for all youths, but teenagers with disabilities face more than the usual array of challenges. Even the conventional dynamics of teenage rebellion can be more complicated. As one boy explains, "For me, one of the hardest things . . . was that I wanted to challenge and defy my parents, as many teenagers do. However, because I was physically dependent on them for personal care, my desire for independence seemed thwarted" (Marshak, Seligman, and Prezant 1999:123).

As early as elementary school, children begin to form gender-segregated small cliques that set themselves apart from other youths. During middle school, these cliques become more identifiable and consolidated, as young teens competing with each other for status recognition become more insensitive to youths who are perceived as lower status (Berger 2009a; Milner 2004). Thus seats at the lunch table, for instance, become public sites of competition for those who are included and those who are excluded from the group. One disabled student recalls his experience this way: "There was an empty seat at the table and when I asked if I could sit there, the kids said no, that the seat was reserved. One of the kids spit on me and pushed me and told me they didn't want me at the table" (Marshak, Seligman, and Prezant 1999:70). More often than not, however, students with disabilities are treated with pity rather than with hostility, but this is not a valued attribution either.

Emily Rapp, whom we introduced in Chapter 4, was not without friends during her adolescence, but she felt as if she was living a "split life," cheerful and gregarious on the outside, but also suffering on the inside because of her missing leg (2007:117). Throughout most of her life, Emily had refused to bare her artificial leg, even to the point of being "unbearably hot" during the summer because she would not wear shorts, "preferring instead to sweat profusely in pants or jeans" (p. 130). But one summer night, when she was sixteen years old, she gave into peer pressure and agreed to wear a miniskirt when she went out with two girlfriends who were also dressed that way. That was the period in her life, she recalls, when

> I agreed to do things I didn't want to do and laughed at jokes that weren't funny. I had just turned sixteen, and what I wanted more than anything else in life was to be beautiful. I didn't care about being smart, successful, or good. In fact, I believed that beauty was the prerequisite for achieving any of these other qualities.
>
> I was wearing a miniskirt because I thought, somehow, that if I dressed like these girls, I would become like them—sleek and pretty, with lithe, tanned legs. Popular. Self-confident. Desired. I

thought I could simply will myself into this type of being, into a different, magical life. (p. 128)

Earlier we noted feminism's analysis of the "politics of appearance," whereby the standardization of what constitutes a socially desirable body leads to the denigration of the disabled body (see Chapter 2). Although it is of course common for teenage girls to feel that their bodies do not meet such standards, the threat to one's self-esteem is greater for those who have disabilities. Indeed, as Emily recalls, "what was a *girl* without her body?" (p. 143). Thus Emily felt that her artificial leg was no match for the tanned, brownish color of her nondisabled friends. Of her friend Melissa, she reminisces:

I looked enviously at Melissa's long legs: . . . two perfectly matched, well-designed calves, the soft impression at the back of each knee; the even brown tan. . . . All of that perfectly constructed flesh taken for granted. And here I stood with my wooden leg and chubby white thigh. Melissa was the girl I aspired to be; the girl who could reach into that open box of cookies and eat one after the other while twirling the cord around her fingers and talking to her boyfriend. And she would not gain one pound because she was blessed with a rich family, a dark tan, a whole, beautiful body, and, of course, a high metabolism. . . . I felt completely fabricated next to Melissa. . . . I coveted her possessions, her body, her life. I envied her because there were so many things I had to assemble in the morning in order to leave the home. There was the cloth sock that rolled onto my stump before it fit into the artificial socket; there was the thick support underwear I wore to avoid sores near my crotch and cuts into my hip if the waist strap rubbed too hard. I buckled the strap below and to the left of my belly button and then adjusted the leg—twist left, twist right—before pulling on my pants and jeans. (pp. 138–139)

And then there were the boys, with Emily thinking that she'd never be able to gain their attention and affection. Thus, Emily thought, "Maybe I would always be running away from boys instead of sauntering up to them with naïve confidence tinged with nervousness as my friends did. I knew . . . that someday someone was going to want to see this leg, with a miniskirt, without a miniskirt, with the leg *off*" (p. 142).

Amy Bleile, whom we also introduced in Chapter 4, says she did not have problems with school or peers until high school. Until then she had been an A/B student; the only issues related to her cerebral palsy had to do with physical mobility, not her intelligence. But in high school she was required to take a battery of tests that were not required of other students to prove she was capable of attending regular classes. Amy recalls that on the first day of class, as she walked into her English class (with braces and using her walker), her teacher told her, "Excuse me, you're in the wrong room." Amy rechecked her class schedule and said, "No, it says this is the right room." The teacher replied, "No, the special ed room is down the hall." Amy was taken aback. "I'm sorry," she retorted, "but I'm not in special ed. This is where I'm *supposed* to be." By now the teacher was visibly upset, obviously not wanting Amy in his classroom. "I said the special ed room is down the hall," he repeated sternly (Berger 2009b:78).

This was only one of many battles that Amy and her mother had to fight at this high school in Dubuque, Iowa. Amy used her walker for half of the school day and her wheelchair for the other half. When she was out of her chair, school policy required her to keep it in a janitor's closet; the chair was a fire hazard, she was told. This created added hardship for Amy when she had to transfer in and out of her chair, which could take her several minutes, as the closet was very crowded. One time a ladder fell on her head and knocked her out for a few minutes. The closet also smelled of cleaning solvents, which made the air unhealthy for Amy to breathe.

Amy also had to endure other harassments from school officials. At the beginning of every school year, she was required to have her doctor write the school nurse a letter verifying that cerebral palsy was not a contagious disease. She also was only allowed to go to the bathroom at certain times of the day, and the teachers would time her to make sure she did not take too long. One time she was called into the principal's office for violating this rule, and the principal actually threw pencils at her and called her a "fucking cripple." An African American friend who had helped Amy in the bathroom was called to the office too; the principal called her a "nigger." During fire drills, Amy was required to stay in the building, because no one was willing to push her outside. When her friend finally did, one supervising teacher got upset and told her to get Amy back into the building.

Additionally, Amy was mistreated by other students who were never reprimanded for their misconduct. Students repeatedly knocked her over in the hallway, just for fun. One student even put rat poison in her lunch food, and another stomped on her foot and broke it. It seems unbelievable that things like this were still happening in the 1990s, but apparently that's how regressive parts of the Dubuque community were in their attitudes toward people who were "different." Eventually, Amy's mother called in the Dubuque Human Rights Commission, which cited the school for more than thirty violations.

Outside of school, Amy and her African American friends were also the victims of hate crimes led by two young men, William and Daniel McDermott. The McDermott gang, as Amy and her friends called them, spit on them, shot at them, nearly ran them down in a car, and burned a cross on their lawn. One of Amy's friends was beaten with a baseball bat and almost died. Amy's mother called the local police who asked her, "Why are you letting your daughter hang out with black kids?" When the federal authorities finally got wind of what was happening, Amy became a witness in one of the first successful hate-crime prosecutions in the country (Berger 2009b:79).

Whereas Emily Rapp and Amy Bleile have congenital disabilities, Melvin Juette (born 1969), whom we introduced in Chapter 2, has an acquired disability, which occurred as the result of a gunshot injury he suffered during a gang dispute when he was sixteen years old. Prior to that time, Melvin had been an active member of Chicago's African American urban gang scene; now he is paralyzed from the waist down.[1] After a period of recuperation at the Rehabilitation Institute of Chicago (RIC), undergoing extensive physical therapy, and becoming acclimated to his new wheelchair, Melvin was transferred from his high school to a different school where the city segregated all the students with disabilities, those with physical and cognitive disabilities alike. Melvin says that he resented being "treated like someone who was mentally disabled" when he was placed in classes with students who "just stared into space" and "didn't seem capable of learning anything" (Juette and Berger 2008:77). Additionally, his new high school guidance counselor told him, "You don't need to go to college. You're just going to be disappointed. Why don't you just collect social security and let the government take care of you" (p. 82).

Melvin did not take the counselor's advice, and he eventually attended and graduated from college. Along the way, his involvement in wheelchair basketball became a driving force in his life, an opportunity to meet new friends and cultivate an empowering bodily experience of disability. He remembers when he was first introduced to the sport while he was recovering at RIC. The therapeutic recreation

FURTHER EXPLORATION

Box 5.1 Hate Crimes Against People with Disabilities

In the early 1990s, a coalition of African American, Japanese American, Jewish, and gay and lesbian groups began advocating for legislation against hate crimes that would identify the acts as a distinct category of crime and would prescribe enhanced penalties for individuals who were convicted. Soon thereafter, disability was added to the minority groups that were covered by this legislation. Although many crimes are motivated by one person's hatred of another, the distinguishing characteristic of **hate crimes** is the bias or prejudice that offenders hold toward *all* members of another group. Often, the purpose of the crime is not just to victimize an individual but to send a message to the entire group the victim represents. From the offender's perspective, the victims are interchangeable, because anyone fitting the description can become a suitable target, leaving victims and those who share similar characteristics with a sense of fear and vulnerability (Jacobs and Potter 1998; Sherry 2010).

Current federal law requires the Federal Bureau of Investigation (FBI) to collect and report hate crimes in the United States. In addition to bias against people with disabilities, hate crimes are reported for racial and ethnic bias, religious bias, and sexual orientation bias, with disability bias making up less than 1 percent of the total (Sherry 2010). The FBI divides disability hate crimes into two categories: **anti–mental disability bias** and **anti–physical disability bias**. In a study of disability hate crimes between 1997 and 2007, Mark Sherry (2010) found that 62 percent were for anti–mental disability bias and 38 percent were for anti–physical disability bias. About 45 percent of the total crimes were for simple assault and 13 percent were for aggravated assault. Another 38 percent were for intimidation, that is, threatening words or conduct that place a person in reasonable fear of bodily harm.

Sherry (2010) notes that disability hate crimes are notoriously underreported. One reason for this is that the people who victimize people with disabilities, such as caretakers who commit sexual abuse, are all too often the very ones who have the responsibility for taking care of them. Additionally, people with disabilities are victims of bullying and violent crimes that are not classified as hate crimes (including domestic battery), and their rate of victim-

continues

Box 5.1 continued

ization from these violations is higher than the rate for the nondisabled population (Hogan 2012; Shakespeare, Gillespie-Sells, and Davies 1996; Sobsey 1994; Thiara, Hague, and Mullender 2011).

In his research, Sherry (2010) also examined postings on the Internet of insidious diatribes against people with disabilities. "It would be a welcome relief," Sherry writes, "to assume that websites which contain this type of animosity toward disabled people are rare and hard to find," but this is by no means the case (p. 33). One common theme on these sites is that people with disabilities "are worthless and do not deserve to live" (p. 35). By way of illustration, Sherry reports on one article entitled "Cripples, Retards, and the Other Untouchables" that encapsulates the hatred that some people hold toward disabled people: "Useless self-pitying cripples and bothersome retarded fucks alike are all extraordinarily worthless. What is their purpose in society? Exhausting our precious resources while annoying the fuck out of us: the hard working American public. I hate crippled people, with their close up parking spots and their defective appendages. . . . . I detest retards immensely. The babbling, drooling, flailing fuck ups irritate me to no end. . . . I also loathe the 'special' Olympics. What the shit is this sorry excuse for an athletic competition for? . . . Screw cripples, screw retards. I hate them all" (pp. 34–35).

coordinator lent him a sports wheelchair and introduced him to the other members of the community team that was sponsored by RIC. "The guys on the team were so full of life," Melvin recalls, "unlike many of the youths I'd met at RIC. It made me feel good just to be around them, to have peers who by their example showed me that a disability didn't have to stop me from leading a physically active life" (Juette and Berger 2008:75).[2]

Melvin went on to become a Paralympic wheelchair athlete, and for him basketball became a way to avoid the social devaluation of disabled men who are denied their sense of masculine competence (Gerschick and Miller 1995; Ostrander 2008). As a gang member, Melvin had been respected as someone who knew how to negotiate the streets. He was tough and agile, a capable fighter, a leader among peers. Gang life had been a means by which he had developed a sense of self-efficacy and masculine competence. After his disablement, Melvin found that the survival strategies he had learned on the street could be transposed to the basketball court, where he could continue to be tough, athletic, competitive, and resolute, still experience his body as a masculine "presence," as "an active power . . . which [could] be exercised on and over others" (Shilling 2003:115). At the same time, Melvin's new body image opened the door to new ways of accomplishing masculine self-efficacy, as he became more emphatic, more considerate of others, a positive role model for youths in need.

Like Melvin, Matt Sanford (born 1965) has an acquired disability, his a result of a car accident he was in when he was fourteen years old, which severed his spinal cord and left him paralyzed from the chest down.[3] Unlike Melvin, Matt returned to his old middle school in Duluth, Minnesota, after an extensive period of recuperation. Even though he had now missed most of the seventh grade, he was allowed to move on to the eighth grade so he could stay with his friends. Matt was a smart kid and was able to "make up for lost time," although it took him about a year to truly catch up (Sanford 2006:132).

Matt had been a popular youth, and he picked up right where he had left off with his old friends. Only now he rolled to their destinations in his wheelchair rather than walk, and "peed into a bag attached to [his] leg rather than into a toilet. . . . We traveled in a pack, my friends taking turns pushing me up the steep hills of Duluth and then fighting to catch a ride standing on the back of my wheelchair while rolling down" (pp. 132–133). Matt thinks he was fortunate not only to have a group of close friends, but also to not have any unsightly disfigurements from his accident.

> At first glance, I looked like an average kid who just happened to be sitting in a wheelchair. This made my immersion into the greater student population easier. Besides bumping into the heels of kids standing in the hallways, I wasn't scary. For the most part, I didn't make people feel uncomfortable.
>
> The other advantage I had was a celebrity status of sorts. Although I was in seventh grade for less than three months, I had made a lot of friends. I had also been elected to the student council and had been the only seventh grader on both the varsity softball and basketball teams. My peers were ready and waiting for the return of the kid who was in that "terrible car accident." (pp. 132–133)

FURTHER EXPLORATION

Box 5.2 African Americans and Violently Acquired Spinal Cord Injury

Proportionally, African Americans have a higher rate of disability than other racial-ethnic groups in the United States, an experience that is correlated with the greater personal and social risks of living in poverty, including inner-city violence, and the general health and health-care disparities that exist in the country (Fujiura, Yamaki, and Czechowicz 1998; Smedley, Stith, and Nelson 2003; Waldrop and Stern 2003). Moreover, homicide is the leading cause of death among African American males ages fifteen to twenty-four; and violently acquired spinal cord injury (VASCI) (mainly from gun violence), the second leading cause of spinal cord injury overall (following motor vehicle accidents), accounts for about half of all spinal cord injuries in the inner city (Hernandez 2005; Ostrander 2008).

Like people of all racial-ethnic groups with a newly acquired disability, African American men face many challenges when learning how to adapt to their new bodies (see Chapter 6). In their research on inner-city African Americans and disability, however, Patrick Devlieger and Gary Albrecht (2000) found that blacks were less likely than whites to identify with the idea of disability culture or the disability rights movement. For those young men who acquired their spinal cord injury from gang violence, identification with disability culture or rights was more likely to occur among those who became alienated from unsupportive family and gang friends and who were immersed in a rehabilitation hospital milieu that allowed them to adopt an alternative narrative of their lives that moved them beyond gang violence (Devlieger, Albrecht, and Hertz 2007). For some of these men, the experience of near death was viewed as a "wake-up call," a second chance to turn to their lives around (Devlieger, Albrecht, and Hertz 2007; Hernandez 2005). As Melvin Juette has said, acquiring his disability was "both the worst and best thing that happened to him," because if he had not been shot, he would have "probably ended up in prison or been killed, like so many of [his] former gang associates," friends and enemies alike (Juette and Berger 2008:3). According to another young man, "I got buddies on death row. Buddies that are doing double life and a lot of buddies that's dead and quite a few that's on [a] wheelchair. The one[s] in jail will tell you it ain't

continues

Acclimating to the physical challenges at school was a different matter, however. The classrooms were located on three floors, and there was no elevator, so one of Matt's friends or a teacher's aide would have to tip him back in his wheelchair and bump him up or down the stairs one step at a time.

In the classroom, it didn't get much better. None of the combination chair/desks worked for a kid in a wheelchair. The school administration found two desks that I could wheel under and have a writing surface. I picked the two classes in which I needed them the most—algebra and English. Situated in the front corner of each room, I sat behind my special desk and tried not to feel conspicuous. In the other classes, I wrote on my lap.

Neither were the bathrooms in the school wheelchair accessible.

This complicated my most stressful problem—managing my bladder and bowels. I was still new at being a paraplegic and had not found my body's new rhythm. . . . The painful consequence was . . . a lot of . . . accidents. . . . Any day, at any time, I might look down and see a big wet spot between my legs, or worse yet, realize that I had involuntarily emptied my bowels. These accidents were so frequent that my mom had to be on call. I would track her down, wherever she was, . . . and [she] would come get me, take me home, help me clean up, redress, and then take me back to school. (p. 143)

In high school and later in college, Matt says he "had a steady stream of girlfriends," maybe too steady, he thinks now, but this was better than having no girlfriends at all (p. 144). At first he was afraid that his paralysis might keep him from having sexual relationships, but he was determined to prove otherwise.

> I sought to make my connections with girls more mature, more meaningful. I listened, I cared, I shared, and I laughed more deeply than most teenagers. I was selective, intuitively looking for depth, along with good looks, in potential girlfriends. When all was said and done, I pursued only one girl who was not ready to date a guy in a wheelchair. The downside of my approach was that I landed myself in some relatively serious relationships for a kid my age. Consequently, I think I missed some of the fun of high school.
>
> I also became sexually active during this time. . . . I can't say it was great sex, but few can as a teenager. It was a bit clumsy and took a lot of communication with my partner about how things were different for me. It's hard for anyone to talk about sex, let alone kids at that age. But this forced communication also put my sexuality on a novel footing. Sex for me was not a lusty, backseat experience. It had to be planned, thought about, and discussed. Even in these first few experiences, I was beginning to learn something that I have carried with me for a lifetime. Sexual expression is a shared exploration of intimacy and bodies. One consequence of my spinal cord injury has been a de-emphasizing of the central role played by sexual intercourse. While I am capable of it and . . . enjoy it, there is so much more to sexual intimacy than an explosion of physical sensation between the legs. I doubt that I would have known this as deeply had I not been a paraplegic. (pp. 144–145)[4]

The Transition to Adulthood

Adolescence and adulthood are best conceptualized as social constructions, not definitive statuses, and the transition between them can be murky. Once a person reaches legal adulthood—in the United States typically at eighteen years of age—the prolonged years of post–high school schooling that many undertake often keeps them in a dependent status vis-à-vis their parents.[5] Nowadays, the complete transition to adulthood takes longer than in the past, extending well into people's twenties. Sue Caton and Carolyn Kagan (2007) argue that it becomes increasingly difficult to identify a "normal" sequence

FURTHER EXPLORATION

Box 5.3 Disability and the Juvenile Justice System

Research indicates that youths with cognitive and emotional disabilities are overrepresented among the ranks of youths who are adjudicated as juvenile delinquent and incarcerated in the juvenile justice system (JJS) in the United States. Studies estimating the prevalence of youths with disabilities in the JJS vary because they employ different criteria for defining disability. In a review of the literature, Kimberly Morris and Richard Morris (2006) found that the percentage of youths in the JJS who have been diagnosed as having a disability ranges from 28 percent to 58 percent. They also found that the most common category of disabled youths in the JJS is for youths with learning disabilities, followed by youths with emotional disorders and then intellectual disabilities. In another review, Christopher Mallett (2013) also notes that disability factors that put youths "at risk" of delinquency are often correlated with other risk factors associated with childhood maltreatment and mental health disorders and that it is this constellation of factors that best explains their prevalence in the JJS.

Morris and Morris (2006) identify three hypotheses that have been advanced to explain the disproportionately high prevalence of youths with disabilities in the JJS. The **school failure hypothesis** posits that students' impairments lead to school failure, which initiates feelings of rejection, frustration, and low self-esteem that are associated with involvement in delinquency. The **susceptibility hypothesis** posits that it is not school failure per se that leads to delinquency, although school failure is a factor, but rather the neurological and intellectual impairments that lead to poor judgment and hyperactivity-impulsivity. The **differential treatment hypothesis** posits that youths with these disabilities are not more involved in delinquency than other youths, but that school, law enforcement, and other public officials treat them more harshly. Morris and Morris note the inconsistencies in the extant studies and conclude that more research is needed to sort out these factors, as well as the factors that insulate disabled youths from delinquent involvement. They also note the ongoing need for educational and mental health services for those youths with disabilities who are under the jurisdiction and supervision of the JJS.

of life course events that people go through. Many people in their twenties, for example, move in and out of their parents' homes after first leaving, experience a period of employment before going to college, both work and attend college at the same time, have children without being married, and raise children while going to school.

It is in this context that the particular challenges facing people with disabilities transitioning to adulthood need to be considered. To be sure, under the provisions of the **Rehabilitation Act Amendments** of 1992, which expanded the provisions of the Rehabilitation Act of 1973, qualifying individuals are entitled to receive vocational rehabilitation services such as career counseling, vocational training, placement services, transportation, equipment and technological aids, and orthotics (Butterworth and Kiernan 1996). At the same time, disabled people and their families often report difficulty locating, accessing, and navigating these services. In her study of the high school transition experience, Valerie Leiter's (2012) informants were especially critical of the lack of help they received from high school guidance counselors, with less than 25 percent of students even talking with their counselors in the year prior to graduation.[6] At the same time, for those going on to college, some of the educational services they received during high school may no longer be available, and the facilities of the institution may not be physically accessible. Similar obstacles are faced by those attempting to move directly into the workforce, where the employment prospects for people with disabilities are much lower than for nondisabled workers.[7] In these ways, the extended transition period characteristic of all youths is even longer for disabled people. Moreover, young people with more serious impairments are less likely to establish independent households, marry, and have families of their own (Caton and Kagan 2007; Marshak, Seligman, and Prezant 1999; Wedgwood 2011).

For those students with disabilities who do attend college, currently more than 11 percent of all undergraduates in the United States (National Center for Education Statistics 2009), those who rely on paid personal assistants (PAs) for independent living face a unique set of challenges. Take a woman named Ella, for example, whose life history is reported in a study by Nikki Wedgwood (2011). Ella was born without limbs, except for a portion of one of her legs, and she is dependent on assistive care for her independence. But during college she had problems with PAs not showing up or not looking after her properly, such as only taking her to the toilet three times a day, which caused her to develop a urinary tract infection. To remedy this problem, Ella found a new PA agency, but even then problems persisted. In fact, Ella was only able to continue in college because her brother Dan was attending the school at the same time, living in the room directly above hers. Ella says that when her PAs "didn't show up in the mornings to get [her] out of bed," Dan would have to help her (p. 444). "He's taken me in emergencies when I've had to go to the toilet and stuff. . . . [I]f the lift isn't working he lifts me and that sort of thing." Ella says she used to be more ambitious about what she wanted to accomplish in her life, priding herself on being a trailblazer for people with serious disabilities. But now she thinks, "Trailblazing sucks! It's not all it's cracked up to be!" (p. 444).

Other college students report more sanguine experiences, however. As Amy Bleile prepared to graduate high school, her guidance counselor told her that she "needed to learn her limitations," that college was not an option because of her disability (Berger 2009b:79). Amy disregarded this advice, however, and enrolled in nearby Clark College in Dubuque, doing very well her first year. During that time she met a student from Wisconsin in one of her classes who told her about the University of Wisconsin–Whitewater (UWW), a completely accessible campus that has been serving students with disabilities as its special mission within the University of Wisconsin System. In addition to its physical accessibility, UWW has a Center for Students with Disabilities, which offers a number of specialized services, including academic and career counseling, instructional aids, transportation assistance, liaison with government and community agencies, and recreational and sports opportunities. The center serves about 700 students a year, about 6 percent of the student body (Berger 2009b).

When Amy arrived on campus, she was thrilled to be in an environment where there were a lot of other students with disabilities. It was an empowering experience for her to not be the "only one," as she had been all her life. She was taken aback, however, by the divisions among different groups of disabled students on campus. She got involved in wheelchair basketball, playing on a fledgling women's team, and got to know the students who played on the men's team, too. The men's wheelchair basketball program at UWW is one of the best in the nation and the place where up-and-coming elite athletes from the United States and even around the globe come to groom their skills so they can compete for a slot on their respective national teams. Amy was surprised to hear some of the men talk disparagingly about students with more serious disabilities who used power chairs. Although Amy hadn't used a power chair before coming to UWW, she did once she arrived on campus. As she says:

> The campus is so large. Me pushing a chair around here isn't too feasible. . . . There's been some [athletes] who've told me, "If it wasn't for you, I would've had real misconceptions about people in power chairs"—thinking that we're lazy and just in power chairs because it's easy, when in reality it's the key to our independence. . . . Then again, I've heard people from the other side who say, "I thought that all the athletes were real jerks." . . . They didn't want to have anything to do with *me* because they felt like I was trying to pretend that I wasn't disabled, that I was better than them because I played sports. . . . But after meeting some of [the athletes] they said, "Now I can see that they're really nice guys. They work really hard." (Berger 2009b:81)

Amy came to view herself as occupying "the middle ground," believing that "both sides hold stereotypes and false ideas about each other. And if there's not someone . . . brave enough to come up and start a conversation, then it can become a real big issue" (Berger 2009b:81–82). But Amy also had experiences with male athletes who refused to date women who use wheelchairs, as if they felt they were "too good" for these women.

> [T]he people who . . . say I'm not going to date you [because you use a wheelchair] . . . that's ridiculous. I have a friend who used to play here . . . [who thought] he'd never date a girl in a wheelchair. . . . After we became friends he told me, "You really changed my view." . . . Well, he got married last year . . . [to] a girl in a chair. "Thank you, Amy, for being right," he said. (Berger 2009b:82)

Ronald Berger (2009b) surmises that some disabled men may try to disavow their stigmatized status by dissociating themselves from women with disabilities, perhaps enabling them to maintain a sense of masculine power and privilege that is often denied to men with disabilities. Male students, on the other hand, may have a different perspective on this matter. Jon Fraser, for example, admits that as a disabled man who uses a wheelchair, he is reluctant to date women who use wheelchairs because it makes a relationship more difficult if both partners have impairments, especially if one of their impairments is severe. "I dated someone who . . . couldn't walk or crawl," he said, "couldn't transfer in and out of her chair very well. And me being in a wheelchair, there's not much I could do for her. . . . So it's just a lot easier to be with an able-bodied person" (Berger 2009b:138).[8] Matt Glowacki, whom we introduced in Chapter 4, adds that the outside world often makes it hard for two people in wheelchairs to date. "A lot of times it doesn't matter one on one. But when you go out in public, people stare, act incredibly stupid. . . . I had one guy in a restaurant come up to us and say, 'What do you guys do, bump wheelchairs together to have sex?' . . . I have to put up with enough in everyday life, so why . . . put myself and my date through that" (p. 138).

Matt also offers some observations on what it has been like for him to date able-bodied women. "You can usually tell right away," he says, if a disability "is going to be a big deal or not—based on when you go out in public." Matt says that it took his current girlfriend a while to get comfortable with the situation, but "she eventually stopped caring about it because she realized it really didn't make a big difference." Matt acknowledges, however, that it "takes a remarkably compassionate individual . . . to say I can love that person" (p. 138).

The World of Work

Elsewhere we noted that people with disabilities are overrepresented among the ranks of the poor and unemployed, with an employment rate of less than 40 percent of the general adult population in the United States (see Chapter 2). On average, the economic prospects of women with disabilities, as well as disabled persons of color, is even bleaker. When employed, people with disabilities tend to be "overrepresented in lower paid service jobs and under-represented in better paid managerial and professional positions" (Wilson-Kovacs et al. 2008:705).

Research suggests several reasons why employers are disinclined to hire otherwise qualified workers with disabilities, reasons having more to do with their perceptions of the disabled than with the qualifications of disabled people. For instance, employers often have reservations about the ability of disabled employees to maintain a high level of work productivity and are more likely to question their work ethic and desire for career advancement in comparison to nondisabled employees. They also think that disabled workers are "more prone to absenteeism . . . and less capable of getting along with others," and they are concerned about the cost of providing for health insurance and an accessible workplace environment (Wilson-Kovacs et al. 2008:706; see also Baker 2011; Cunningham, James, and Dibben 2004; Stevens 2002).

Sara Lane, who contracted polio when she was an infant, studied journalism in college, where some of her professors told her that her reliance on a wheelchair would restrict her ability to become a reporter, advising her to settle for "what she considered to be a less desirable desk job as a copyeditor" (Engel and Munger 2003:23). Following graduation, Sara did spend some time as a copyeditor, but she was also able to pursue her ambition of becoming a reporter. Over the years, some of her employers have been cooperative about providing the accommodations she needs, such as an accessible bathroom and special parking place, but others have been more resistant. In the latter cases, Sara has been reluctant to invoke her legal rights under the Americans with Disabilities Act (ADA) because she feels that to do so would create an impression of her as a dependent person rather than as a "normal" professional and thus hurt her chances for career advancement.

Similarly, Sid Tegler, who was paralyzed in a skiing accident, also encountered people who were skeptical about his employability as a tax accountant, the profession for which he is highly trained, because some positions require him to go out into the field to meet clients and inspect their facilities. One prospective employer even expressed concern about Sid's ability to fit into the organization and about how the company's clients would react to an accountant with a disability. He eventually decided to become self-employed to avoid dealing with these prejudicial attitudes (Engel and Munger 2003).

Unlike Sara and Sid, Jim Vargas's learning disability is not visible to his employers, but this invisibility poses special challenges to his work as a licensed physical therapist. Providing physical therapy to clients is no problem for Jim, but he does have trouble keeping up with the paperwork aspects of his job, which requires him to work extra unpaid hours to complete these tasks. Unlike his experience in college, where accommodations to his learning disability were made, Jim is reluctant to reveal his impairment to employers. Although he is entitled to accommodations under the ADA, in his case the assistance of a stenographer and transcribing equipment, he is reluctant to request it.[9] On the other hand, to remain silent about his disability runs the risk of employers thinking that he lacks the discipline, aptitude, or intelligence to be a competent physical therapist. Jim has dealt with this dilemma by trying to conceal his learning disability until, paradoxically, he has proven "himself without the accommodations he actually requires" (Engel and Munger 2003:128).

Pamela Reed Gibson and Amanda Lindberg (2007) studied the problems faced by employees who have chemical sensitivities to low levels of incitants in ambient air. These sensitivities cause allergic-like reactions that range from mild to life threatening and affect one or more bodily system, including the "respiratory, digestive, neurological, endocrinological, musculoskeletal or cardiovascular" systems (p. 719). Gibson and Lindberg interviewed people who were denied accommodations by their employers, sometimes in outright violation of the ADA. One person who worked for a chemical company was told that "it was a conflict of interest for her to get sick from chemicals when the chemical industry was paying her salary" (p. 726). Another person who worked for a religious organization "was told by the pastor that she was just thinking negatively and . . . if she would just cheer up" her symptoms would go away (p. 726). Employees with chemical sensitivities also encountered a host of indignities, including "eye rolling, disgusted looks, verbal abuse, increased use of perfume, perfume spraying outside their doors, being 'tested' in various ways to see if chemicals really did make them sick, laughter when they wore masks and ostracism" (p. 727). One health-care worker was told by the head physician of a medical facility that he thought she had a mental illness. Another employee said that a manager had actually sprayed cleaning solution in his face.

Robert Wilton (2008) discusses similar problems in his study of service-sector workers. One worker with chronic back pain reported that it was difficult for her to stand all day, as was expected of her retail position, and that she needed to periodically sit down when there were no customers present, only being able to do this when her supervisor was not around. Another worker who needed periodic rest for a condition that was not readily apparent had coworkers question the legitimacy of her impairment. As she said, "People kind of think that you are being lazy, . . . [and] say, 'What do you mean you're disabled?' You feel like you have to defend yourself constantly" (p. 369). Workers with hearing impairments also reported instances when they could not hear what a boss or coworker was saying, and when they asked them to repeat themselves, they received responses of annoyance such as "it's not our fault that you don't hear" or "Oh, God . . . What is it now?" (p. 369).

In a study of blind and vision-impaired employees, Mala Naraine and Peter Lindsay (2011) also document the social isolation of disabled employees that inhibits their occupational success. Even when employers make workplace accommodations, visually impaired employees often have difficulty networking with other workers, socializing after work, and attending work-related social events that would enable them to become integrated into the workplace culture. One woman reported that while her workplace is accessible, employee social gatherings such as potluck dinners are not. Another said she would walk into a room at events unable to recognize people's faces and be ignored by her coworkers. Another woman said that because she cannot see and interpret body language, she frequently misunderstands social situations. She said there are times when she might still be talking to someone at a gathering and not realize the person is no longer there.

Lastly, in a study of disabled professionals, Dana Wilson-Kovacs and colleagues (2008) highlight the obstacles faced by employees who seek promotions and advancement in their careers. One way that opportunity is limited for disabled professionals is not being given challenging assignments by employers, which would otherwise allow them to demonstrate their advanced competencies (see also Jones 1997). As one employee explained, "You are not necessarily given the cutting edge stuff . . . so you're not stretching . . . and therefore . . . you're not necessarily learning" (p. 709). Another said, "I don't feel that I've got that opportunity to be pushed in my ability and to recognize the risk of it all going horribly wrong" (p. 709). Wilson-Kovacs and colleagues note that "[r]ealizing one's full potential means having one's potential recognized in the first place" (p. 710). When employers have lower expectations of disabled employees, these expectations become self-fulfilling prophecies. As one of the informants said, "Just because you can get your wheelchair in the building doesn't necessarily mean you can still participate" (p. 712).

Sexual and Emotional Intimacy

Our earlier discussion of adolescence and the transition to adulthood raised some preliminary issues regarding dating and sexuality. In this section we consider matters of sexuality and emotional intimacy further. Nondisabled people are often curious about disabled sexuality. Recall John Hockenberry's (1995) observation about an episode of *The Oprah Winfrey Show* in which Winfrey asked a wife, whose previously able-bodied husband was disabled in an accident, "can he do it?" (see Chapter 2). More often than not, however, the public tends to view disabled people as asexual, and they have trouble imagining that an able-bodied person would choose a disabled person as a sexual partner. It is one thing to stay with an able-bodied partner who becomes disabled, but it is an entirely different matter for a nondisabled person to become intimately involved with a disabled person they could have chosen to avoid (Hockenberry 1995; Rainey 2011; Shakespeare, Gillespie-Sells, and Davies 1996).

Having internalized these societal attitudes, disabled people often struggle with their body image, doubtful if others will view them as sexually desirable partners (Mairs 1996; Rapp 2007). Nondisabled people struggle with this too—hence the interest in cosmetic surgery to refashion one's body in the image of an unobtainable yet socially desirable norm (see Chapter 2). But this broader normative context poses particular challenges for people with disabilities. As Jane Elder Bogle and Susan Shaul observe: "It's very easy to consider one's body as the enemy when you're getting all negative input from the outside world. . . . Most of us need to rely on some hardware to get around, such as braces, crutches, wheelchairs, and catheters. They can be very difficult to incorporate into our concept of being sexually desirable people, . . . [as] warm, squeezable, and lovable" (1981:92).

Of course, as we have also seen in our previous discussion of dating, it is more common for nondisabled women to partner with disabled men than for nondisabled men to partner with disabled women, and this is a likely consequence of the more nurturing aspects of conventional female socialization (Rainey 2011; Shakespeare, Gillespie-Sells, and Davies 1996).[10] As one woman with spina bifida notes, of even the men she knows who are disabled: "I've gotten into some heated conversations with people. . . . 'How can you say you're not going to date anyone in a wheelchair? . . . Even though you like me

FURTHER EXPLORATION

Box 5.4 Mothers with Physical Impairments

Just as people with disabilities are often considered to be asexual beings, the public often assumes that they should forgo the responsibilities and pleasures of parenting (Shakespeare, Gillespie-Sells, and Davies 1996). This is especially true when it comes to disabled mothers. For many disabled women like Heather Kuttai (2010), however, pregnancy and childbirth makes them feel feminine, sexual, and whole. As she says, "My pregnancies enabled me to feel truly 'female' because I was experiencing something that many women also experience. I felt as though my body was 'showing' more societal worth than it did when I was not pregnant. I also often felt a strong sense of positive femininity and a brand new sense of sexuality" (p. 70). At the same time, Kuttai also experienced disapproving stares, difficulty with inaccessible medical facilities, and obstetricians who had no "interest in how [her] paraplegic body was being affected during pregnancy" (p. 67; see also Collins 1999; Lipson and Rogers 2000; Prilleltensky 2003).

In a review of the literature on mothers with physical disabilities, Ora Prilleltensky (2004) found that a common theme focused on the question of children's well-being, with an emphasis on the adverse consequences of being overburdened with responsibilities for providing caregiving to the parent, and even a reversal of roles, whereby the child becomes the parent and the parent the child. At the same time, she also found studies that showed a lack of adverse consequences and even positive ones associated with the family's ability to reflect on its circumstances and make appropriate adjustments without overburdening children.

In her own research on this subject, Prilleltensky found no evidence that children were being burdened "with excessive, developmentally inappropriate responsibilities" and that parents made an effort "to shield their children from the burdens of care" (2004: 219). At the same time, she does make a distinction "between a teenager who has little choice about providing intimate care to a parent and one who may be expected to assist more with household chores than some of [her or his] peers" (pp. 219–220). There also was a case of a seven-year-old daughter who helped out with the laundry, but "this was instituted with the goal of promoting the [child's] independence and sense of self-efficacy rather than as a necessity related to the mother's disability" (p. 214). And even

continues

Box 5.4 continued

when assistance with personal care of the parent was needed, this did not mean that a reversal of roles had occurred.

Some mothers with physical impairments who are unable to provide traditional caregiving to their children find ways to support their children in other ways. In her memoir, Nancy Mairs explains that she tries to find "alternatives to the traditional modes of tendering care. . . . Since most physical acts are denied to me, my efforts must take largely intellectual and emotional form. I've become a closer and more patient listener, and I spend time giving information, counsel, and encouragement" (1996:83). Similarly, one of the mothers in Prilleltensky's study said, "From a young age I taught [my children] that if they listen to me I can keep them safe . . . like if a fire alarm goes, if they just listen to what I tell them they'll be safe, . . . they're not going to burn to death. . . . I don't want them to feel anxious . . . if they're home alone with me that there's more of a threat to their security than if they're home alone with their dad. Because even though there are things I can't do, they still see that I get it done somehow. Like I know who to call or what to do or I can teach them to do things themselves" (2004:213).

you won't date me because I'm sitting.' . . . They have such high standards for *their* women. . . . They want them perfect. They have to be this pretty. They have to have this good of a body" (Berger 2009b:93). Similarly, another disabled woman says: "I've often felt that disabled women who want to relate to men are at a terrible disadvantage because men do buy into the good looks syndrome. Women don't so much. I don't choose a man for his looks. A disabled man has a much better chance in this world of finding partners" (Chapkis 1986:151).[11] And one disabled gay man adds:

> [It] has affected me . . . no points for political correctness when it comes to dating men. In the past I've nearly always ended up going out with so-called non-disabled people, I've gone out with a few disabled people as well, but very few. I would say that probably because of this body beautiful image, it gets to us all, like I still tend to go for a nice good-looking six foot two, not necessarily six foot two, but just nice and good looking, who's not bald. (Shakespeare, Gillespie-Sells, and Davies 1996:72)

It is not just men, however, who reject sexual partners who are disabled. As one lesbian reports:

> At clubs I've been patronized or used as a token disabled person. At parties I've been chatted up when I was sitting on a couch or chair and when people see me getting into my wheelchair they are suddenly called away. Once a woman gave me her phone number and begged me to come for dinner, I said "I'll think about it." When she saw me get in my chair her face fell and she said, "On second thought, I'm very busy [the] next few weeks." (Shakespeare, Gillespie-Sells, and Davies 1996:162)

Another lesbian describes her experiences this way:

> Issues of equality are not fashionable in the majority of the . . . able-bodied, white, middle-class lesbian and gay communities. To them, our disabilities preclude us from having, or wishing to express, an independent sexuality. We are therefore not considered "proper" lesbians and gays. Most of us do not look, act, move or communicate in what is considered to be a lesbian or gay way. We are outsiders in our own community, and no-one hesitates to let us know that. The message may be shrouded in patronage or ignorance, but we know exactly what is meant by the space created by our absence. (Hearn 1991:34)

These testimonies notwithstanding, there are many disabled people who defy societal attitudes that diminish their sexuality. In Chapter 2, for instance, we noted a woman who tries to compensate for a facial difference by projecting a look of self-confidence, as "friendly, upbeat, energetic, a little in your face, a little pushy" (Zitzelsberger 2005:396). Similarly, another woman says she tries "to project the image of being in control, or being assertive" (Shakespeare, Gillespie-Sells, and Davies 1996:78). And one man explains: "Personally I am not ashamed of my body. I have adjusted to the fact that I am different, . . . [to take] pride in what I am as a disabled man, and I accept that my body has given me access to a whole set of experiences, whether negative or positive, which make me different, which gave me a different outlook, a different awareness of life, which is something positive which I can give" (Shakespeare, Gillespie-Sells, and Davies 1996:78–79).

In this way, as we noted of Matt Sanford earlier in this chapter, disabled people with physical paralysis strive to put their "sexuality on a novel footing" by exploring other ways to share emotional and bodily intimacy (2006:144). Milton Diamond believes that disabled people would do well to dispense with a narrow view of sexuality that "states that the only satisfactory means of expressing oneself sexually and achieving satisfaction is with an erect penis in a well-lubricated vagina" (1984:99). As Miriam Kaufman, Cory Silverberg, and Fran Odette candidly write:

> Watch any one of the thousands of mainstream porn films (or even regular films with sex scenes) released each year and you'll get some idea of how sex is "supposed" to work. "Real" sex progresses from light activities like kissing to the "real" thing, penis-in-vagina intercourse. . . . You should also be able to have sex in a variety of positions all in the same night. Everything we do sexually is supposed to progress toward that goal, and none of it is as important as the result itself. Thus "foreplay" is nothing more than a prelude to the main event. Oral sex is hot, but it's not as good as the "real" thing. (2003:3–4)

Thus, Diamond argues that sexual satisfaction, for both disabled and nondisabled people, "is possible without these practices and . . . may even be more satisfying" when parts of the body other than genitalia—mouths, hands, feet, any part of the body—become more hypersensitive to touch (1984:100; see also Rainey 2011; Shapiro 1993; Zola 1982).

In a study of intimate relationships between disabled and nondisabled partners, in which the latter also serve as part-time caregivers, Sarah Smith Rainey (2011) interviewed couples for whom caregiving was not a burden, as the public often misconstrues, but an expression of love, including erotic love.[12] The routine task of assisting a partner with bathing, for example, can become an occasion for emotional intimacy and erotic pleasure (see also Kondracke 2001). Nancy Mairs adds that without her disability to regularly bring her husband and her together through caregiving, "our bodies might spend their days racing separately from one activity to another, coming across each other only in time to tumble into sleep" (1996:54). Another man puts it this way, "There are times when . . . [the act of caring] increases intimacy, and I'm talking both sexual intimacy and just the closeness. In fact, I think we get a lot more closeness out of those up-close and personal moments that we have together" (Rainey 2011:150).

Health Care and Personal Assistance

Like everyone else in society, people with disabilities need health care, and while disabled people are generally healthy, their health-care needs are typically greater than those of the nondisabled population. For one, people with disabilities require access to specialists who are familiar with the particulars of their impairments and the medical treatments that are available to improve their functioning, if they so desire. Additionally, as we noted in Chapter 2, people with physical impairments may experience secondary health effects, such as earlier onset of chronic health conditions such as coronary heart disease and adult diabetes due to fewer opportunities for aerobic exercise needed to maintain good cardiovascular health and weight control, arthritis and osteoporosis due to poor orthopedic and muscular health, and renal disease due to a neurogenic bladder; and people with mental illnesses may require ongoing medications (DeJong and Basnett 2001; Heller and Marks 2006; Pope and Tarlov 1991). People with disabilities may also need access to assistive service animals (primarily dogs) as well as technological devices such as wheelchairs (manual and powered), orthotics and prosthetics, synthesized speech devices, vans with lifts, and hand-operated vehicle controls (Litvak and Enders 2001).[13]

In the United States, where millions of people are uninsured or underinsured, coverage for this range of health-care needs is problematic for disabled people and nondisabled people alike. While people with disabilities may be covered through Medicaid (for the poor) or Medicare (for the elderly), their ability to maintain eligibility for these government programs forces them to limit their income through paid employment. Moreover, insurance coverage may not be available for ongoing physical therapy, continued access to specialists, long-term stays in hospitals, or purchase of the best available assistive technology products (Baker 2011; Fleischer and Zames 2001; Kohrman and Kohrman 2006; Litvak and Enders 2001). As we also noted in Chapter 2, a disabled person's financial ability or inability to obtain these needed resources will have a significant impact on their quality of life.

With the rise of the independent living movement, people with disabilities advanced their cause of living in their communities rather than in institutional settings, defining independent living in terms of the quality of life they could achieve *with or without* assistance (see Chapter 1). Short of living with family members, who provide about 80 percent of the care that is given to disabled people in their homes, the matter of funding for personal assistance that would enable those with serious impairments to realize this goal becomes paramount (Heller and Marks 2006).[14]

In 1965, the federal Medicaid program authorized grants-in-aid to states for the establishment of medical assistance to low-income individuals, including funding for long-term institutional care in nursing homes. With the creation of the **Home and Community-Based Services** waiver program in 1981, states were also granted the *option* of providing these services in the home if the costs did not exceed the cost of nursing-home care. Insofar as the waiver program is an option, not an entitlement, there is considerable disparity in the availability of home-based services around the country, and many poor disabled people are still forced into institutional settings, deprived of the opportunity to receive personal assistant services in their homes. Currently only 25 percent of Medicaid dollars are allocated for community-based care (Hayashi 2005; Heller and Marks 2006).

For those seriously disabled adults who are able to stay in their homes, the experience of relying on paid PAs to meet their daily needs is fraught with potential dilemmas, not the least of which is the absence of privacy regarding an individual's most personal bodily functions—eating, dressing and undressing, toileting, bathing, and so forth.[15] In their interviews with disabled people who receive personal home care, Michelle Meyer, Michelle Donelly, and Patricia Weerakoon (2007) learned it was important for recipients of care to maintain their autonomy and control, which requires willingness on the part of the PA to respect and follow their choices and preferences. It also was important for recipients of care to take a proactive and assertive approach by setting the ground rules when they first meet with PAs (see also Karner 1998). As one man explains:

> It [is] difficult at first to be strong in your own home because the carers always feel that it's their job—they know how to do it—why should I be telling them all the time. So I explain to them that I'm part of the scene, that they're taking the place of my hands. Once they get the message that it's not a personal criticism of them—this is just the way that I like things done. I have to explain that I'm

actually taking part in the proceedings. (Meyer, Donelly, and Weerakoon 2007:599)

Some of the informants describe this process as a matter of "training" their PAs. One woman emphasizes the need to pay attention to detail, such as making sure "there are no creases in the bed linen and clothes" to prevent pressure sores (Meyer, Donelly, and Weerakoon 2007:600). She also provides directions on how she wants to be washed and dried thoroughly, telling the PA to "give the towel a bit more of a brisk rub" (p. 600). Another woman says that her PAs are sometimes inhibited about completing certain hygiene tasks involving intimate parts of the body. "Some carers go about it a bit more comprehensively, and others definitely are more tentative. I guess part of my role is to be comfortable to say, 'Just go 'round there a bit more, rinse the wash cloth off because it smells from there, and remember go front to back.' I have to say those things, and do say those things" (p. 600). Similarly, another informant explains that he has to be diligent about reminding his PAs to empty the urine from his leg bag:

> They seldom forget, but sometimes they do forget. . . . Like sometimes at night-time, they have to connect my leg bag to the night bottle, which carries, or catches the urine, and if it's not connected once the leg bag fills up, you could be in dire straits. That's happened quite a few times, when they've forgotten to connect it. So I've remembered to say "Have you connected the night bottle?" They'll say "Oh thanks for reminding me," "Yep. Just about to do it" or "No, it's all done." (p. 601)

Some informants say that a few PAs get defensive about being constantly reminded about what to do, feeling that their competencies are being called into question. As one man explains: "I repeat myself daily, day in [and] day out, because if something is forgotten, then I can blame myself. I can't blame them. [Most] don't have a problem with it really. One thinks, that I think she's stupid. But I don't think they're stupid. It's just a habit that I've got myself into, that I repeat myself all the time. Like brush my teeth, brush my hair, wipe my eyes . . . and stuff like that" (p. 602).

Informants also indicate that they actually prefer PAs who have not been professionally trained, because they are more open to receiving direction (see also Morris 1993):

> I have more control [with nonprofessionals] because I can tell them what to do without having any objections, because I know what I need for my personal care. The last thing I need is some young upstart nurse that says "Well that's not how you put in an enema, I've been taught this way." Well I just say ". . . I don't care how you've been taught, this is how it works for me. You may use that system on someone else, but I've been doing this for ten years." I don't particularly like to experiment unless I . . . have to, or if I've got some chance of improving my personal care. But generally if they're untrained, they're more receptive to being able to just do what you want them to do. (pp. 603–604)

Of professionally trained PAs, another woman says, "What's happening is that they're being trained to work as screws, and when they come into my home, it's like they spin out. The new ones I mean that have just come out of the courses. I'd rather pick Joe Bloggs out of the City Mall, I could train them easily—anyone who has no experience with disability. Clean slate, I'll have them up and running in a week" (p. 604). Still another man explains:

> What concerns me about the whole professionalization of the industry is that we're going . . . towards having to have a certain certificate to do things. And [PAs] are going to think that they know how to do it, whereas everyone's different. Rather than teaching people exact ways to do things—recogniz[e] that people with disabilities are individuals, just like everyone else. They have individual needs that might not follow your textbook way of doing things. (p. 604)

In the last analysis, however, it is the establishment of trust between two people, the caregiver and the recipient of care, who are able to keep the lines of communication open that is the key to an effective PA experience.

Summary

This chapter continued our examination of disability across the life course, focusing on adolescence and adulthood. We first looked at adolescents' relationships with peers, both good and bad, and their experiences in school, including the challenges of physical accessibility and problems with teachers and other school officials. We then

FURTHER EXPLORATION

Box 5.5 The Graying of Disability and Alzheimer's Disease

In Chapter 1, we noted that most anyone who lives long enough can expect to have an experience of disability before they die. Moreover, as people on average live longer, we are witnessing a process of what Jeffrey Kahuna, Eva Kahuna, and Loren Lovegreen (2011) call the "graying of disability." Although this population is generally "retired and not likely to rejoin the workforce, . . . [they] desire to maintain social connectedness and to function independently in their communities" (p. 1). At the same time, this group is more likely to identify themselves as elderly rather than as people with disabilities (Darling and Heckert 2010). Likewise, the disability rights movement has tended to ignore the needs of this constituency when advocating on behalf of the disability community (Jönson and Larsson 2009), a constituency that accounts for about a third of all those reporting a disability in the United States, about half of those who are sixty-five years of age or older, and about 70 percent of those who are eighty years or older (Moore 2009; Pincus 2011; see also Box 1.1).

Of all the debilitating conditions experienced by the elderly, Alzheimer's disease (AD) has arguably received the most attention, and managing the burdens of AD patient care poses significant challenges to both families and society in general. AD is an irreversible condition and the fourth leading cause of death among elderly Americans, surpassed only by cardiovascular disease, cerebrovascular disease, and cancer. While the causes of AD are unclear, it is likely due to a mix of genetic, environmental, and lifestyle factors (Cabin 2010; National Institute of Aging 2011).

The discovery of AD is credited to Alois Alzheimer, a German psychiatrist and neuropathologist, who first wrote about the condition in 1906. In his autopsy of a fifty-one-year-old woman, Alzheimer found "atrophy and lesions in the area of the cerebral cortex and an unusual clumping and distortion of cortical neurofibrils" (Holstein 1997:1). These are now known to be amyloid plaques and neurofibrillary tangles that progressively attach themselves to and destroy cells in certain parts of the brain, causing *cognitive symptoms* that may include "memory impairment, speech

continues

Box 5.5 continued

and language comprehension problems, and impaired judgment," and *behavioral symptoms* that may include "personality changes, irritability, anxiety, depression, delusions, hallucinations, aggression, and wandering" (Cabin 2010:2). AD is also accompanied by *functional symptoms* that may include "difficulty with eating, dressing, bathing, toileting, walking, grooming, getting in [and] out of bed, meal preparation, shopping, moving within and outside the house, money management, and using the telephone or computer" (2010:2; see also National Institute of Aging 2011).

Alzheimer did not actually believe he had discovered a new disease outside of what is commonly referred to as senile dementia, and it was not until the 1970s that a medical consensus emerged that recognized AD as a special category of dementia (ten Have and Purtilo 2004). Still, the diagnostic criteria that distinguish AD from dementia remain unclear, with dementia being considered both a broad diagnostic category covering AD and a symptom of AD and other diagnoses associated with cognitive impairments. Nevertheless, researchers estimate that AD represents about 50 percent to 70 percent of all cases of dementia in the United States. AD progresses with age, with an estimated 10 percent of all persons over age sixty-five, and 50 percent of all persons over age eighty-five, exhibiting the condition (Cabin 2010; National Institute of Aging 2011). In a study of 100 randomly selected, autopsy-confirmed AD patients, B. C. Jost and G. T. Grossberg (1995) found that the average age of diagnosis was 74.7 years, with an average age of institutionalization of 77.6 years. The average length of time between the onset of symptoms and death was 32.1 months.

considered the period of transition to adulthood, including the challenges of college and dating, followed by an examination of the work experiences of adults with disabilities, including workplace accessibility barriers and resistance to accommodations, as well as problematic relationships with employers and coworkers. We also discussed matters of adult sexuality and emotional intimacy, and lastly, the dilemmas of health care and the experiences of severely disabled adults who require paid personal assistance in order to remain in their homes.

Notes

1. The bullet that entered Melvin's body lodged in his tailbone and damaged the nerves around his spine. The doctors decided against removing the bullet because they were concerned that to do so would cause further damage.

2. We will discuss wheelchair sports further in Chapter 6.

3. The accident killed Matt's father and sister.

4. Men with paralysis who have no feelings in their genitals can still get reflex erections (Hockenberry 1995).

5. Only 65 percent of youths with serious disabilities graduate from high school, compared to 79 percent of those with mild disabilities, and 89 percent of those without disabilities (Hogan 2012).

6. Not surprisingly, students and families from more privileged backgrounds who attended private high schools reported better experiences.

7. Sheltered paid employment is an option for people with disabilities who are unlikely to be successful in the labor market. Sheltered employment offers a more protective environment of less responsibility, a slower work pace, and fewer hours. It is offered by private, nonprofit, and voluntary organizations, and may include commercial or subcontracting ventures like car washes, janitorial services, and food services. They may also be used for the development of skills that would enable participants to move into the regular workforce (Krupa 2006).

8. Another man who uses a wheelchair notes the logistical barriers faced by two disabled people: "Like getting out to . . . a meal, you have got to book two taxis. . . . Going on a holiday is a logistics nightmare, we try to find a place which allows you to have wheel-in showers—it's almost impossible, and the very cost of taking two personal assistants away . . ." (Shakespeare, Gillespie-Sells, and Davies 1996:94).

9. Beth Omansky (2011), who is partially sighted but legally blind (see Chapters 4 and 6), reports that her rehabilitation counselor advised her to not disclose her disability when she applied for a job at a pie shop. After she was offered the job, she informed her employer about her visual impairment and requested two accommodations: that he enlarge the print of the menus, and that she be allowed to place raised marks supplied by her rehabilitation counselor on the baking equipment, so she could measure ingredients and adjust temperatures more accurately. Her employer agreed to her request, but only after he reduced his initial wage offer by 50 cents an hour. Although Omansky thought this might be in violation of her legal rights, she agreed to the lower wage, and during the year and a half that she worked there, she never reached wage parity with her sighted coworkers.

10. Regarding relationships that were formed prior to one in the couple becoming disabled, "disabled men are more likely to maintain their relationships, while disabled women are more likely to find themselves abandoned by their erstwhile partner" (Shakespeare, Gillespie-Sells, and Davies 1996:95).

11. Still another woman points to a normative hierarchy that exists even within the disabled community about "what is beautiful, what is ugly. . . . At the top is someone who sits in a wheelchair but looks perfect" (Chapkis 1986:19).

12. Rainey notes that feminist critiques of caregiving as exploitative unpaid or underpaid labor (Glenn 2010; Kittay and Feder 2002; Meyer 2000) miss the "pleasures of care" that are associated with an experience of inter-corporeality between the carer and cared-for. Berger and Feucht (2011) make a similar point regarding parental care of disabled children.

13. We will discuss issues pertaining to disability and computer technology in Chapter 8. For comparative analyses of the role of markets and non-market mechanisms in the provision of health care, see Albrecht and Bury (2001) and DeJong and Basnett (2001).

14. With longer life expectancies of people with disabilities, there is a greater likelihood that a disabled family member will outlive his or her family caretakers; and parents of disabled children face the dual challenge of "dealing with their own aging in addition to the aging of their adult children" (Heller and Marks 2006:74). Group homes, particularly for people with intellectual disabilities and mental illness, are another community-living option. The residence, where up to about fifteen people live, may be an apartment building or a freestanding home. Some provide live-in care providers, while others provide shift workers. Some expect the residents to assume primary responsibility for household chores, while others allow for the staff to perform these duties (McDonald 2006).

15. Nursing home residents, of course, experience this lack of privacy, too (Hayashi 2005). But whether in home or institutional settings, Jon Feucht thinks that it is dignity, not privacy, that is the real issue. "Being disabled," he says, "doesn't lessen dignity. . . . It's how [others] treat people with disabilities that defines dignity" (Berger and Feucht 2011:83).

6

The Bodily Experience of Disability

EARLIER IN THIS BOOK WE INTRODUCED THE PERSPECTIVE OF phenomenology, which takes the lived experience of embodied human beings, or what Tobin Siebers (2008) calls complex embodiment, as a central focus of disability studies (Chapter 2). This perspective complicates the distinction between *impairment*—the physiological loss of physical, sensory, or cognitive function—and *disability*—the inability to perform a personal or socially necessary task because of that impairment or the societal reaction to it (Chapter 1). In doing so, impairment and disability are understood not as meeting in the body "as a dualistic clash of inner and out phenomena," but rather as impinging upon each other as a fully integrated embodied whole (Hughes and Paterson 1997:337).

In this chapter, we pursue a phenomenology of the body, or rather the bodily experience of disability from the vantage point of those who live with a physiological impairment. We seek to understand, as best as is possible, what it is like for disabled people to live in an ableist world that is designed for nondisabled people. We begin with a consideration of the ways in which people perceive the world without sight and sound, turning next to the phenomenology of sign language and then to the ways in which people with mobility impairments navigate the physical environment. We also examine the experience of rehabilitation after a newly acquired spinal cord injury, concluding the chapter with an examination of disability sport and athleticism.

Perceiving the World Without Sight or Sound

People who are vision impaired are not always completely without sight, and those who are hearing impaired are not always completely without hearing. As with any other impairment, sightedness and hearing exist along a continuum that consists of varying degrees. With this in mind, we will begin with the case of Helen Keller, who did in fact live in a phenomenological world that was fully without both sight and sound. Keller described her subjective perceptions in her book *The World I Live In* (1908), where she wrote: "To the blind child the dark is kindly. In it he finds nothing extraordinary or terrible. It is his familiar world; even the groping from place to place, the halting steps, the dependence upon others, do not seem strange. . . . Not until he weighs his life in the scale of others' experience does he realize what it is to live forever in the dark" (cited in Hermann 1998:156).

The testimony of those who were sighted until later in life indicates that people with complete vision loss do not actually inhabit a world of blackness, but rather, a world of neutral gray.[1] But due to the effectiveness of Annie Sullivan's teaching methods (see Box 3.1), and Keller's keen appreciation of the natural world, she was able to attach symbolic meanings to colors.

> I have talked so much and read so much about colors that through no will of my own I attach meanings to them, just as all people attach meanings to abstract terms like hope, idealism, monotheism, intellect, which cannot be represented truly by visible objects, but which are understood from analogies between immaterial concepts and the ideas they awaken of external things. . . . The force of association drives me to say that white is exalted and pure, green is exuberant, red suggests love or shame or strength. (p. 157)

In the absence of both vision and hearing, Keller developed an acute sensitivity to the vibrations in her environment. "Every atom of my body is a vibroscope," she wrote. "I derive much knowledge of everyday matters from the jars and jolts which are to be felt everywhere in the house" (cited in Hermann 1998:157). By the manner of one's walk on the stairs or floor, she could sense the difference between a child and an adult, and a man and a woman. She was able to recognize the flight of airplanes passing in the vicinity of her home, the difference in the vibrations produced by different carpentry tools, the thud of a book falling on the floor, and the flutter of papers blown off her desk.

As for music, Keller was unable to distinguish one composition from another, but she could feel the pulsating of air on the organs in her ears. "I love the instrument by which all the diapasons of the oceans are caught and released in surging floods," she wrote about her favorite instrument—the organ (cited in Hermann 1998:158). "If music could be seen, I could point where the organ-notes go, as they rise and fall, climb up and up, rock and sway, now loud and deep, now high and stormy, anon soft and solemn, with lighter vibrations interspersed between and running across them. I should say that organ-music fills to an ecstasy the act of feeling" (p. 158). The violin was another instrument Keller enjoyed, which seemed "beautifully alive as it responds to the lightest wish of the master. The distinction between its notes is more delicate than between the notes of the piano" (pp. 158–159). As for the piano, she liked it most when she could touch it: "If I keep my hand on the piano case, I detect tiny quavers, returns of melody, and the hush that follows" (p. 159). In her later life, Keller also enjoyed concerts on the radio, with her fingers touching a specially made loudspeaker, and she was able to differentiate types of instruments. She did not like jazz, however. "When it continues for some time," she said, "I have a wild impulse to flee" (p. 160).

Keller, of course, relied a great deal on touch to make her way around her environment, and she thought she could tell a great deal about a person from the feel of their face or hands. But she also had an acute sense of smell, able to distinguish different types of flowers, men from women, and qualities and identities of people.

> The odors of wood, iron, paint and drugs cling to the garments of those that work in them. Thus I can distinguish the carpenter from the iron-worker, the artist from the mason or the chemist. When a person passes quickly from one place to another, I get a scent impression of where he has been—the kitchen, the garden, or the sick-room. . . . Human odors are as varied as and capable of recognition as hands and face. The dear odors of those I love are so definite, so unmistakable, that nothing can quite obliterate them. If many years should elapse before I saw an intimate friend again, I know that I should recognize his odor instantly. (cited in Hermann 1998:161)

Lastly, Keller's appreciation of the world was powerfully enhanced by her imagination. As she wrote: "Without imagination, what a poor thing my world would be! My garden would be a silent patch of earth strewn with stick of a variety of shapes and smells. But when the eye

FURTHER EXPLORATION

Box 6.1 Temple Grandin

Temple Grandin, who gained recognition for her contribution to animal psychology and development of humane methods of handling livestock, is perhaps the best known contemporary figure with autism. She has published six books, including her memoir *Thinking in Pictures*, first published in 1995 and updated in 2006, and has become a leading equipment designer for the livestock industry. *Temple Grandin*, a film about her life starring Claire Danes, was released in 2010.

As the title to her memoir suggests, Grandin says she "thinks in pictures." For her, words are a "second language"; when someone speaks to her, the "words are instantly translated into pictures" (2006:3). She also says that this facility with "visual thinking as the primary method of processing information" can lead to the remarkable ability of many autistic people to solve jigsaw puzzles, find their way around a city, or memorize "enormous amounts of information at a glance" (p. 10). Grandin also writes about the difference between "normal" brains, which tend to ignore details and focus on the larger context, and "autistic" brains, which focus on details at the expense of context.

Grandin describes her mind as working "like an Internet search engine that has been set to access only images. The more pictures I have stored in the Internet inside my brain the more templates I have of how to act in a new situation" (p. 31). She has been able to learn to enhance her perceptual strengths and compensate for her perceptual deficits by acquiring more and more information that "can be placed in more and more categories with many subcategories" that she can access as needed (p. 31).

Grandin also provides insight into the developmental appearance of autism in young children. "The first sign that a baby may be autistic is that it stiffens up and resists being held and cuddled. It may be extremely sensitive to touch and respond by pulling away or screaming. More obvious symptoms . . . usually occur between 12 and 24 months of age, . . . [with the] most common symptoms in young children [being] no speech or abnormal speech, lack of eye contact, frequent temper tantrums, oversensitivity to touch, the appearance of deafness, preference for being alone, rocking or other rhythmic stereotypic behavior, aloofness,

continues

Box 6.1 continued

and lack of social contact with parents and siblings. Another sign is inappropriate play with toys. The child may spend long periods of time spinning the wheel of a toy car instead of driving it around on the floor" (p. 35).

When Grandin was two years old, she says she "showed the symptoms of classic autism: no speech, poor eye contact, tantrums, appearance of deafness, no interest in other children, and constant staring off into space. I was taken to a neurologist, and when a hearing test revealed that I was not deaf, I was given the label 'brain-damaged.' . . . I can remember the frustration of not being able to talk at age three. This caused me to throw many a tantrum. I could understand what people said to me, but I could not get my words out. It was like a big stutter, and starting words was difficult" (pp. 33–34).

Grandin adds that "one of the perplexing things about autism is that it is almost impossible to predict which toddler will become high-functioning. The severity of the symptoms at age two or three is often not correlated with the prognosis. . . . I am lucky in that I responded well when my mother, teachers, and governess kept encouraging social interaction and play. I was seldom allowed to retreat into the soothing world of rocking or spinning objects. When I daydreamed, my teachers yanked me back to reality. . . . Almost half of all very young children with autism respond well to gently intrusive programs in which they are constantly encouraged to look at the teacher and interact" (p. 43).

of my mind is opened to its beauty, the barge ground brightens beneath my feet, and the hedge-row bursts into leaf, and the rose-tree shakes its fragrances everywhere" (pp. 161–162).[2]

Unlike Helen Keller, most people who are legally blind are not completely without sight. According to medical criteria, **legal blindness** entails visual acuity of 20/200 or less (seeing at 20 feet away what a fully sighted person sees at 200 feet), and/or a peripheral visual field of 20 degrees or less, in the better eye with corrective lenses. Beth Omansky (2011), whom we introduced in Chapter 4, describes the experience of being legally blind as living in the borderlands of blindness, neither fully sighted nor fully blind, yet most of her life she has been pushed to identify herself as one or the other, often finding herself falling between the cracks with respect to disability accommodations she needs but is denied.

Depending on the nature of the visual impairment, people who are legally blind vary considerably in what they can actually see. As Omansky observes: "No matter how much time I spend with legally blind friends and colleagues, I can neither assume nor accurately guess how they view and see. I have met only one other person with the same eye disease I have, and her description of what she sees is different from mine because the progression of her disease process is not at the same stage" (2011:154). Moreover, any one individual may have varying vision function depending on subtle differences in the environment. One man named Larry who was interviewed by Omansky says that his vision changes with even subtle variations in the weather, with rainy days affecting him differently than misty days, and cloudy days affecting him differently than foggy days.[3] Sunshine is Larry's least favorite weather condition, especially in conjunction with snow, because the laser treatments he has undergone have left scars that make him painfully sensitive to brightness and glare. As Larry explains, "Every single thing you do . . . when you're blind, no two scenarios or situations are exactly alike. . . . [E]ven if the damned knife is five inches over to the right from where it was last time, and the lighting isn't as bright, . . . maybe you're cutting a carrot instead of a tomato" (p. 157).

Or take the case of Georgina Kleege (1999), who became visually impaired due to macular degeneration.[4] Kleege has retained her peripheral vision but has a blind spot in the central part of her visual field. When she looks at a painting, she can generally make out the edges of the canvas, but she has to move her face within a few inches of the canvas in order to see "the details of texture, depth, and illumination" (p. 94). What this means, of course, is that she is unable to see the composition as a whole. As she writes:

> To get a general sense of the overall composition, I scan the painting systematically, moving my oversized blind spot around it, allowing different regions to emerge in my peripheral vision. My brain slowly identifies the forms and assembles the picture bit by bit. In effect, my mind sketches an outline, or a map: "To the left, there's a table with a basket of fruit. To the right, there's a window with a view of the sea." (pp. 93–94)

Moreover, different textures are more or less difficult for Kleege to see. She can't see straight lines, and solid objects may "dissolve or shimmy, insubstantial shadows and patches of light acquire solidity and form" (p. 101). She finds herself having to sense what is there, using her imagination, rather than assuming that what she is seeing is all that others with vision see.

When walking about on the street, Kleege says she can't see her "feet or what's directly in front of them," so she has to use her peripheral vision to "get a general sense of an obstacle here or directions there" (1999:104). Mostly, she relies on predictability, what she expects to be there. If something unusual appears in the environment, she is less likely to perceive it. One time she encountered a rabid raccoon on a sidewalk near her house; she only learned what it was from a neighbor who was watching nearby. All she "saw was an indistinct, grayish mass, low to the ground and rather round. It was too big to be a cat and the wrong shape to be a dog" (p. 106). At the grocery store, she is able to distinguish the Cheerios from the Wheaties, but only "because one hazy blur is yellow and the other is orange" (p. 107).

People who are blind report relying on their memories to orient themselves to their environment and protect themselves from physical injury (Kleege 1999; Kuusisto 1998). They count the number of steps it takes to get from one place to another. They memorize the locations of the curbs and bus stops, relying on the contours of the land, the landscaping, and the architectural features of the environment, because they can't read street names. They try to "memorize telephone numbers, credit card information, and membership identification numbers" because they have trouble seeing small printed material (Omansky 2011:160). They memorize the menus of fast-food restaurants because they are located behind the counter high on the wall and in font sizes they cannot see. But some environments—such as dimly lit restaurants, bars, and nightclubs—are just not amenable to memorization, and cocktail parties are "social death" because the visually impaired "cannot scan a room to see people's faces" and approach them for conversation (p. 138).[5]

Omansky (2011) reports on an incident at an outdoor amphitheater after calling in advance to request accessible seating close to the stage. She was told that the only place to accommodate her request was in the wheelchair section, even though this section was halfway

FURTHER EXPLORATION

Box 6.2 John Nash

In *A Beautiful Mind*, the 2001 Academy Award–winning film based on the best-selling book by Sylvia Nasar (1998), the life of Nobel laureate John Nash was brought to the big screen. Nash, born in 1928, was a brilliant mathematician, some have called him a genius, who worked in both pure and applied mathematics, making discoveries that had significant impacts on economics, computer science, and game theory, among other scientific fields. Always perceived as an eccentric and arrogant intellectual, a solitary thinker who was obsessed with originality, Nash was diagnosed with schizophrenia when he was thirty-one years old.

The symptoms of schizophrenia, a mental illness that affects about 1 percent of the US population, most often appear between the ages of sixteen and thirty (National Institute of Mental Health [NIMH] 2012). Nash's symptoms, which included delusional and paranoid thinking, involved the hearing of voices that were alerting him to a nefarious conspiracy. According to Nasar's (1998) account, Nash believed that inhabitants of another galaxy, and perhaps foreign governments, were communicating with him through encrypted messages in the *New York Times* that were meant only for him to decipher. When his behavior became increasingly erratic, "simultaneously grandiose and persecutory, . . . irritable and hypersensitive one minute, eerily withdrawn the next," he was hospitalized against his will (pp. 248, 258).

The causes of schizophrenia are not well understood, but it does run in families and appears to have a genetic component. (Nash's son has schizophrenia, too.) Scientists now think that a chemical imbalance that causes an overstimulation of neurotransmitters in the brain may be involved. The risk of violence to other individuals from schizophrenia is low, but about 10 percent of people with schizophrenia do commit suicide. Ironically, the suicide risk may be greatest when the course of treatment is successful, perhaps because "the absence of delusions allows other feelings, including very painful ones, to emerge" (Nasar 1998:308; NIMH 2012).

After his diagnosis, Nash spent the next decade of his life in and out of mental hospitals, where he was treated with antipsychotic drugs and insulin shock therapy. Nowadays people can learn to manage their condition and live in the community by taking the

continues

Box 6.2 continued

proper medication. But while most people need to stay on their medication for their entire lives if they expect to control their symptoms, Nash dealt with his through the sheer power of his will. Describing his condition "in terms of a persistent dreamlike state, . . . of being preoccupied by delusions, of being unable to work, . . . of withdrawing from the people around him, . . . [and] as an inability to reason," Nash compared "rationality to dieting, implying a constant, conscious struggle, . . . a matter of policing one's thoughts, . . . trying to recognize [delusional] ideas and rejecting them, just the way somebody who wants to lose weight has to decide consciously to avoid fats or sweets" (Nasar 1998:351). In this way, Nash learned to live with his illness without drugs. Intellectually, however, he was never the same, having completed all of the work for which he received the Nobel Prize before the onset of his illness. Although a predisposition to schizophrenia may have been implicated in Nash's brilliance and creativity as a mathematician, the full-blown manifestation of his disease essentially put an end to his seminal career.

up the hill from the stage, and when she sat in this section anyway, some of the wheelchair users complained that she didn't belong there and should move. Similarly, at movie theaters and concert halls the only "handicapped" seats are for wheelchair users, and those are typically located at the ends of aisles and far back from the stage, which are of no use to blind patrons.

Omansky also discusses the pros and cons of legally blind people using a white cane, which is both an adaptive aid and a universal symbol of blindness. On the upside it makes it easier for people to understand that you have a disability, eliminating the ambiguities inherent in interactional settings in which others do not know you cannot see very well at all. On the downside it is a cultural artifact associated with stigma, fear, and avoidance of blind people (see also Kuusisto 1998; Michalko 1998).

Lastly, Omansky notes that the phenomenology of borderland blindness can include living with pain (see also Kleege 1999; Kuusisto 1998). Some legally blind people suffer from chronic neck and posture-related back pain from trying to position their line of sight to enhance their limited vision. Omansky says that when she holds "a book or magazine two inches from [her] face for more than a few minutes, [her] forearms and hands go numb, and [she has] to shake . . . and shake them to get [the] feeling back" (pp. 163–164).

The Phenomenology of Sign Language

Unlike legal blindness, there is no such thing as legal deafness, but there are of course variations among the hearing-impaired as to how much sound they can hear, depending on which part of the ear is affected. In her book *Dancing Without Music*, Beryl Lieff Benderly (1990) notes the two elements of hearing that mark these variations: *intensity* and *frequency*. Intensity involves the amount of energy driving the sound waves that impact the ear; this controls the volume or degree of loudness that a person perceives. Frequency has to do with the shape of the waves, "whether they are large or small, jagged or smooth, simple or complex"; this controls the degree to which sounds will appear clear or distorted (1990:28). Richard Rosenthal (1978) compares these two elements to listening to a radio, with low intensity the equivalent of listening to a radio with the volume turned down, and jagged frequency the equivalent of listening to a poorly tuned-in station with muffled and garbled sound.

In our early discussion of disability in historical perspective (see Chapter 3), we noted the conflict between oralists and manualists regarding the teaching of language to deaf people, with oralists believing that verbal articulation was necessary for deaf people to be educated and achieve social acceptance, and manualists believing that educating them through the natural language of sign was superior. We also noted the emergence of American Sign Language, derived from French Sign Language, as an evolving language with its own syntax, abbreviations, and gestural expressions. It is this language that constitutes the lingua franca of contemporary Deaf culture in the United States (see Chapter 2).

Benderly offers a useful description of the phenomenology of sign, noting that sign language "is a symbolic communication medium specifically designed for transmission by the human body to the human eyes" (1990:168). She observes that "ASL uses space the way spoken language uses sound," with the user sculpting space to communicate the message (p. 175). Whereas English is linear, sign is three-dimensional. The location of the body from where the sign is formed, the shape and motion of the hands, the position of the hands in relation to the body, whether the two hands move similarly or differently—all these combine in multiple ways to constitute a language as complex as any spoken language in the world. "No English translation can express the sum of undertones and overtones in a sign language phrase," which has its own nuances of meaning that may get lost in translation, anymore than it can for another spoken language (p. 178).

Over the years, deaf educators have developed alternatives to the either/or approach of manualists versus oralists. One approach employs **signed English**, which essentially uses the structure and syntax of English to sign, as a bridge between ASL and spoken English. Proponents of Deaf culture, however, think it is one thing to teach signed English as a second language to ASL, but quite another thing to require children to think linguistically in English *before* thinking linguistically in ASL (Deaf Linx 2012; Edwards 2001; Fleischer and Zames 2001).

Another approach is called **cued speech**, which aims to help deaf people visually interpret the speech of English speakers. As developed by R. Orin Cornett in the 1960s, cued speech is a variation of lip reading. The problem with conventional lip reading, Cornett believed, is that "most mouth shapes can stand for more than one sound. The speechreader who [does] not already know the language has no way of telling which of several visually identical possibilities the speaker [is] pronouncing at any given moment" (Benderly 1990:192). To remedy this problem, "Cornett developed a system of eight hand shapes that can be held in any of four positions relative to the face. These by themselves do not stand for sounds; they have meaning only when combined with information from the speaker's lips" (p. 192).

Finally, there is a method called **total communication**, which is an eclectic approach that borrows techniques from multiple methods, often using them simultaneously. For people with some residual hearing, or for those who lose their hearing later in life, verbal communication may become part of this mix. Needless to say, any approach that attempts to displace ASL as the primary language of deaf people has been vigorously opposed by those committed to maintaining the vitality of Deaf culture in the United States (Benderly 1990; Deaf Linx 2012; Fleischer and Zames 2001).

Navigating the Physical Environment
with a Mobility Impairment

In their research with people with mobility impairments, Heather Ridolfo and Brian Ward (2013) shed light on the phenomenology of moving about in an ableist world designed for nondisabled people.[6] Many of the people they interviewed in their study say they either receive help from others for the performance of routine tasks or have made accessibility modifications to their homes, for example, by installing ramps, railings, automatic doors, lower kitchen cabinets, and bathroom modifications such as raised toilet seats and hand rails adjacent to toilets and in baths and showers. However, many others do not own their own homes and/or cannot afford these modifications, leading to much difficulty accomplishing basic daily tasks that nondisabled people take for granted. One fifty-four-year-old woman with multiple debilitating conditions, for instance, who has no grab bars in her bathroom, describes the challenge of "trying to get from the toilet to the sink": "I pulled one sink off the wall and the water—WHOOSH! Had to get an emergency plumber to come. So when he came he put in a cabinet; he put in a new sink, a new wall, the whole thing, . . . but still when I raise up I have to put one hand on the tub and lightly pull up on the sink. Not pull up, but just balance myself and put my weight on the tub and stand up" (p. 63). Two other informants describe the challenges of bath management this way:

> I hold onto the towel bar that's on this wall, and I'll reach over and hold onto the sink. And I'll put my left leg in the tub first, and then I just sit on the side of the tub or sit in the shower chair and wash myself up. (p. 64)

> I have fallen once or twice. Getting [in the shower] one time, and the one time I was hobbling to the bathroom and fell into the shower. I was like I got to catch my balance and then BOOM. Yeah right on the back of my head. . . . I think I was out for about a minute. (p. 65)

Few of the informants in Ridolfo and Ward's study were able to afford kitchen modifications, leaving them unable to reach items in cabinets. Some say they have to climb up on counters to get what they need, and even for those who have cabinets low to the floor, some have trouble bending over to reach them. Others have problems reaching the kitchen sink from their wheelchairs. One man who uses a wheelchair says he cannot see the pots on the stove, so he has to remove the pots in order to monitor his cooking. This also places him at risk of getting burned.[7]

Difficulty gaining entrance to homes is the most common problem cited by Ridolfo and Ward's informants, with a majority having trouble with steps. This problem is particularly acute for those who live in rental apartments. Informants also report having trouble opening and closing heavy exterior doors, particularly when carrying bags upon returning from the grocery store. Others say they have difficulty passing through interior doorways in their homes, needing to get out of their wheelchairs to get into the bathroom, for instance. Some also have problems accessing the different levels of their homes, needing to abandon use of the second floor or the basement altogether. One woman says she has to crawl up the stairs to get to the second floor.

Once out in the community, things do not get any easier. Uneven sidewalks, potholes in streets, steep ramps, inadequate or absent curb cuts, and slippery surfaces are all barriers to mobility. Hills that form the natural contour of the landscape are the most commonly cited difficulty. As Ridolfo and Ward note: "For respondents who wear prosthetics or who have ankle injuries, flexing the ankle to walk up an incline can range from difficult to impossible. For others, fatigue, pain, and balance issues pose a challenge to walking up and down hills. For those who use wheelchairs, simply having the strength to wheel oneself up hills and steep ramps pose challenges" (2013:72). One fifty-nine-year-old woman with degenerative arthritis and a bulging disk in her back describes walking up the hill to the bus stop as "devastating. It's like a day's work" (p. 72). Another woman says she has to walk in the street because of the buckled sidewalks, fearful that she will twist her ankle. One man who uses a wheelchair says there are times when he has to push himself down the road in traffic because there are no curb cuts.[8]

Ridolfo and Ward's informants also describe social barriers related to others' impatience with their slower pace. One man who walks with a cane says it's common for people to shout, "Hey, move out of my way!" (2013:74). Others simply don't pay attention. As this man explains: "They talk on their cell phone, walking down the street, and you have to stop and kind of put your cane out and poke them. . . . you have to be like, 'Wait a minute, pay attention to where you're going.' Because they will walk right over you or just stand there. . . . They're behind you, they get impatient. They're in front of you, they act like you're not there" (p. 74). Another man says that one of the reasons he even uses a cane is to communicate that he can't move as quickly as others.

> People look at me and if I don't have the cane, they don't realize that I'm slowed down. . . . The cane's almost a warning device. . . . There are times when if I was crossing a wide street that you're not going to make it on the light without having to move quick. . . . I use the cane partially for . . . a warning . . . to drivers or to other people . . . because I'm a big guy and people look at me and they can't understand . . . why I'm not moving quick. (pp. 74–75)

Informants in Ridolfo and Ward's study note improvements in the availability of paratransit vans for people with disabilities, and many rely on these services for their primary means of transportation. They also appreciate that more buses nowadays have lower ground-level entrances or automated lifts, as well as priority seating for seniors and people with disabilities and transportation stops located closer to their homes. At the same time, these two modes of transportation—paratransit vans and buses—are not without problems. The paratransit drivers all too often pick them up too early or too late, or do not pick them up at all. Informants report that they are "a headache" and "pain in the butt" to use, "the luck of the straw" in terms of reliability, and the "last form of transportation" they rely on (2013:77).

Those who use buses or subways also report problems with other passengers, with nondisabled passengers unwilling to give up seats reserved for seniors and the disabled, and bus drivers refusing to help them. These nondisabled passengers also raise questions about their disability. For example, one woman with a prosthetic leg that is covered by her pants says there are times when she's been asked to get up from the reserved section. Informants also note problems with elevators at subway stations. One man says that elevator outages are so common at the station he uses that he has learned how to use the escalator with his wheelchair. Others report having to compete for space with nondisabled people in elevators. As one woman explains: "[S]ometimes [you're] waiting and waiting for the elevator. And when it comes there are about six people on there, sometimes teenagers, sometimes business people who just didn't want to walk the stairs. . . . The escalator might be broken in the station so they use the elevator and they don't give people in wheelchairs priority to get on" (2013:79).

For those who drive to their destinations, Ridolfo and Ward's informants report having difficulty finding accessible parking places. One forty-eight-year-old woman who suffers from bursitis, rheumatoid arthritis, and diabetic neuropathy says she gets so fatigued from having to walk from her parking place in a public garage to her destination that she has to stop four times to rest. Others mention difficulty getting in and out of their cars, particularly vehicles that are low to the ground. Once they arrive at their destination, they also have trouble with entrances into buildings. One woman who uses crutches says she has problems with doors closing too fast and then catching her arm in the door. Others do not have the arm strength or ability to push the door open, hold it in place, and maneuver through the doorway. Once inside the building, they may find that there are no elevators and that the bathrooms are inaccessible. Such are the experiences that represent the phenomenology of navigating the environment with a mobility impairment.

Recovery from Spinal Cord Injury

John Hockenberry (1995) severed his spinal cord in a car accident when he was nineteen years old. He lost all physical sensation in his body from his nipples down, but he describes the numbness he feels not as an absence of feeling but as a "distinct feeling" (p. 42). "Just as zero gives meaning to all numbers," he writes, "numbness is a placeholder of the flesh, the boundary where consciousness and body divide, where life becomes the inanimate vessel we live in" (p. 42). Hockenberry adds that the "body is your body whether you can feel it or not. There is actually no reason to believe that loss of feeling makes you any different from the same old bag of water and flesh you have always known. The bag fills. The bag empties. Life goes on" (p. 98).

To more fully understand the nature of spinal cord injury (SPI), it is first necessary to say something about the spinal column. From top to bottom, the spine consists of five regions: the cervical (neck), thoracic (chest), lumbar (lower back), sacral (hip), and coccygeal (tailbone) regions. The cervical (C) region consists of seven verte-brae, descending from C1 to C7, while the thoracic (T) descends from T1 to T12, and the lumbar (L) from L1 to L5. Below the lum-bar region are five fused vertebrae of the sacral region and four fused vertebrae of the coccygeal region. In general, the higher the level of impairment, the greater the loss of sensation and movement function. But there are also variations in the places where one may feel pres-sure but not temperature, or temperature but not pressure, and there are those who retain sensation but who have no motor control (Hock-enberry 1995). There are also people like Melvin Juette, whom we introduced in Chapters 2 and 5, who has what he describes as an "incomplete" SPI, because his spinal cord was not completely severed and he retains use of his hip muscles and sensation through his lower buttocks (Juette and Berger 2008). Thus Hockenberry observes, "The trace of each paraplegic and quadriplegic's sensory border zone is as unique as a fingerprint. Each person has a different answer to the question: What does paralysis feel like?" (1995:98).[9]

In her research on SPI, Christina Papadimitriou has examined the phenomenology of recovery from SPI, which she describes as "the creative process of **re-embodiment**," the process by which one becomes acclimated to and learns how to maximize the abilities of their new body (2008a:691). In one of her studies, Papadimitriou focuses on "the co-production of 'work' in a clinical setting among spinal cord injured adults and their physical therapists" (2008c:365). She notes that the cardinal task of rehabilitation is the transformation of what is deemed "a compromised, limited and injured body" into a "newly abled" body (p. 365). Phenomenologically speaking, this is experienced by the newly disabled person as a transformation from "I cannot do" to "I can do."

According to Papadimitriou, the rehabilitation that takes place in medical settings entails the treatment of the newly disabled person as a **patient**, which requires "the surrendering of one's own routines, rhythms, preferences, and decision-making to the institution's poli-cies, structures, and regulations. Everyday practices such as waking, getting out of bed, washing, eating, napping, entertaining visitors, taking medication, [and] sleeping" are governed by an external med-ical authority (2008c:368).[10] From the perspective of the medical staff and hospital-clinic, having others "determine one's everyday

FURTHER EXPLORATION

Box 6.3 Living with Traumatic Brain Injury

Traumatic brain injury (TBI) refers to an injury to the brain from a shock or blow to the head that "results in impairments in cognitive, physical, or emotional functioning" (Lorenz 2010:1). An estimated 5.3 million people in the United States are currently living with TBI, which is caused mainly from falls (28 percent), motor vehicle accidents (20 percent), sports-related injuries (20 percent), and criminal assaults (11 percent) (Davies, Connolly, and Horan 2001; Langlois, Rutland-Brown, and Thomas 2004; National Center for Injury Prevention and Control 2005). The two age groups most at risk for TBI are persons fifteen to twenty-four years old and those sixty-five years and older (Kraus and Chu 2005). Recently, the large number of Iraq and Afghanistan US war veterans incurring TBI, mainly from improvised explosive devices—the "characteristic injury" of these wars (Jones, Fear, and Wessely 2007:1641)—has increased interest in this type of disability (Lorenz 2010; see also Box 8.3).

Depending on the part of the brain that is affected, people with TBI experience symptoms that include impairment of memory, problems with attention and concentration, and difficulty processing information and initiating and completing activities (Ownsworth and Oei 1998; Sherry 2006; Zhang et al. 2001). In her research on TBI, Laura Lorenz (2010) found that people expressed a range of emotions, including confusion, frustration, embarrassment, anger, and depression, particularly over the impairment of memory (including forgetting what they just said or where they just put something) and loss of former competencies. One informant named Peggi says she "forgets where she is driving, despite placing a note with the destination on her car's dashboard. She is distracted by 'constant background noise'—the television, someone walking past, people talking—that prevents her from focusing 'on what's in front of me'" (p. 84). She has difficulty completing tasks that require multiple steps or careful planning and says she feels like she's "treading water, or slipping around" as daily tasks multiply "like rabbits" into "moving furry targets" (p. 95). She also suffers from fatigue, needs to use a cane for balance, and cannot stand without the aid of (expensive) medication.

continues

Box 6.3 continued

Recovery from TBI entails forging new pathways in the brain, but living with the condition requires accepting that things will never be the same as they were before. It also involves reconciling oneself to the loss of one's former self and the development of a new sense of self. As Peggi describes it, "The 'new self' concept is very true . . . because when you get stuck wanting to be your old self, it only leads you to frustration, and takes away from acceptance" (2010:110). David, another of Lorenz's informants, says, "Acceptance is like facing the truth. . . . I'm not going to lie to myself that I should be doing what I did before. . . . How can I move forward if I'm lying?" (p. 118). In the last analysis, however, those living with TBI want to be known as "survivors" rather than as "tragic victims," as forward-looking individuals who are seeking a new way of being in the world (Sherry 2006:209).

routine and tasks may sound constricting and oppressing to many self-sufficient adults, but for the newly injured, a pre-determined schedule comprised of pre-structured activities is viewed as allowing patients to concentrate on their therapy instead of worrying about daily living management" (p. 368). In this way, the rehabilitation setting is viewed as providing "a safe, accessible, and supportive environment for patients" (p. 368).

Papadimitriou notes that medical personnel, including physical therapists (PTs), also make moral assumptions about what constitutes a "preferred" or "good" patient. As she observes:

> SPI patients are perceived as needing to go through several psychological stages of adjustment before they are "ready" for physical therapy. . . . "[P]atients who are motivated," as one physical therapist said, "are easier to work with than those who are depressed or bored." . . . "Motivated patients" involve those . . . who seem to be able to keep a light and presumably non-depressed attitude; are on time for therapy; are open and cooperative to suggestions, corrections and innovations from staff; are not rude to staff; are not violent when they disagree or dislike an aspect of therapy; are friendly and courteous; and gracefully and stoically accept pain, discomfort and adversity. (2008c:368; see also Bishop and Scudder 1990)

At the same time, Papadimitriou argues, to define the rehabilitation process primarily as an oppressive or constrictive practice is to misconstrue "the caring, committed, coaching and collaborative aspects" of the patient-PT relationship (p. 369).

The process of rehabilitation following SPI entails special exercises designed to strengthen the body and enhance flexibility and coordination. It also involves the teaching of daily life skills under new constraints, use of a catheter and bag to manage bodily waste, techniques for transferring in and out of a wheelchair, and techniques for maneuvering a wheelchair. As the facilitator of the rehabilitation process, an effective PT must be able to manage the disabled person's emotions, for they are undergoing not just physical changes but psychological changes as well. But some PT's are not trained or comfortable trying to do so. As one PT said, "Ask me about transfers, about passive or active range [of motion]. . . . [But] I am not a psychologist or a social worker" (Papadimitriou 2008c:369). As such, Papadimitriou found that PTs distinguish between the "work" of physical therapy and the "talk" of psychology and social work. At the same time, PTs cannot ignore the emotional aspects of their relationships with patients, because the establishment of trust between patient and PT is an essential part of the rehabilitation process. As one PT named Susan said, "if they don't trust me, they are not gonna believe me when I tell them 'you can do this, try harder.' . . . So, yeah, we talk during physical therapy, but you know, got to keep it light and easy, 'cause physical therapy is about working hard and concentrating. It's hard work, for both of us really" (p. 370).

Papadimitriou offers an exemplary vignette between Susan and a twenty-eight-year-old SPI patient named Roy to illustrate her portrayal of the collaborative work that takes place in the rehabilitation setting. The session begins with Roy wheeling into the therapy room in his wheelchair, his upper body supported by a brace and his knees locked into a straight position with a metal knee-immobilizing device. Susan and a PT aide transfer Roy to a matted exercise bed about two feet off the ground.[11] Susan's goal for this session is to get Roy to transfer from the bed to the wheelchair on his own, "without bending his knees or his back and without using a sliding board" (an assistive aid used in transfers), relying primarily on his shoulders, arms, and hands (2008c:370).

Susan helps Roy move his legs closer to the chair, while the aide stands by to catch him should he fall. As Roy lifts his upper body, he loses his balance, falls backwards, and is caught by the aide. Seeing that Roy is alarmed, Susan immediately apologizes and says, "it won't happen again." In turn, Roy says, "I can't do more," but Susan retorts, "Yes you can, you are doing fine" (2008c:370). This time, with Susan holding Roy by his torso brace, Roy pushes himself up again and positions himself "sitting partly on the wheelchair and partly on one wheel" (pp. 370–371). Susan then moves his legs and Roy slides his body onto the chair. "How was that?" Susan asks. "Hard!" Roy murmurs. "It was hard but you did it," Susan replies, adding: "It was hard because you did most of the work. I did not help so much, which means that you are doing better. When I don't do as much and you do all the work, it is not as hard for me, but it is harder for you. But this means that you are improving. . . . The less work I do, the better you are" (p. 371).

In her analysis of this vignette, Papadimitriou notes how Susan skillfully deflects Roy's concern about falling. Although she apologizes for what happened, she immediately returns to the task at hand, encouraging Roy "to reach beyond [his] current limitations, work harder, and be motivated to take responsibility for [his] own rehabilitation" (2008c:371). In doing so, she helps him move from an existential position of "I cannot do" to a position of "I can do." More generally, Papadimitriou observes, the rehabilitation process is not simply a matter of acquiring new physical skills; it is also a matter of changing attitudes. To be sure, some patients require more assurance and coaxing than others, but when they do, the interpretive and communicative skills of a PT come importantly into play—knowing when and how to "push" a patient to try harder.

For some people facing the challenge of a newly acquired SPI, a positive, forward-looking attitude comes more easily than it does for others. In the immediate aftermath of his paralyzing gunshot injury, Melvin Juette felt like he was "a little child. . . . I had lost control of my bladder and had to learn to use a catheter to urinate. I needed help bathing, getting dressed, and transferring in and out of my wheelchair. . . . I realized that I would have to learn all the little things I had once taken for granted all over again" (Juette and Berger 2008:70).[12] Juette describes his rehabilitation experience as his "therapeutic boot camp. . . . The work was hard, grueling at times, but I could see that I was making a lot of progress" (p. 71). But Juette was one of those individuals who exhibited remarkable resiliency in the face of adversity. As he says:

> It would have been easy for me to give up at the time, and today when I tell people my story, they often assume that I must have fallen into a deep depression. But this is not what happened because I decided early on that I wasn't going to give in to self-pity or despair. I remembered how my friends and I had reacted to James, a neighborhood youth with muscular dystrophy, who was the first person I'd ever known who had a disability. Although James used a power wheelchair, we all tried to include him in everything we did. We even changed the rules for touch football to accommodate him; if the passer hit James with the ball, it was counted as a catch. But James would at times feel sorry for himself, and some of the kids began to tire of his negative attitude. Eventually, when we made plans to do something, someone would inevitably ask, "What about James?" Someone else would reply, "Naw forget about him." I was determined not to end up like James. (Juette and Berger 2008:70)

While Juette was recovering in the hospital, he had an epiphany of sorts. He was hanging around in the lobby when another young patient pushed by him in his wheelchair, popped a wheelie—balancing the wheelchair on its two rear wheels—and took off. Juette thought it would be "really cool" if he could do that too: "Everyone would be impressed if I could pop a wheelie and do tricks in my chair. I started to think that if I was going to be in a wheelchair, I wanted to get really good at using it" (Juette and Berger 2008:73). Juette's epiphany is related to a phenomenon that Papadimitriou also studied in her research on SPI, noting that the creative process of re-embodiment entails a process of becoming **en-wheeled**, that is, "learning to live through (the use of) a wheelchair in order to become newly abled" (2008a:695).[13] In phenomenological terms, "the chair becomes a part of one's way of being in the world, part of the 'I can' or 'I can do again'" dimension of the recovery experience (p. 696). Becoming en-wheeled entails the process by which a paraplegic becomes someone who is not "in" a chair, but rather someone who "uses" a chair and for whom "the chair is experienced as an extension and integral part of the lived body" (p. 699). As one man explains, "I put my chair on along with my clothes. . . . It's part of me." Another man says, the chair "is a part of me. It's my other half. My mind is one half, the wheelchair is my body." Thus Papadimitriou found that patients who were most positive and forward-looking in their attitudes were those who came to view their wheelchair not as a stigmatizing symbol of disability but as the vehicle of their independence (see also Sapey, Stewart, and Donaldson 2005). As Mike Frogley observes, of his recovery from SPI after a car accident he was in when he was twenty-one years old:

> It would have been easy for me to look at myself and say, "being in a wheelchair is not as good as walking." It's true that in some places it's not as good. In a society filled with stairs, a wheelchair is not your number one choice. But if you're going to be in a shopping mall, which is 100 percent accessible, it's one of the best ways to get around. . . . The point is that being in a wheelchair is not worse or better, it's just different. (Berger 2009b:59)[14]

Disability Sport and Athleticism

In Chapter 5, we noted Melvin Juette's introduction to the game of wheelchair basketball while he was recovering at the Rehabilitation Institute of Chicago (RIC), and how he found it inspiring to meet peers who showed him that being disabled didn't have to stop him from leading a physically active life (Juette and Berger 2008).[15] Similarly, one of Papadimitriou's informants said that learning about rock climbing at a disability sports center caused "a big [light] bulb" to go off in her head (Papadimitriou and Stone 2011:2127). She had always wanted to try rock climbing, even before her SPI, and was thrilled to learn she could still do it. As she explains, "that was one of those things when I found out that I could still rock climb, I get it! I can still do a lot of stuff. There are things I simply cannot do and that I miss, like dancing, and I had a motorcycle before, they have bikes, but it's not the same . . . and once you realize it, that you can do things, it makes it easier" (2011:2127).

Juette describes his palpable excitement the first time he played wheelchair basketball with the RIC community youth team.

> While I used a conventional hospital chair, [the other players] all pushed lightweight sports chairs. When [the coach] put me in the game, I trailed behind the others the entire time. My chair was heavier and I wasn't in as good condition. By the time I got to one end of the court, the shot had already been taken and everyone else was heading the other way. No one would pass me the ball. When [someone] finally did, I threw up a shot as I fell backward in my

chair. Miraculously the ball went in! That night, as I lay wide awake, my mind was racing about the prospects of playing competitive sports again. (Juette and Berger 2008:74–75)[16]

A few weeks later, Juette had the opportunity to watch more experienced and talented players at a men's tournament sponsored by RIC.

I was simply amazed when I saw the Chicago Sidewinders, one of the best teams in the country at the time. How quickly they propelled their chairs up and down the court as my head ping-ponged back and forth in disbelief. On a fast break, a player would throw a behind-the-back pass to a teammate who'd lay it up into the basket with an underhand scoop or over-the-head shot. They maneuvered their chairs so skillfully, stopping and pivoting on a dime and then shooting or passing the ball to the open man. It was at that moment that I knew what I wanted to do—to be as good as these men, to be like Mike, one of the best in the world. Later I would read about the legends of the game in *Sports 'N Spokes* magazine, the premier publication for disability sports. Watching and reading about these players opened up a whole new world for me. (Juette and Berger 2008:80)

An extensive body of research supports the proposition that participation in sports provides an array of benefits for people with disabilities. For many, the primary benefit is the intrinsic satisfaction, the reward felt for playing the game, accomplishing the task itself. Others enjoy the camaraderie and affirmation they get from teammates and peers. Participants gain improved physical conditioning and a sense of bodily mastery, the pleasure of "feeling athletic" (Cooper and Cooper 2012:59). They also gain a heightened sense of self-esteem and personal empowerment that spills over into other social pursuits, as they learn to view "challenges as possibilities rather than as obstacles," to deal with defeat not as failure but as an incentive to do better (Blinde, Taub, and Lingling 2001:163). These enhancements are not simply therapeutic or rehabilitative, for they are the same ones enjoyed by the nondisabled who participate in athletics (Ashton-Shaeffer et al. 2001; Greenwood, Dzewaltowski, and French 1990; Guthrie and Castelnuovo 2001).[17]

The most notable venue for elite competition in disability sports is the international **Paralympics**—with the first summer Paralympics being held in 1960, the first winter Paralympics in 1976, and women first included in 1968. The term "Paralympics" initially referred to the word "paraplegic," but later came to mean "parallel," as the com-

FURTHER EXPLORATION

Box 6.4 The Sport Wheelchair

For four decades, from 1937 to 1977, the Everest & Jennings (E & J) company held a wheelchair patent that gave them a virtual monopoly in the wheelchair industry. The E & J adult model, which was made out of chrome-plated steel and weighed 45 to 55 pounds, had a number of features such as hard rubber tires and fixed armrests that were not conducive to sporting activities. In 1977, however, a US Justice Department antitrust lawsuit and a newly emerging wheelchair industry eroded the E & J monopoly, leading to a period of innovation in wheelchair technology (Fleischer and Zames 2001).

As early as the 1950s, wheelchair basketball players initiated a period of experimentation with the design of the wheelchair to make it more suitable for competitive athletics. One of the first innovations was the development of the pneumatic (air) tire to replace the hard rubber tire that was used on the conventional wheelchairs of that era. Players found that the hard tires would at times separate from the rims while they were turning their chairs, and they also provided a rougher ride and would break down after about three months of play. With the aid of a $1,800 grant from the *Chicago Sun-Times* Veterans Association that was secured by Timothy Nugent, the director of rehabilitation services at the University of Illinois at Urbana-Champaign (U of I) and a key figure in the development of competitive wheelchair basketball in the United States (see Box 6.5), designers at U of I developed a pneumatic tire that was more durable and provided a more comfortable ride. Additionally, players began removing the armrests and push handles from their chairs and lowering the backrest to eliminate unnecessary bulk and weight. They attached anti-tip casters to the underside of the rear frame, several inches off the ground, so if the front end of the chair lifted off the floor, the casters prevented it from tipping over. The players also angled the wheels, making them farther apart at the bottom than at the top, giving the chairs more stability and making them easier to turn. By the late 1960s, the manufacture of tubular stainless steel chairs lowered the standard weight to about 30 to 45 pounds (LaMere and Labanowich 1984).

The next innovation, the contemporary lightweight sports wheelchair, came in the late 1970s and is credited to Marilyn

continues

Box 6.4 continued

Hamilton, who became a paraplegic after suffering a spinal cord injury in a hang-gliding accident in 1978. Prior to her injury, Hamilton had been an avid tennis player, and she found the conventional hospital chair, even the stainless steel models, too heavy and bulky for tennis. She asked two of her hang-glider friends who designed gliders to build her a lighter chair. The 26-pound aluminum chair they came up with was light and sturdy. It had a sleek and sporty look, with a low-slung back and compact frame that resembled a multispeed racing bicycle. Hamilton and her friends started their own business, manufacturing and selling their Quickie brand wheelchairs as fast as they could. The chairs came in a variety of colors and transformed an unappealing medical apparatus into a symbol of fun, sport, and disability pride. Today, several manufacturers design lightweight sports chairs for use in a variety of sports and recreational activities (Berger 2009b; Shapiro 1993).

petitions (since 1988) have been held just following and in the same venue as the regular Olympics.[18] Although the Paralympics is separated from the able-bodied Olympics, it bears little resemblance to the **Special Olympics** held for people with intellectual disabilities in the United States. Paralympians are at times disgruntled that the Special Olympics seems to receive more publicity and that the public often confuses the two sport competitions. Founded by Eunice Kennedy Shriver in 1968, the Special Olympics is better funded through charitable contributions than are sports programs for the mobility impaired, particularly through subsidies from the Joseph P. Kennedy Jr. Foundation (DePauw and Gavron 2005). With more than 2 million people participating worldwide, the Special Olympics is the largest sports program for people with disabilities in the world (Roswal and Damentko 2006). Although the Special Olympics are competitive, and individuals take great pride in winning and showing off their medals, they strike some as reflecting a "charity" orientation to disability sports, as exemplified by the practice of positioning people to give hugs at the finish lines of races (Baker 2011; Leiter 2011). The Paralympics, on the other hand, is intended for elite athletes who train and compete with the same level of dedication as their able-bodied Olympics counterparts (Berger 2009b; Medland and Ellis-Hill 2008; Nixon 2002).

Nevertheless, as competitive opportunities for disability sports grew, critics began to question whether disabled people actually benefit from "able-bodied achievement values" and whether the competitive athletic model is an appropriate one to emulate (Nixon 2002:429; see also Hahn 1984). Jay Coakley (2004), a leading sport sociologist, notes that the **performance ethic** of competitive sport entails several elements of what it means to be an "athlete": sacrificing other interests for "the game," striving for distinction, accepting the risk of defeat, playing through pain, and refusing to accept limits in the pursuit of excellence. While overconformity to this ethic can lead to the taking of performance-enhancing drugs, the development of an attitude of hubris toward others, and a desire to humiliate or even physically harm an opponent during a game, Coakley thinks that under optimal conditions the competitive ethic can have positive benefits, including the building of "self-esteem, responsibility, achievement orientation, and teamwork skills required of occupational success" (2004:485). Thus, while complaints about so-called supercrip athletes are often used to bolster the critique of competitive disability sports (see Chapter 2), others believe that on balance competitive sports offer an affirmative experience for people with disabilities (Berger 2009b; Cooper and Cooper 2012; Hardin and Hardin 2004; Medland and Ellis-Hill 2008).

Howard Nixon observes that "disabled athletes have shown that they want opportunities to compete" at the elite level of their respective sports, and he thinks the best way to accommodate this interest is to develop differentiated sport structures that allow for a "continuum of options . . . ranging from relatively uncompetitive recreational sports where 'everyone is a winner' to highly competitive elite sports where only a very talented few are selected or earn the right to compete" (2002:429). This approach is the one taken in nondisabled sports, and in spite of the stress of elite competition (Campbell and Jones 2002), there is little reason to expect or desire disabled athletes to forgo comparable opportunities to excel (Berger 2009b; Cooper and Cooper 2012).

More broadly, disability sports raise the question of what is a "real" sport, because the public does not typically consider disabled athletes to be "real" athletes. This question, too, suggests the need to rethink the phenomenology of athleticism, about what sorts of sporting activities actually constitute admirable physicality (DePauw 1997). According to Coakley (2004), a conventional definition of sport includes the following criteria: physical activity, competition, and an institutional structure in which rules are established and standardized over time, with flexible parameters that allow for change. This latter element involves the emergence of regulatory bodies that oversee the sport and a cadre of experts who develop, disseminate, and teach specific training regimens that enhance participants' skills (see Box 6.5). Although disability sports meet all of these criteria, their defining feature is that they are designed for and intended to be practiced by people with disabilities. In some cases, such as wheelchair basketball or wheelchair tennis, players need adaptive equipment to participate; in other cases, such as swimming or wrestling, they do not. But because disability sport structures are segregated from able-bodied sports, they are relegated to second-class status, as if only "natural" bodies play natural sports and "unnatural" bodies play unnatural sports (Berger 2009c; Brittain 2004; Shogan 1999).

Disability sport, especially as practiced at the elite level, moves us beyond the conventional phenomenology of athleticism. The ability to effortlessly maneuver a wheelchair in wheelchair basketball, for example—as Melvin Juette noted of the Chicago Sidewinders— and the ability to shoot the ball into a 10-foot-high basket from the three-point line, the free-throw line, or even closer, *while sitting in a chair,* is a skill whose mastery takes hours and hours of practice over an extended period of time. Merely wanting to be an elite player, to be good enough to be selected for a national team, is not enough. One has be dedicated to this goal, be willing to put in the time to acquire new skills and achieve a high level of physical conditioning that enables one to sustain maximum effort for a 40- or 48-minute game (Berger 2009b; Juette and Berger 2008; Womble 2012).

Mike Frogley, whom we introduced earlier, is a former elite player on the Canadian national wheelchair basketball team and one of the most respected coaches in the game. He thinks that in order to elevate the status of competitive disability sports, a total transformation of public perception will need to take place. Speaking of wheelchair basketball, he says:

> This is not the Special Olympics . . . [or] human interest. . . . It's a competitive sport. It's about winning. . . . The key [is] . . . getting people to see these guys as athletes, projecting an image of what a

FURTHER EXPLORATION

Box 6.5 Wheelchair Basketball in the United States

The game of wheelchair basketball in the United States emerged in the aftermath of World War II, at a time when improved battlefield evacuation methods and medical technologies dramatically increased the survival rate of the wounded. These soldiers, including those with spinal cord injuries, would have died in previous wars. Many of them, who were often warehoused in Veterans Administration (VA) hospitals throughout the country, had previously enjoyed participation in competitive sports and would not tolerate inactivity. They started playing pool, table tennis, and catch, and then progressed to swimming, bowling, and pick-up games of water polo, softball, touch football, and basketball. Of all these sports, wheelchair basketball proved to be the most popular (Berger 2009b; DePauw and Gavron 2005; Fleischer and Zames 2001).

In 1948, several VA teams were organized under the auspices of the Paralyzed Veterans of America, and the Birmingham Flying Wheels from California made the first of several cross-country tours, competing with teams around the country and spreading the word about the sport among disabled veterans and nonveterans alike. An immediate result was the formation of the Kansas City Wheelchair Bulldozers, later called the Rolling Pioneers, which was the first wheelchair basketball team to be formed outside of the VA system (Berger 2009b; DePauw and Gavron 2005; Labanowich 1987).

The first *collegiate* wheelchair basketball team composed of nonveterans was established in 1948 at the Galesburg extension campus of the University of Illinois (U of I) under the leadership of Timothy Nugent, director of the university's student rehabilitation services. When the state of Illinois soon closed its Galesburg campus, Nugent moved the team to the U of I's flagship campus at Urbana-Champaign, where he also developed the prototype for disabled student services that was later adopted throughout the country.

In 1949, Nugent organized the first National Wheelchair Basketball Tournament, which was held in Galesburg. During that tournament, the participating athletes decided to organize the **National Wheelchair Basketball Association** (NWBA), the sport's first national governing body. The NWBA's mission included working

continues

Box 6.5 continued

on the standardization of rules, determining the eligibility of participating individuals and teams, conducting tournaments, and "foster[ing] the concept of the participant as an athlete in his own right, and by doing so, establish[ing] the validity of the sport as a legitimate avenue of athletic expression for all disabled individuals" (cited in Berger 2009b:25).

In general, the rules of wheelchair basketball are similar to the ones used in stand-up basketball. In the case of the wheelchair sport, however, players are allowed two pushes of the wheelchair before they must shoot, pass the ball to a teammate, or dribble the ball at least once. At one time, before the rules were refined, ramming into an opponent's chair was part of the game. Today, although some incidental physical contact is allowed, the wheelchairs are considered part of the player and general basketball rules prohibiting charging and blocking are applied (Crase 1982; Smith et al. 2005).

Currently, the NWBA organizes men's, women's, youth, and collegiate divisions and sponsors more than 200 teams. Although the NWBA is an amateur organization, a number of its teams receive financial support from, and bear the names of, professional National Basketball Association teams. The NWBA is also the official body that governs the selection, training, and fielding of US teams that compete in international competitions, which include the Paralympics and the Wheelchair Basketball Championship, or Gold Cup, which is held every four years in the off years between the Paralympics. Since 1993, the NWBA has been affiliated with Wheelchair Sports USA, formerly the National Wheelchair Athletic Association, the broader organization that facilitates US participation in international competitions (Berger 2009b; NWBA 2012; Smith et al. 2005).

wheelchair athlete looks like, getting people to recognize players of differing ability, just as they do in able-bodied sports. So they can say, wow, [that player] is a phenomenal athlete. He's just spectacular. Or [that player], he's pretty good. He can play with some of the better players, but he's not one of them. He just doesn't have the same athleticism. (Berger 2009b:140)

Brad Hedrick (2000), another highly regarded coach, thinks that major amateur athletic organizations like the US Olympic Committee and the International Olympics Committee (IOC) could help change the conventional mindset that undermines the legitimacy of wheelchair sports. But up to now these sport bodies have been impediments to change. While they have given their seal of approval to the Paralympics as "para" Olympics, they have rejected even minimal integration of wheelchair events into the regular Olympic games. But why, Hedrick asks, did the IOC elevate recreational sports like beach volleyball and mountain-bike racing to Olympic status in 1996, while wheelchair basketball was deemed unworthy of inclusion, in spite of persistent efforts by Hedrick and others? Why do Olympic sport organizations view wheelchair basketball as a less legitimate sport than, say, badminton or table tennis or curling? Why do they continue to preserve the "complete programmatic separation" of athletes with disabilities from athletes without disabilities (p. 74)? Is it because they think that wheelchair athletes are not really athletes after all? Do they think that inclusion of wheelchair sports would somehow diminish the Olympic games? How long will the "separate but (un)equal" model of the Olympics/Paralympics be maintained?[19]

The answers to these questions are as yet uncharted territory for the disability rights movement. Outside of the wheelchair sport community, these questions have not even been raised. But there is another side to this issue as well, which also challenges the conventional phenomenology of sport—the participation of nondisabled people in wheelchair sports. At first glance, some might wonder why nondisabled people would even be interested in playing disability sport. But the fact of the matter is, as Joan Medland and Caroline Ellis-Hill's (2008) research shows, this is a phenomena that occurs with regularity (see also Berger 2009b; Kirkby 1995). Medland and Ellis-Hill therefore ask not whether the nondisabled would be interested in playing wheelchair sports, but why it is that they do? In most cases, the nondisabled first get involved in order to support and share in an activity with a disabled friend or family member. But as they get further into it, they also find the sport to be intrinsically fun and enjoyable. One bodily experience that both disabled and nondisabled participants find particularly compelling is the mastery of a piece of equipment—the wheelchair. As one participant says, the challenge of mastering the maneuverability of a wheelchair "puts a different spin" on disability sports (Medland and Ellis-Hill 2008:111). In this way, Ronald Berger (2009b) views the contemporary sports wheelchair—

lightweight and sleek in design—as a piece of equipment anyone can learn to use, just like a bicycle, bobsled, hockey stick, or baseball glove and bat are used in any other sport.[20]

All this, of course, raises the question of competitive fairness—do nondisabled players have an unfair advantage when competing with disabled players? To a large extent, this issue is not limited to nondisabled versus disabled players, because players with disabilities themselves differ in the degree of their impairments, which gives the less impaired an advantage over the more impaired. In wheelchair basketball, for example, eligible players who are missing some toes, a foot, or part of their leg still have full use of their upper bodies and have an advantage over SPI players who have restricted upper-body movement. Some players are able to lean out of their chairs to shoot or pass, grab a rebound, receive a pass, or pick up the ball from the floor. Others have little or no sitting balance without using leg straps or supporting themselves with the back of the chair, or they need to hold on to at least one arm of the chair in order to move their trunk frontally or laterally (Berger 2009b; Labanowich 1988; Smith et al. 2005).

Without any rules to regulate this imbalance, there is nothing to stop teams from stacking their rosters with less-impaired players, and in order to address this issue, wheelchair sports organizations have developed player classification systems to insure competitive balance. Under the rules of a classification system, each player is assigned a particular number of points, with those with less-serious impairments being assigned higher points than those with more-serious impairments. Then the rules specify a maximum number of points a team can put on the floor or field at any given time. Not only have such rules increased the participation of more-impaired athletes, but a coach's decision about which players to use at any given time becomes part of the strategy of the game (Berger 2009b). With this in mind, those who advocate the inclusion of nondisabled players in some disability sports, which is referred to as **reverse integration** (Nixon 2002), propose that nondisabled players could be classified in the same category as the least-impaired disabled players as a way to maintain competitive balance. As Tracy Chenoweth, another highly regarded wheelchair basketball coach, explains:

> So much of the game is moving a wheelchair, and there's really no difference between a disabled Class III player [the highest classifi-

cation] and a completely able-bodied person like me, functionally speaking, in a wheelchair. He can bend over and pick up every ball I can. He can . . . use his abs, trunk, and hip flexors for stability, speed, and balance. I actually think able-bodies are at a disadvantage because they don't know how to use a wheelchair. And if they want to learn, why not let them play? I'm not going to take anybody's opportunity unless I work harder than them. It would actually increase opportunities for lower-classification players, because if you have more Class III's wanting to play, you'd need more I's on the team. It would also create more teams, which would be good for the sport. (Berger 2009b:141; see also Medland and Ellis-Hill 2008)

With such a classification system in play, wheelchair sports could also move from the notion of reverse integration to **genuine integration**. According to Nixon, genuine integration entails interaction between disabled and nondisabled players in a way that "is not affected, stigma, prejudice, or discrimination," where "disabled competitors do not feel deviant, inferior, or specially favored because they are disabled," and where "disabled athletes' impairments . . . are recognized and accepted but do not [disadvantage them] . . . in competition . . . with their able-bodied counterparts" (2002:428).

Summary

Taking a phenomenological view as a point of departure, this chapter explored the bodily experience of disability from the perspective of those who live with a physiological impairment. We first looked at the ways in which people experience the world without sight and sound, drawing on the lives of Helen Keller and others who are legally blind. Next we considered the phenomenology of sign language and its role in the education of deaf youths. We then turned to the experiences of people with mobility impairments and the obstacles they encounter while navigating a physical environment designed for able-bodied people. We also considered the process of recovery from spinal cord injury and the collaborative work between patients and physical therapists that takes place in rehabilitation settings. Lastly, we examined disabled people's participation in disability sports and athletics and the ways in which this participation disrupts conventional assumptions about what a disabled body can do and the types of sporting activities that constitute admirable physicality.

Notes

1. One man described his condition as if he had stepped "into a London fog" (cited in Hermann 1998:162).

2. Research finds that the congenitally blind, as well as those who lose their vision before the age of five, do not experience vision in their dreams. Children between the ages of five and seven vary in their capacity for dream vision, but those who become blind after age seven have dreams that "are scarcely distinguishable from those of the seeing" (Kirtley 1975:308).

3. One man describes his progressive blindness as "an on-going phenomenological experiment" (Omansky 2011:159).

4. Macular degeneration, the leading cause of blindness among older Americans, is a disease that destroys the cells of the macular, the part of the eye that allows one to see details in the center of one's vision field.

5. Stephen Kuusisto (1998) writes about people shouting at him, assuming that because he's blind, he also cannot hear.

6. The thirty participants in their study ranged from eighteen to sixty-seven years of age. The mobility criteria used for inclusion in the study were use of assistive aids such as canes, crutches, walkers, scooters, or wheelchairs, or difficulty with any of the following functional activities: walking for a quarter mile or ten steps without rest, reaching out to grab a door handle or to get something off a shelf, performing housework or preparing meals, or toileting or bathing. The book was "in press" at the time of this writing, and the referenced page numbers are from Chapter 3 of the original manuscript.

7. In his memoir, John Hockenberry (1995) describes an incident early in his postparalysis life when he burned himself with a hot ceramic pot that he placed on his legs. The pot was cool to the touch of his hands but still hot underneath. He could not feel it on his legs as he continued to stir in more ingredients for about two minutes. It was not until he saw "a slight outline of fluid on [his] pants leg that [he] suspected something terrible might have happened." He noticed his legs twitching and when he removed his trousers he saw that his "skin was gathered into a leathery, shrunken depression," with the hairs on his leg "cooked into a blistered white wound" that was indicative of a third-degree burn (p. 45).

8. Hockenberry (1995) describes an incident when he was nearly killed by a bus as he was crossing the street in his wheelchair. The bus driver could not see him as he made a sharp right turn. Hockenberry narrowly escaped death when he jumped out of his chair just before the bus tire crushed it.

9. Spinal cord injury can also involve living with pain and difficulty controlling one's body temperature (Donahue and Spiro 2007).

10. Talcott Parsons (1951) coined the concept of the "sick role" to describe this view of the patient.

11. The aide was Papadimitriou.

12. Similarly, one of Papadimitriou's informants said, "I've often equated this whole experience to sort of being born again. When it happens . . . it's like . . . everything is left in disarray and you are left without knowing the

things that you knew moments before it happened. How to sit, how to touch your feet, how to balance, how to stand, I mean how to do all those things as an adult you're supposed to know how to do and you are left having to learn it all over again" (Papadimitriou and Stone 2011:2128).

13. From the PTs' and medical staff's point of view, the ability to do a wheelie is a symbol of therapeutic progress for those who are capable of using a manual wheelchair, a sign that they are able to perform maneuvers such as jumping curbs without curb cuts (Papadimitriou 2008a).

14. Like Juette, Frogley did not give in to despair. He says that when he first realized he would be unable to walk again, he "took a deep breath, literally for a moment," and then pulled himself together (Berger 2009b:59). "Life is too short," he says, "to feel sorry for oneself." He asked the hospital rehabilitation staff to tell him what he needed to do to get better. If his PT told him he needed to do 500 push-ups a day, he did not do 300 or 400 or 490. He did 500 and then asked if it was okay to do more.

15. Papadimitriou also notes the role of peer mentors in sharing "information about services, resources, and equipment" that enables one to live successfully with a disability (Papadimitriou and Stone 2011:2127). Similarly, Cynthia Schairer (2011) found that prosthesis users shared knowledge about prosthetic use that went beyond what was provided by their physical therapists or prosthetists.

16. Juette had played sports—baseball, football, and basketball—all his life. From as early as a young child, that's what he did every day. During high school, before his injury, he played on the varsity football team.

17. For a more complete list of references, see Juette and Berger (2008:166–167, note 41).

18. In addition to the Paralympics, international competitions for individual sports are also held every four years in the off-years between the Paralympics. For historical background on international disability sports before the Paralympics, see Berger (2009b), DePauw and Gavron (2005), Labanowich (1987), Nixon (2002), and Smith et al. (2005).

19. This is an entirely different matter than, say, the case of South African Paralympic runner Oscar Pistorius wanting to compete in the regular Olympics. Known as the "Blade Runner" and the "fastest man on no legs," double-amputee Pistorius races with high-tech artificial legs. Pistorius caused controversy in 2008 when he requested to participate in both the Olympics and Paralympics and the International Association of Athletics Federation ruled that "his prosthesis gave him an unfair advantage over non-disabled athletes and were therefore illegal" (Dyer et al. 2010:595). Consequently, Pistorius was not allowed to compete in the Olympics, although this decision was later overturned and he was able to compete in 2012. It also differs from the case of golfer Casey Martin, who suffers from a degenerative leg condition that prevents him from traversing a golf course without a cart. Martin caused controversy in 2001 when he wanted to use a cart to participate in Professional Golf Association (PGA) events. Although the US Supreme Court ruled that the Americans with Disabilities Act required that Martin be permitted to use a cart, the PGA and the rest of the

golf establishment refused to accord him social legitimacy (Berger 2009c; Burkett, McNamee, and Potthast 2011).

20. In the game of wheelchair rugby, a sport popularized in the 2005 documentary *Murderball,* the wheelchair is designed to be more rugged, with armor-like lower frontal trim that enables players to crash into each other, as is allowed by the rules of the game (Boebinger 2012). For an analysis of wheelchair rugby as a way for disabled men to assert their masculinity, see Barounis (2008).

7
Representing Disability in Literature and Film

IN CHAPTER 1, WE NOTED THE CONTROVERSY PROVOKED BY the ending of the film *Million Dollar Baby* (2004), in which the main character is euthanized at her request after an accident that rendered her quadriplegic. This is not the only film that has portrayed disability in this way,[1] but voluntary euthanasia is by no means the most common representation of disability in popular culture. In this chapter, we will examine a range of such representations, and the evolution of these representations over time, by drawing on selective examples from classic literature and Hollywood films. My aim is not to cover every literary or film portrayal imaginable—this would take volumes—but rather to give readers a sense of the main themes that have emerged over the years. For the most part, we will focus on fictional works, though we will consider a few noteworthy films "inspired by" or "based on" true stories. In offering a critical reading of this body of literature and film, I do not wish to imply that these works have no redeeming qualities. Rather, my aim is to draw attention to the ways in which people with disabilities have been portrayed, with an eye toward understanding that these depictions both reflect and influence societal attitudes toward people with disabilities.

We will begin with a consideration of the classic folk literature of *Grimms' Fairy Tales*, moving next to classic literary figures and the films made about them. We then turn to a historical overview of dramatic filmmaking, beginning with the emergence of the horror genre in the 1930s, followed by the emergence of the recovery/

overcoming disability genre in the late 1940s, and continuing with other dramatic representations until the end of the twentieth century. Finally, we consider comedy films about disability from the silent era to the present day.

Lessons from *Grimms' Fairy Tales*

John Money observes that folk wisdom penetrates our consciousness in subtle and not-so-subtle ways: "We assimilate its . . . meanings, make them our own, and then, through failing to recognize what we are doing, may put them to our own use" (1989:15). Believing that images of disabled characters in these tales provide us with "archetypes that augment and explain our experience," Beth Franks sought to examine the portrayal of disability in a sample of 100 stories taken from the more than 200 *Grimms' Fairy Tales*, the set of German folk tales that were first compiled by Jacob and William Grimm in 1812 (2001:244).

The first question Franks sought to address in conducting her study was the number of the Grimms' tales in which human characters with disabilities played a major role, finding this was true of nearly half of the stories. Among these characters, nearly half had a physical disability, a fifth had a cognitive disability, with the rest divided among characters who had communication, sensory, emotional, or multiple disabilities.[2] A second question Franks considered was the role of the character's disability in the storyline of the tale. Expecting that she would find a predominance of negative portrayals, Franks was surprised to discover that the disabled characters were portrayed as heroes or heroines in about 40 percent of the stories. In contrast, the characters were portrayed as villains or villainesses in just 15 percent. The rest of the characters were distributed among an assortment of other roles. In only one instance—of doves blinding one of Cinderella's selfish stepsisters—was disability used as a punishment for negative behavior.

In a follow-up to her research, Franks developed an exercise for students in her college course titled "Portrayal of Special Populations in Texts" to examine how they interpreted the Grimms' tales. Over the years she conducted this exercise, Franks observed a consistent pattern: "students express their surprise at the presence of disability in the Grimms' tales, never expecting it to be a feature, much less a focus" (2001:254). The exercise included a lecture Franks gave to her students that was based on her content analysis of the tales, with representative examples. Several weeks later she gave them a quiz and asked them to describe how disability was portrayed in the stories. Franks describes her findings: "Every student remembered how surprised [they were] to find disability present in fairy tales, but only one student remembered a positive character having a disability. One-quarter of the students remembered both positive and negative characters as having a disability, while three-quarters remembered disability being the marker of only a negative character" (p. 254). Surprised at this finding, Franks asks: "How was I to understand my students' responses? In the lecture I had emphasized that disability was primarily a feature of characters who played positive roles and that it was used as a punishment in only one tale. While students had obviously remembered something from this part of the course, they did not take away the message I expected." Franks has no definitive answer to this quandary, but she surmises that even when exposed to positive portrayals of disability, what people remember most are the negative ones.

> We remember messages that conform to our expectations and dismiss evidence to the contrary. . . . Despite the association with heroes and heroines, my students remembered disability as being linked with villains and villainesses. Most students also remembered that disability functioned in a predominately negative way and cited the instance of disability punishing Cinderella's stepsister. My students remembered the exception as the rule. (p. 254)

Franks concludes by noting the "invisible legacy" of disability in fairy tales: We don't remember these characters well, but when we are reminded of them, our perceptions are guided by preconceived notions—that disability is a negative trait.

Classic Literary Characters

Franks's research serves as a caveat for those attempting to uncover the symbolic meaning of disability representations—that readers or moviegoers may take away a message that is at variance from what might be intended or expected. Nevertheless, the weight of the evidence is that the most memorable disability characters in literature and film are those who are negatively portrayed. In this section, we consider five iconic disability characters—Richard III, Quasimodo, Captain Ahab, Captain Hook, and Tiny Tim—that illustrate this truism.

We begin with the play *Richard III*, written by William Shakespeare in the late seventeenth century, which set the standard for things to come. Leonard Kriegel (1987) characterizes Richard as an instance of the **demonic cripple**, a self-loathing, limping hunchback, who describes himself as "deformed, unfinish'd, sent before my time / Into the breathing world, deformed by not enough time in the womb" (cited in Davis 2002:53). He is a jealous and ambitious man, who will stop at nothing (including murder) to get what he wants. He is, in his words, "determined to prove a villain."

The stooped hunchback is also the central character in Victor Hugo's French novel *Notre-Dame of Paris*, better known as *The Hunchback of Notre Dame* (1831). Quasimodo, the novel's central character, is not only physically grotesque but also deaf and half-blind. According to Lennard Davis, as a person constructed with multiple disabilities, Quasimodo "is not a *person* with disabilities, but the icon of the disabled person" (1995:116).[3] And this icon was seared into public consciousness through Hollywood renditions of the novel. The first version was a silent film that appeared in 1923, starring Lon Chaney. Chaney had previously (and subsequently) acted in disability character roles, one as the villainous blind pirate Pew in a film based on Robert Louis Stevenson's *Treasure Island*, which the Scottish author published in 1883.

Martin Norden credits *The Hunchback of Notre Dame* with being "one of the first feature films of physical disability to replicate a disabled person's point of view . . . [by] photographing and editing a considerable amount of the film from Quasimodo's perspective" (1994:91).[4] At the same time, Norden notes, "the director never allows this strategy to go on too long without positioning the audience, often through title cards, to treat Quasimodo primarily as an object of spectacle" (p. 91). Importantly, the parts of the film that do present Quasimodo's perspective do so from the towering heights of the church bell tower from where he performs his responsibility as the bell ringer. This, Norden argues, represents an ableist understanding of the disabled as isolated from society, with "Quasimodo high up in his Notre Dame perch" looking down upon the tiny dots of the townspeople below (p. 92).

In 1939, the first talking version of *The Hunchback of Notre Dame* was released. This film starred Charles Laughton, who insisted upon being made up to look as grotesque as possible. A leading Hollywood make-up artist was hired to make Laughton "look as if half his head were melting," which the actor enhanced "by letting his mouth hang open, revealing missing teeth and a protruding tongue, and wildly flicking his 'good' eye back and forth" (Norden 1994:139).[5]

Arguably the first iconic disability character in US literature was Captain Ahab of Herman Melville's *Moby-Dick* (1851), considered by many to be one of the greatest American novels. The novel focuses on Ahab's obsessive quest to extract revenge on Moby Dick, the gigantic white whale that had severed Ahab's leg. Ahab represents a tormented man who is marked by a "permanent insufficiency," unable to live with or without his prosthetic whalebone leg (Kriegel 1987:34). Taking on the character of the demonic cripple and what Norden calls the **obsessive avenger**, Ahab leads a group of sailors on a quest that will lead all but the narrator of the novel to their deaths.

The 1930 film version of *Moby Dick* was "one of the first full-length talking films to feature a disability theme" (Norden 1994), and like the film version of *The Hunchback of Notre Dame*, seared an iconic image of disability on the public consciousness.[6] In 1956, John Huston's classic remake starring Gregory Peck further cemented Ahab's image in popular culture. In addition to highlighting Ahab's diabolic nature, Huston emphasized his sense of isolation from the rest of society. When Ahab walks outside a tavern at the beginning of the film, all goes quiet when the once boisterous occupants hear "an odd tapping sound and stare out a window (as does the audience) to see the lower half of Ahab walk by, his whalebone prosthesis prominent" (p. 217). Indeed, the distinctive sound of Ahab's walk becomes a kind of motif that symbolizes Ahab's ominous presence.[7]

In 1911, Scottish writer J. M. Barrie published *Peter Pan*, based on a children's play he had written a few years earlier, introducing the world to Captain Hook. Like Ahab, Hook had lost a limb—in his case, a hand to an arch-rival crocodile, which he compensated for by wearing a hook. The obsessive avenger theme characteristic of Ahab is also part of Hook's modus operandi. Among the several versions

FURTHER EXPLORATION

Box 7.1 The Story of Quasimodo

As is often the case, a film production of a great novel can never do justice to the original work. Victor Hugo's *The Hunchback of Notre Dame* is one of the great works of Western literature. The full story of Quasimodo goes like this: In the early fifteenth century in Paris, a malformed baby boy is abandoned on the doorstep of the church of Notre Dame. His mother then abducts a more beautiful baby to replace the one she just abandoned. The baby with the grotesque face and humped back is raised by a priest and ultimately becomes the bell ringer of Notre Dame. That duty and his appearance socially isolate him, and he earns his keep at the expense of his hearing, as the bells' noise deafens him. As a deaf, disfigured, and rather grotesque young man, Quasimodo becomes the central character in the novel's plot.

All of the other characters in the book respond only to his physical appearance. None can see beyond the outer trappings to Quasimodo's intelligence or his ability to care and love. In his childhood he develops a strong, one-sided attachment to the priest who took him in, but the priest is uncaring, calculating, overly critical, and eventually lustful over an object of Quasimodo's affection: a young Gypsy woman named Esmeralda. In the course of a local celebration, Quasimodo becomes the butt of people's scorn without realizing he is being humiliated, and after a minor transgression he is lashed with a whip in a public flogging. Esmeralda, secretly the grown infant his mother had abducted, takes mercy on him and gives him water when he cries out in thirst and pain. Quasimodo experiences the first pangs of kindness in his life and is enchanted by the young woman.

Esmeralda is a self-absorbed adolescent who is oblivious to the effect she has on Quasimodo. Instead, she is smitten with a dashing officer in the local militia. He, in turn, is attracted to her but is troubled by her low social status. Later, a rumor is heard that something dire has happened to the officer and local officials assume that Esmeralda has done him harm. In lynch mob fashion, they quickly sentence her to death. Quasimodo understands the crowd's intentions and manages a dramatic rescue. He carries her off to the church seeking sanctuary, where the priest feels stirrings in his loins and begins to lust after Esmeralda.

Meanwhile, the rabble and local constabulary attempt to storm the church to lynch her. From the safety of the bell tower, Quasi-

continues

Box 7.1 continued

modo protects Esmeralda by flinging heavy objects down on the crowd below. Political pressure is applied to the priest to give her up, and when Esmeralda rebuffs his advances he blames her for enchanting him and turns her over to the crowd. She is summarily and grotesquely hanged. Quasimodo is distraught by the treachery of the priest, his ersatz father, and flings him to his death from atop the cathedral. Some years later, in a building in which the hanged and the indigent of Paris are left to rot, a skeleton of a hunchbacked man is found embracing the remains of a young woman with a broken neck. Quasimodo is loyally united in death with the object of his love.

   The potboiler that is *The Hunchback of Notre Dame* served as a vehicle for Hugo to lampoon the Catholic church, the sexual predilections of the priesthood, the dimness of the monarchy and the body politic, and social systems that foment the creation of underclasses, bigotry, mob mentality, and uncaring and unthinking people in general. Quasimodo, an innocent without guile, was the only character in the novel capable of love and caring. But the trueness of his heart was obscured by his appearance.

Source: Adapted from William E. Powell, "Becoming Quasimodo: The Shaping of a Life," in *Storytelling Sociology: Narrative as Social Inquiry*, eds. Ronald J. Berger and Richard Quinney (Boulder, CO: Lynne Rienner, 2005).

of the story that have been made into film, Walt Disney's 1953 animated feature film and Steven Spielberg's 1991 *Hook* are arguably the most well known, but it was Herbert Brenon's 1924 silent film that first accentuated Hook's prosthesis, which was not a central element of the original story (Norden 1994).

   Our final classic literary character, Tiny Tim (or Tim Cratchit), of Charles Dickens's *A Christmas Carol* (1843), is by no means a demonic cripple or obsessive avenger. Rather, he is a pitiable figure, what Kriegel (1987) characterizes as a **charity cripple** and Norden (1994) as a **sweet innocent**. Anchoring the opposite stereotype spectrum of what we have been describing so far, the charity cripple/sweet innocent is portrayed as almost entirely dependent on the good graces of others for their every need. Tiny Tim, the "crutch-bearing cherub" who comes from a poor family, is the prototype of this disability genre (Norden 1994:11). As Kriegel explains:

> The Charity Cripple soothes [polite] society because he refuses to accept his wound as the source of rage. Indeed, he refuses to acknowledge rage. His purpose is never to make "normals" . . . uncomfortable or guilty. He inspires pity, not fear. He plays with the heartstrings of the world. Or rather he plays on them. In updated versions, on telethons and billboards and letters appealing for alms, . . . his picture is intended to destroy the isolation of the giver. He enables the audiences to avoid the coldness of its own potential fate by becoming givers of alms. Of course, Dickens is offering a Christian message. And the giving he is so enamored of springs from a specifically Christian sentimentality about the poor and maimed. . . . For the poor and halt and lame are not only forever with us, they can also be called upon—and called upon consistently—to help [us] justify [our] own virtue. (1987:37)

There have been countless movie adaptations of the novel in Great Britain and the United States, most called *A Christmas Carol*, but some called *Scrooge*, that go back to the beginning of the twentieth century. A line from Tim's father in the 1935 version of *Scrooge* best illustrates the charity theme. Speaking of Tim, the father tells Tim's mother, "He told me coming home that he hoped the people in the church saw him because he was a cripple, . . . and if it might be pleasant for them to remember, upon a Christmas day, who made lame beggars walk and blind men to see" (quoted in Norden 1994:133).

The Emergence of the Horror Film Genre

In addition to the 1923 version of *The Hunchback of Notre Dame*, predatory hunchbacks willing to commit unspeakable crimes was a common theme of the silent-film era, and it was these films that paved the way for the horror genre that emerged in the 1930s (Norden 1994). Arguably, the seminal film of that period was the first of a series of *Frankenstein* films, which was released in 1931. Based on Mary Shelley's novel that she published in 1818, *Frankenstein* starred Boris Karloff as the "Monster," the victim of an experiment gone awry. The demonic cripple in the film is Fritz, who is not a character in the original book, the assistant to Dr. Henry Frankenstein, the Monster's creator. A scruffy man with a twisted spine, Fritz assists Dr. Frankenstein in "robbing graves and stealing bodies still dangling on the gallows" to use in his experiments (Norden 1994:113). Dr. Frankenstein treats Fritz like a slave, calling him a fool and barking out orders that Fritz follows obediently. But away from his master, Fritz vents his frustration on the Monster, cracking a whip at the Monster's feet. After learning that the Monster fears fire, Fritz terrorizes him with a torch.[8] On one occasion, however, the Monster gets loose and kills Fritz, hanging him from the rafters.

In later versions of the Frankenstein series, *Son of Frankenstein* (1939) and *Ghost of Frankenstein* (1942), the Fritz character is replaced by Igor, another villainous figure with a disability. An evil shepherd who escapes the gallows, Igor emerges with "a contorted body as a result of a broken neck" (Norden 1994:141). In *Son of Frankenstein*, in the manner of the obsessive avenger, Igor manages to befriend the Monster and seeks to use him to extract revenge on the jurors who sentenced him to the gallows. In *Ghost of Frankenstein*, Igor plots to kidnap one of Dr. Frankenstein's sons to transplant his brain into the Monster's.

It is interesting to note, on the other hand, a more benevolent disability theme that appeared in the second film in the series, *Bride of Frankenstein* (1935). Here we are introduced to a disability type that Norden (1994) describes as the **saintly sage**, whereby a blind hermit befriends the Monster, welcoming him into his home.

> Eyes alight with a mystic glow, his bearded visage often turned heavenward, the hermit looks as if he just stepped out of a Bible story. . . . [He] shares his food, drink, and lodging with the Monster and even [begins] a modest socialization program for him. His humane treatment leads to a strong irony later in the film when a hunter, startled at the sight of the Monster living with the hermit asks incredulously, "Good heavens, man, can't you see?" Though sightless, the hermit does "see." [Indeed], he is the only character in the film who understands the Monster will behave as a human being if so treated. (p. 132)

The success of the first *Frankenstein* film, produced by Warner Brothers, led an envious Irving Thalberg, a studio executive at Metro-Goldwyn-Mayer (MGM), to want to make a film that "out-horror[ed] Frankenstein" (quoted in Norden 1994:115). For this job he hired director Tod Browning, who subsequently made *Freaks*, which was released in 1932. *Freaks* was unique in that it used actual people with physical and cognitive disabilities to play major and minor roles. Setting the film in a circus with freak show exhibits (see Chapter 3), Browning assembled a cast of characters that MGM described in its advertisements as "creatures of the abyss," "strange children of shadows," and "nightmare shapes in the dark" (cited in Norden 1994:115–116).

The storyline of *Freaks* follows a variation of the obsessive avenger theme, focusing on Hans, played by a real midget, who is in love with Cleopatra, an able-bodied trapeze artist. Hans's love is unrequited, but when Cleopatra learns that he stands to inherit a sizable fortune, she plots with her lover Hercules, the circus strongman, to marry Hans and then poison him and steal his money. The plot is averted when the other "freaks" learn of the scheme, and they decide to "exact a cold-blooded revenge; in a nightmarish sequence replete with thunder and lightning, [they] slay Hercules and mutilate Cleopatra to such an extent that she becomes a 'freak,' too, a grotesque 'chicken woman'" (Norden 1994:116).

Perhaps to the public's credit, *Freaks* was a box-office failure. And film critics of the day denounced the revenge-taking scene as misguided, a major flaw in the film. Up until that point in the story, Browning had presented the "freaks" as basically "normal" people who were even more likable than the two able-bodied antagonists. But by finally resorting "to the popular image of circus freaks as being strange and sinister creatures he destroyed all his previous good work, laying himself open, at the same time, to the charge of exploitation" (Brosnan 1976:66).

In spite of the critical reaction to the film, Browning went on to make other horror films for MGM. One of these films, *The Devil-Doll* (1936), is worth mentioning because it was a rare instance of an actress, Rafaela Ottiano, cast in a central role as a demonic cripple. Ottiano plays Malita, the crutch-using wife of Marcel, a "mad scientist" who has been "experimenting with a method of reducing humans to doll size and then commanding them to do his will" (Norden 1994:120). Malita is mad, too, and after Marcel's death, she seeks to carry out their plans to shrink the entire world. "Inexplicably eager to follow *Freaks* with another film that featured multiple disabled characters," Browning also populates the film with a saintly blind woman, a cognitively disabled sweet innocent, and a young woman described as "an in-bred peasant half-wit" (p. 121). There is also a banker who is paralyzed after being stabbed by a doll with a poison knife. Of this man, the attending physician says, "He'll be hopelessly paralyzed for the rest of his life. A brilliant mind imprisoned in a useless body" (p. 121).[9]

Postwar Recovery Films

Following World War II, the experience of disabled war veterans initiated a new direction in films about disability, the genre of recovery/overcoming adversity films, the most famous of which is *The Best Years of Our Lives* (1946). This film follows three returning veterans, one of whom is a sailor who has lost both of "his hands as a result of a fire on board his attacked ship" (Norden 1994:165).[10] The handless character, Homer Parrish, is played by Harold Russell, a veteran who in real life had lost his hands, too. Homer is understandably having difficulty adjusting to his condition, learning how to use his prosthesis and dealing with the awkward reactions of others. Homer also has a prewar girlfriend in Wilma Cameron, who wants to continue their relationship and offers him love and support. When Wilma's parents want to send her away in the hopes that she and Homer will forget about each other and move on with their lives, Homer offers to end their relationship. But Wilma remains steadfast about making the relationship work. Although nowadays the film has its critics, particularly for "its avoidance of social issues insoluble beyond the individual level," Norden believes that *The Best Years of Our Lives* is "one of the most forthright, sensitive, and honest depictions" of the disability experience in the history of filmmaking (pp. 166–167).

Though not a film about war veterans, another noteworthy disability film of that era, *Johnny Belinda* (1948), featured a lead female character played by up-and-coming actress Jane Wyman. The film centers on a deaf-mute woman, Belinda McDonald, who the townspeople of a remote fishing village think is retarded.[11] Belinda is befriended by a newly arrived physician who senses her intelligence and teaches her sign language. Although Belinda is portrayed as a sweet innocent, what makes the film memorable is that Wyman prepared for the role by learning to sign and by spending months working with deaf people to understand their perspective. Because of her efforts, *Johnny Belinda* "allowed audiences unfamiliar with sign language to appreciate its expressive beauty while still participating fully in the characters' conversations" (Norden 1994:176).

Still another significant postwar recovery film was *The Stratton Story* (1949), based on the life of Monty Stratton, a Texas farm boy who became a star pitcher for the Chicago White Sox in the 1930s, lost a leg in a hunting accident in 1938, and returned to successfully pitch professional baseball again (though in the minor leagues) during the 1946 and 1947 seasons. In the film, Monty, played by James Stewart, becomes bitter after his accident, refusing to wear a prosthesis or help around the house. He's eventually brought around by his wife who tells him, "I've made out much worse than you. You lost your leg, but I lost you." With the help of his wife and best friend, Monty gets himself back into shape to play ball once again.

Film critics applauded the film "for its restraint and sense of triumph that went beyond the world of sports" (Norden 1994:189). Producer Sam Wood said that baseball "was merely backdrop for the more important story of a man's faith in himself and a woman's faith in a man, plus the sympathetic understanding of his best friend" (quoted in Norden 1994:190). As one of the most notable "inspirational" disability films of that era, however, critics of the overcoming disability theme, like critics of the so-called supercrip phenomenon (see Chapter 2), read a conservative message into the film: In refusing to seek help outside of family and close friends, *The Stratton Story* reinforced the view that people with disabilities can make it on their own; it is they, not society, that need to change. As Irving Zola explains:

> In almost all the success stories that get to the public, there is a dual message. The first one is very important—that just because we have polio, cancer, or multiple sclerosis or have limited use of our eyes, ears, mouth, and limbs, our lives are *not over*. We can still learn, be happy, be lovers, spouses, parents, and even achieve great deeds. It is the second message [that troubles me]. . . . It states that if a Franklin Delano Roosevelt or a Wilma Rudolph[12] could OVERCOME their handicap, so could and should all the disabled. And if we fail, it's *our* problem, *our* personality, *our* weakness. . . . And all this masks what chronic illness [or disability] is all about. For our lives and even our adaptations do not center around one single activity or physical achievement but around many individual and complex ones. Our daily living is not filled with dramatic accomplishments but with mundane ones. And most of all, our physical difficulties are not temporary ones to be overcome once-and-for-all but ones we must face again and again for the rest of our lives. (1984:142–143)

Zola's admonition notwithstanding, however, few would deny that the inspirational theme is far superior to the demonic or pitiable themes, and *The Stratton Story* set the pattern for such films to this very day.

The Uneven Progress of Disability Filmmaking

As we move forward in our account, we see uneven progress in the ways people with disabilities are portrayed in Hollywood films, with some breaking new ground and some rehashing old themes. There was little new in the 1950s, which brought us *Peter Pan* (1953) and *Moby Dick* (1956), as well as a few other films that do not raise additional issues for us here (see Norden 1994). But a few films of the 1960s are worth noting, beginning with two true-story films about celebrity "supercrips": *Sunrise at Campobello* (1960), a film about Franklin Delano Roosevelt, and *The Miracle Worker* (1962), a film about Helen Keller and Annie Sullivan, both of which were successful plays before being brought to the big screen (see Chapter 3). Additionally, two fictional films about blind women employing the sweet innocent theme are worth mentioning: *A Patch of Blue* (1965) and *Wait Until Dar*k (1967).

In the midst of the civil rights revolution of the 1960s, *A Patch of Blue* portrayed a relationship between Selnia D'Arcey, a poor, uneducated, white blind woman, played by Elizabeth Hartman, and black journalist Gordon Ralfe, played by Sidney Poitier, the leading black actor of his generation. In this film, the power differential between blacks and whites is reversed, as Gordon takes pity on Selnia and helps her break out of the dismal conditions of her life. In an era charged with social controversy about race, Selnia is a sweet innocent who is able to "see" beyond race and develop an emotional attachment to a black man. The film also showed how negative social attitudes, not Selnia's disability, "were the main factors in holding her back and keeping her socially isolated" (Norden 1994:227).

In *Wait Until Dark*, leading film actress Audrey Hepburn tries to present a sympathetic portrait of a blind woman, Susy Hendrix, but in Norden's opinion she goes a little too far "with her almost perpetual upbeat and happy demeanor," especially when she says she wants to become the "world's champion blind lady" (1994:228). Nevertheless, although a sweet innocent, Susy is also "tough, resilient, and resourceful in her fight against the criminals who have misrepresented themselves to her and have broken into her apartment" (p. 228).

John Wayne's portrayal of the eye-patch–wearing Rooster Cogburn in *True Grit* (1969),[13] and Dustin Hoffman's seedy, orthopedically impaired Ratso Rizzo in *Midnight Cowboy* (1969), closed the decade of the 1960s. Wayne's curmudgeonly character was a likable sort, while Hoffman's was a creep. During the 1970s, these films were followed by several featuring an assortment of disabled villains, with a notable exception being *Butterflies Are Free* (1972), a film inspired by the life of Harold Krents, a visually impaired (though not completely blind) man who had graduated cum laude from Harvard Law School. The fictional character is Don Baker, who suffers from a misguided and overprotective mother. The storyline eschews conventional narratives having to do with "self-pity, rehabilitation struggles, [or] the uphill return to former glory," and focuses instead on Baker's resolve to puncture, often with gentle humor, other's misconceptions about blind people (Norden 1994:248).

By the late 1970s, films about Vietnam were starting to be released, and for our purposes the most significant of these early films is *Coming Home* (1978). The film has an antiwar message and focuses on the relationship between Luke Martin, played by Jon Voight, and Sally Hyde, played by Jane Fonda. Luke is a disabled war veteran who is recovering in a VA hospital when he meets Sally, a bored military wife who only recently started volunteering at the VA. Luke has been paralyzed from the waist down, and we are made privy to his use of a catheter bag, including a scene where he spills urine on Sally. We also watch Luke and the other disabled veterans playing wheelchair basketball and throwing around a football and Frisbee.

Although the storyline of *Coming Home* is in some ways typical of other recovery films—in this case Luke vents his frustration by becoming an antiwar activist—it is unique in another respect. As the film progresses, Sally becomes increasingly detached from her husband and enters into an intimate relationship with Luke. According to Sarah Smith Rainey (2011), the portrayal of Luke and Sally's relationship as based on equality and mutual respect, where Luke is not a dependent cripple, creates an opportunity for an honest portrayal of Luke's sexuality. In a critical sequence, Sally bails Luke out of jail after he is arrested for protesting the war, and they go back to his apartment with the mutual intent of consummating their relationship sexually. Luke excuses himself to the bathroom and says he will only be a few minutes. He returns naked, with only a hand towel draped over his lap, and asks Sally to place a sheepskin in the center of the bed. She then helps him transfer into the bed and asks Luke, "What do I do?" Luke replies, "Everything. . . ." In some ways, Rainey observes, the ensuing sex sequence "looks and feels much like a typical Hollywood film," but, she adds, "The dialogue lets the audience know that people with paralysis are still sexually aroused by touch in the numb areas [of their body] because they can see the touching and feel through body memory. It also suggests that the rest of the body becomes hypersensitive to touch. . . . I know of no other Hollywood film that treats disabled sexuality this way" (2011:43–44).

A passionate relationship between a disabled person and a nondisabled person is also a theme in *Children of a Lesser God* (1986). In this film, the lead female character, Sarah Norman, is played by the hearing-impaired Marlee Matlin, who won a best-actress Academy Award for her performance. Sarah is a former honors student who remains at the school for the deaf that she attended as a youth. She is stubborn, feisty, and independent, refusing to read lips or speak, instead choosing to communicate through sign language. The lead male character is James Leeds, played by William Hurt, an idealistic speech teacher and advocate of oralism, who finds Sarah, in his words, "the most mysterious, beautiful, angry person [he] ever met." As their relationship develops, James is bent on getting Sarah to speak, which becomes a major point of contention between them. In the final analysis, however, *Children of a Lesser God* is a love story, as the conflict revolving around issues of deafness becomes a metaphor for any number of things that may separate two people trying to maintain an intimate relationship. While the film had its critics among deaf advocates—it does not, for example, confront issues of discrimination—most felt that the film had a positive impact. As Kevin Nolan, a guidance counselor at the Clarke School for the Deaf in Massachusetts, observed, "This movie is . . . a very important work for the deaf because it educates the hearing. Hearing people have so many misconceptions—like deaf people can't read or dance or cry or laugh. The movie shows that we have the same worries and feelings, abilities and aspirations as anyone else" (quoted in Norden 1994:290).

Another notable film of the 1980s was *Places in the Heart* (1984), a depression-era story that includes a blind World War I veteran, Mr. Will, played by John Malkovich. There is an adjustment theme in this film, as Mr. Will comes to live as a boarder with his struggling in-law, Edna Spaulding, played by Sally Field, and her two young children. Mr. Will initially goes about contributing to the household by making brooms and caning chairs, but he is rather bitter and isolated from the others, spending his time listening to recorded books. He eventually comes around, and Edna and he develop a mutual respect for one another and work together to make ends meet. Critics praised Malkovich's performance, with Sheila Benson of the *Los Angeles Times* writing, Malkovich's "slow humanizing of this intelligent, aloof and bitter man is without sentimentality, . . . rich, intelligent and many-layered" (cited in Norden 1994:286).

The 1980s also witnessed increased interest in true story films, most notably *The Elephant Man* (1980), *Mask* (1985), *Born on the Fourth of July* (1989), and *My Left Foot—The Story of Christy Brown* (1989).[14] *The Elephant Man* tells the story of John Merrick (1860–1890), who suffered from a condition called neurofibromatosis, a nervous system and skin disease, which causes tumors to develop beneath the skin.[15] *Mask* is about Roy "Rocky" Dennis (1961–1978), a boy who suffered from craniodiaphyseal dysplasia, also known as lionitis, which causes an enlargement of the cranium. In both films, a good deal of emphasis is placed on the prejudice and discrimination faced by those whose appearance is at variance with the norm and on people's inability to see the humanity behind the visible deformity.

Born on the Fourth of July, directed by Oliver Stone and starring Tom Cruise, is another antiwar film. It tells the story of Ron Kovic, a hawkish prowar soldier who becomes an antiwar activist after becoming paralyzed in the Vietnam War. In many respects, the success of the film lies in Stone's ability to transmute the story of Kovic's disablement into the story of the country's "terrible legacy of Vietnam" (Norden 1994:302). As for the real-life Kovic, he said:

> When Oliver called me up and told me that we were going to do this film, . . . it was like being given a second life. I could never quite reconcile being in a wheelchair after Vietnam. I could never quite understand how my sacrifice could have any kind of meaning at all. Working on the script with Oliver was the first time that I began to understand that my sacrifice, my paralysis, the difficulties, the frustrations, the impossibilities of each and every day would now be for something valuable, something that would help protect the young people of this country from having to go through what I went through. (quoted in Norden 1994:302)

Regrettably, the country did not learn the lesson that Stone and Kovic hoped to impart.[16]

My Left Foot is about the life of Christy Brown (1932–1981), who grew up in Dublin, Ireland. Born with cerebral palsy, Brown was unable to walk or use his hands. In spite of this handicap, he became a successful writer and painter, a "supercrip" of sorts, by using his left foot. Arguably the key element of the film that made it so powerful was the stunning performance of Daniel Day-Lewis, a British actor, who received a best-actor Academy Award.[17] Day-Lewis had a late stepfather who had been paralyzed, so he already had an intuitive grasp of the experience of using a wheelchair. He also spent several months researching the role, including time spent observing children with cerebral palsy at a clinic in Dublin and learning how to write and paint with his left foot. Of Day-Lewis's performance, film critic Richard Corliss observed, "Day-Lewis' triumph is nearly as spectacular as Christy's: to reveal the blind fury in his eyes and stunted gestures, to play him with a streak of fierce, black-Irish humor. Brilliantly, Day-Lewis shows a mind, and then a man, exploding [forth] from . . . Christy's body" (cited in Norden 1994:306).[18]

Two other films of this era—*Rain Man* (1988) and *Sling Blade* (1996)—are also worth mentioning as we conclude this part of our review, because they raise bleak prospects for people with mental disabilities living on their own and the potential for harm to come to themselves or others if they are allowed out of the confines of a custodial institution (Whittington-Walsh 2002). In *Rain Main*, Dustin Hoffman plays the role of an autistic savant by the name of Raymond Babbitt.[19] Raymond is living in an institution for the mentally disabled when he is reunited with his estranged brother Charlie, played by Tom Cruise, who discovers that their now deceased father has bequeathed all of his multimillion-dollar estate to Raymond. Over the course of the film, Charlie develops a genuine affection for Raymond and wants to help set him up to live on his own. But Raymond has trouble adjusting to the outside world, and after he triggers a smoke alarm when he leaves his toaster oven on too long, Charlie realizes that Raymond is better off in an institution.

Sling Blade is the story of Karl Childers, played by Billy Bob Thornton, who has been confined to a state mental hospital since his young teens for murdering his mother and her lover with a sling blade. Karl is befriended by a young boy named Frank, and through their conversations we learn that Karl had been severely abused by his parents. Frank's mother Linda takes Karl in and lets him move into the garage. But Karl is angered by the abuse heaped upon Linda and Frank by Linda's boyfriend Doyle, and when Doyle refuses to leave, Charlie kills him with a lawnmower blade in a violent seven-and-a-half-minute barrage that surpasses even the brutality of the ending in *Freaks*. In some ways, this film is a version of the age-old demonic cripple, though in this case it is a mental disability rather than a physical disability that is the source of the violence (Whittington-Walsh 2002).

Disability and Humor

Thus far we have not considered disability comedy films, a genre that raises complex questions about the nature of humor. In undertaking this part of our inquiry, we need to make a distinction between humor that denigrates and humor that enlightens. D. Kim Reid, Edy Hammond Stoughton, and Robin Smith (2006) characterize the former as **disabling humor** and the latter as **disability humor**. It is essentially the difference between laughing *at* them or laughing *with* them, and whether nondisabled characters or ableist attitudes are ever positioned to be the source of humor in situations with disabled characters (LeBesco 2004; Shannon 2005).

Disability comedy is a genre that goes back to the slapstick days of the silent-film era, where a common theme was to have the lead character impersonate a disabled person, such as in *Blind Man's Bluff* (1903), where a purportedly blind and one-legged beggar, after seeing that a passerby has given him a bogus coin, strikes the passerby with his wooden leg. While some observers of the day thought that making fun of the physically disabled was acceptable only if the characters were not really disabled, the theme had adverse consequences for beggars who were truly disabled. In New York City in 1896, for example, Police Chief Peter Conlin justified the crackdown on beggars with disabilities as a way to get the sham ones off the street, but he made no distinction between those who were disabled and those who were not. As Chief Conlin proclaimed: "The law is clear about the mendicants who pretend to be deaf or dumb or inflicted in any way, and there is no reason why they should not be sent to prison. [But there] are a number of beggars who are really afflicted or deformed, and who thrust their deformities forward to the

FURTHER EXPLORATION

Box 7.2 *Avatar*

Science fiction is another film genre that features disabled characters (Anders 2009), most notably James Cameron's *Avatar* (2009), the highest-grossing film in the history of filmmaking. *Avatar* tells the story of Jake Sully, a disabled war veteran who is assigned a mission that involves becoming an able-bodied avatar. The story takes place in 2154 on the planet Pandora in the Alpha Centauri star system. An American mining company is there to extract valuable minerals, but the tall, blue-skinned humanoid occupants, the Na'vi, are resisting. The mining company wants Jake to infiltrate the Na'vi and subvert the resistance. As a reward for his efforts, the company offers to pay for an expensive new treatment that will restore the use of his legs.

According to Alison Wilde (2010), "There is no apparent reason for this character to be disabled in the first place, other than to frame [his] moral dilemma: whether to put the good of the Na'vi before the evil of the invaders. Making a decision to side with the native people means Jake will remain disabled, . . . spurning [the] reward of 'new' legs." In the end, Jake decides to side with the Na'vi, but he is rewarded by being fully converted into his avatar, his legs, masculinity, power, and sexuality fully restored.

Michael Peterson, Laurie Beth Clark, and Lisa Nakamura (2010) draw attention to an element of the plot that is generally ignored by the audiences that have seen the film. We learn that Jake's spinal injury is reparable, but he simply cannot afford it— "Though technology can fix many things in Pandora and our world, it still apparently cannot or rather chooses not to fix human beings." Moreover, we are shown that "the bias against disabled people is exactly the same in the future as it is at present—one passing soldier refers to Sully as 'meals on wheels' and another replies 'that's just wrong,' apparently referring to Sully's very presence on Pandora." He is there only because he has a particular genetic structure suitable to the avatar; otherwise his "disabled body is viewed as 'waste.'"

public gaze, much to the disgust of ladies. They are impudent and persistent, and will be attended to also" (quoted in Norden 1994:16).

Another theme that emerged in the silent-film era was what Norden (1994) calls the **comic misadventurer**, whereby a disabled person gets into trouble because of his or her impairment.[20] In *The*

Invalid's Adventure (1907), for example, a wheelchair user escapes from his attendant and initiates a wild chase that entails a number of ludicrous accidents in which the "invalid" manages to maintain his balance. Similarly, W. C. Fields's *It's a Gift* (1934), a talking remake of his silent *It's the Old Army Game* (1926), includes a scene that is incidental to the plot in which an elderly visually- and hearing-impaired woman makes a mess in a grocery store.

Charlie Chaplin, the preeminent comedian of the silent-film era, also employed disability themes in his films as a counterpoint to the famous Tramp character that he cultivated during his career. In *City Lights* (1931), one of his best-remembered pictures, the Tramp sets his mind on winning the heart of a beautiful blind flower-seller, a sweet innocent. By happenstance, she thinks he is wealthy, and when the Tramp learns that her sight can be restored by an operation she cannot afford, he goes about finding the money to help her. Throughout the film the woman remains nameless; even in the credits she is simply referred to as "A blind girl," her only signifying trait. The part was played by Virginia Cherrill, and Chaplin remarked that one of his goals in casting her "was to find a girl who could look blind without detracting from her beauty" (quoted in Norden 1994:126). But it is only when her sight is restored—when they can return each other's gaze—that their relationship can be truly consummated.

Just as Chaplin combined comedy with the sweet innocent theme, director Stanley Kubrick is noteworthy for combining comedy and the demonic cripple theme in *Dr. Strangelove or: How I Learned to Stop Worrying and Love the Bomb* (1964). There is no doubt that *Dr. Strangelove*, as a sardonic comedy about the dangers of nuclear war, has many redeeming qualities, but the film's depiction of the ridiculous but villainous Dr. Strangelove, played by Peter Sellers, as a disabled character troubles some disability advocates (Longmore 2003). In the film, Dr. Strangelove is a strategic military adviser to the president of the United States, but he is depicted as an ex-Nazi who has never abandoned his devotion to the führer. He also uses a wheelchair and has a biotic hand covered by a leather glove, which is prone to malfunctioning as it attempts to raise the "Heil Hitler" salute and at times to strangling his own neck.[21]

An entirely different angle, this time about people with mental illnesses, is pursued in *One Flew Over the Cuckoo's Nest* (1975). In this film, based on the 1962 Ken Kesey novel, Randle McMurphy, played by Jack Nicholson, is a rebellious criminal serving a short sentence for the statutory rape of a fifteen-year-old girl. When he is transferred to a mental institution for evaluation, he hopes to stay there to avoid going back to prison. The film portrays the institution, with its mind-numbing daily routines and unpleasant medical treatments, as a major source of the residents' grief. It also presents the staff, especially the hard-nosed, inflexible, and at times sadistic nurse Mildred Ratched, as even more "crazy" than the residents.[22]

Mental disability is also the subject matter of *Being There* (1979), another film starring Peter Sellers, who plays the role of Chance, a simple-minded gardener. Chance has the intellectual capacity of a child and has lived a totally dependent and isolated life. All he knows of the outside world is what he sees on TV. For reasons unexplained, Chance has been living with a wealthy benefactor, and when the benefactor dies, he is forced to leave his home for the first time. After wandering around the city for a while, he is struck by a car owned by a wealthy businessman. This happenstance leads Chance into the world of the super-rich and their high-powered associates—including the president of the United States—who are eager for sage wisdom and think that Chance's observations about gardening are intended as a metaphor for incisive advice about business and politics. In some respects, the storyline is a variation of the saintly sage theme, now transmuted as the **wise simpleton**, along with a dose of the sweet innocent. Fifteen years later, the portrait of an intellectually disabled man as a wise simpleton is the subject of *Forrest Gump* (1994), in which Tom Hanks plays the role of a naïve man who witnesses, and in some cases influences, some of the defining events of the latter half of the twentieth century.

The potential for a humorous critique of society's treatment of people with disabilities is not part of two subsequent films starring Richard Pryor, whose stand-up routines offered trenchant commentary on race relations in the United States. In *Bustin' Loose* (1981) and *See No Evil, Hear No Evil* (1989), the latter with Gene Wilder, all these talented comedians could offer was a regurgitation of the comic misadventurer theme. In *Bustin' Loose*, Pryor plays "an ex-con who guides a busload of physically and emotionally disabled youths through" an assortment of misadventures that includes the almost obligatory scene for comedies with blind characters: driving a motor vehicle (Norden 1994:284). In *See No Evil, Hear No Evil*, Pryor and Wilder play two disabled men, one visually impaired and one hearing impaired, who enact "an unending series of slapstick gags that trade on the characters' disabilities" (p. 292).

Throughout the 1990s and 2000s, no comedic directors were as preoccupied with disability themes as Peter and Bobby Farrelly, better known as the Farrelly brothers. In an analysis of five of the films they directed between 1994 and 2003, Kathleen LeBesco (2004) characterizes their contribution to the disability genre as a mixed bag; some entail the standard fare of making fun of disabled characters, while some actually function to challenge ableist assumptions about people with disabilities.

LeBesco is rather critical of *Dumb and Dumber* (1994), the first of these films, because the treatment of "a pair of dim-witted friends" is at the expense of disabled people and has "none of the humanity that infuses" their disability characters in some of their later films such as *Stuck on You* (2003), a story about two conjoined twins (2004:1). What LeBesco finds appealing about *Stuck on You* is the storyline that portrays social stigma and discrimination, not the characters' impairment, as the cause of their problems. In fact, she suggests, the film portrays the conjoined brothers as "able to function more effectively in a number of areas (sports, food preparation, trick or treating) than any of us singletons do, and . . . their main difficulty comes in encountering cruel and close minded people" (p. 2). LeBesco also appreciates the fact that the cast includes "a relatively large number of disabled people. Actors using wheelchairs, actors with intellectual or developmental disabilities, actors with congenital variations—all seem to find a place here, whether as extras in a crowd scene, as featured extras, or as important minor characters" (p. 2). In doing so, she argues, *Stuck on You* counters the all-too-often societal expectation that people with disabilities, in real life, should be concealed.[23]

What LeBesco also likes about *Me, Myself and Irene* (2000) and *Shallow Hal* (2001), films about a schizophrenic and a very obese woman, respectively, is their use of nondisabled people's "treatment of disabled people as the barometers by which they can be morally evaluated" (2004:3).[24] She finds it noteworthy, however, that the Farrelly films that did the best at the box office—*Dumb and Dumber* and *There's Something About Mary* (1998)—do no such thing. In the latter film, people with disabilities are stereotypically made the butt of the joke—we are laughing at them, not with them. For example, Mary has a brother Warren who has an emotional disability that causes him to react violently at the slightest touch of his ear. In another scenario, Ted, one of Mary's suitors, bends over backwards moving heavy furniture for a grouchy and unappreciative disabled man, whose wheelchair bumper sticker reads, "How's my driving? Call 1-800-eat-shit." And Healy, another of Mary's suitors, tries to impress her by lying about working with people with intellectual disabilities. "My passion is my hobby," he says. "I work with retards." In this scene, it is interesting to observe the film's self-consciousness about "political incorrectness," although it does so in a way that trivializes the issue. When Mary calls Healy on his use of the term "retards," Healy replies, "To hell with that—no one's gonna tell me who I can and can't work with."[25]

Like their previous films, the Farrellys' *The Ringer* (2005), which they produced but did not direct, has brought forth mixed reaction from the disability community. In this film, the lead character Steve Barker, played by Johnny Knoxville, reincarnates the disability scam artist storyline by faking a mental disability so he can enter the Special Olympics and win a gambling bet. Barker proceeds to amuse the audience by practicing his impersonations of "retarded" stereotypes (where we are supposed to laugh *at*, not *with*, disabled people). Upon entering the competition, he meets the other participants, most of whom "are played by actors who have the disabilities they display" (Cherney 2006:2). In another example of the wise simpleton theme, these characters come across as "savvy, quick-witted, . . . and full of insightful wisdom" (Snider 2005:2). To the plot's credit, Barker ultimately realizes the error of his ways and we're "told in no uncertain terms that mocking the handicapped is wrong" (Snider 2005:2). James Cherney (2006) finds it commendable that *The Ringer* makes an attempt to question ableist assumptions but notes that it's telling that it didn't do as well at the box office as the Farrelly films that more consistently pander to the public's inclination to disparage people with disabilities.

Summary

In this chapter, we drew upon selective examples from classic literature and Hollywood films to examine ways in which disability has been portrayed in popular culture. Beginning with the representation of disability in *Grimms' Fairy Tales,* we then looked at five iconic lit-

FURTHER EXPLORATION

Box 7.3 Comedians with Disabilities

In making a distinction between disabling humor and disabled humor, D. Kim Reid and colleagues (2006) argue that it is disabled people themselves who are best positioned to employ affirming rather than derisive humor about disability. Geri Jewell, who has cerebral palsy, was a pathbreaker in this regard, appearing in a dozen episodes of the popular sitcom *Facts of Life* from 1980 to 1984. Just as the sitcoms *Ellen* and *Will and Grace* "paved the way for greater acceptance of gays and lesbians years later, Jewell's affable" character increased viewers' comfort level with people with disabilities (Long 2012:2).

In 1994, Jewell was featured in a documentary about "stand-up" disability comedians entitled *Look Who's Laughing* that was broadcast on Public Television. The other comics in the documentary included Kathy Buckley (who is deaf), Chris Fonseca (who has cerebral palsy), Alex Valdez (who is blind), J. D. England (who has paraplegia), and Bret Leake (who has multiple sclerosis).

One element in some of their routines is the use of "self-deprecating humor to shatter stereotypes and preconceived notions about people with disabilities" (Long 2012:2). In doing so, they also demonstrate that disabled people "are not so fragile as to need constant condescension through mock sentiments of political correctness" (O'Connor 2002:3). Buckley tells a joke about not having dates because she is flat-chested and too tall, but then she says she may have fewer dates because she "didn't hear the phone ring." Fonseca, who speaks in a slow, methodical cadence, plays on stereotypical attitudes when he jokes, "I'm handicapped and I'm Mexican, so you know what that means: If you piss me off, I'm gonna pull a knife and we're both gonna get hurt." In another bit he capitalizes on his unsteady arm movements by recounting his experience at a shooting gallery at a state fair: "Last year I won a teddy bear. . . . Ok, I didn't win it. They gave it to me so I would put down the rifle. . . . It works every time" (Reid, Stoughton, and Smith 2006:633, 637).

Some nondisabled comedians competing for stage time at comedy clubs think that disabled comedians have an advantage because they have a "gimmick." But in the final analysis it is the audience that renders judgment about these comics, not on the basis of their disability but on the basis of whether they are truly funny. As one night-club owner observes, "A [disabled] guy has a gimmick for two minutes, after that he has to win the audience on his own merits. A gimmick doesn't mean a thing. He has to have substance and quality" (Reid, Stoughton, and Smith 2006:633).

erary characters: Richard III, Quasimodo, Captain Ahab, Captain Hook, and Tiny Tim. Next, we considered the representation of disability in the horror genre of filmmaking, representations that portrayed disabled characters in a negative light. We also reviewed "inspirational" post–World War II recovery films that marked a notable improvement in disability film representations, although we noted some criticism of the way this genre reinforces the societal expectation that disabled people should be able to "overcome" their impairments on their own, without the aid of social reforms.

As we turned to dramatic films in the latter half of the twentieth century, we saw uneven progress in disability filmmaking, with some films rehashing negative themes and others portraying disabled people in a positive light. We also considered the comedy genre of disability films, from the silent-film era to the present day, noting the difference between disabling humor and disability humor, with the former involving representations that encourage viewers to laugh *at* disabled characters, and the latter involving representations that encourage viewers to laugh *with* them.

Notes

1. Other films with this theme include the fictional *Whose Life Is It Anyway?* (1981) and *The Sea Inside* (2004), the latter based on a true story.

2. Three-quarters of the characters were male.

3. The condition causing a hunchback is known as Scheuermann's disease, "a hereditary condition of the spine in which growing children, usually male, develop vertebrae in wedge shapes that bend and curb the spine, most particularly in the upper back and neck" (Powell 2005:98).

4. The discussion of films in this chapter draws heavily from Norden's (1994) seminal examination of hundreds of cases.

5. Other versions of *The Hunchback of Notre Dame* include a 1957 French film, a 1982 British made-for-TV film, a 1996 Disney feature film animation, and a 1997 US made-for-TV film.

6. In this sanitized version, Ahab kills the whale and returns safely home.

7. In 1998, a version starring Patrick Stewart as Ahab aired on TV, with Gregory Peck playing a minor supporting role.

8. Fritz is also portrayed as responsible for the Monster's viciousness. When he breaks into a medical school to steal the "normal" brain Dr. Frankenstein ordered him to get, he drops that brain and takes the one marked "abnormal" instead.

9. Arguably the most notorious modern successor to the diabolical disability theme is Freddy Krueger, the villain of the *Nightmare on Elm Street* film series, who was turned into a hateful, sadistic killer after being disfig-

ured "by a fire that left him more monster than human being" (Shapiro 1993:31).

10. The plight of injured war veterans was first brought home to the American public in *All Quiet on the Western Front* (1930), the classic film about World War I.

11. In the film, Belinda is raped and gives birth to a boy she names Johnny.

12. Wilma Rudolph (1940–1994) was considered at one time the fastest woman in the world, competing in two Olympics in 1956 and 1960. She was born prematurely at 4.5 pounds, contracting infantile paralysis (from polio) as a young child. She recovered, but wore a brace on her left leg for three years to correct her twisted left leg and foot. She also survived an assortment of serious diseases, including scarlet fever and double pneumonia.

13. Jeff Bridges played Rooster Cogburn in a remake of *True Grit* released in 2010.

14. Another true story film that did not get much attention but is worth seeing is *Gaby—A True Story* (1987), which recounts the life of Mexican writer Gabriela Brimmer, who was born with cerebral palsy.

15. *The Elephant Man* was directed by David Lynch, who also has made other films with disability themes. For a discussion of these films, see O'Connor (2002).

16. The feature-length documentary *Body of War* (2007) is a powerful portrait of Tomas Young, a paralyzed Iraqi war veteran turned antiwar activist.

17. Four other actors also have earned a best-actor Academy Award for their performance in a film about disability, two for fictional characters and two for real-life figures. Dustin Hoffman won his for *Rain Main* (1988), a film about an autistic savant; Al Pacino for *Scent of a Woman* (1992), a film about a cantankerous blind war veteran; Jamie Foxx for *Ray,* a film about blind singer Ray Charles; and Colin Firth for *The King's Speech* (2011), a film about the stuttering King George VI.

18. For a more critical assessment of *My Left Foot,* see Whittington-Walsh (2002).

19. Hoffman prepared for this role by meeting with an actual autistic savant, Kim Peek, a number of times (Haller 2010).

20. The misadventures of the animated character, the near-sighted Mr. Magoo, is another example of the comic misadventurer.

21. In the first James Bond film, *Dr. No,* the villainous Dr. No is similarly depicted with two bionic hands. Dr. No was just the first in a line of disabled villains to battle the dashing secret agent (Norden 1994).

22. The film also brings to mind D. L. Rosenhan's (1973) study "Being Sane in Insane Places," a field experiment in which eight pseudopatients faked symptoms of mental illness to gain admission to a mental hospital, and when they reverted to "normal behavior," they were still treated by the staff as ill.

23. Beth Haller (2010) and Jeff Shannon (2005) offer a similar observation about the Timmy Vulmer character in the animated TV series *South*

Park. The producers of *South Park,* Matt Stone and Trey Parker, also produced a feature-length documentary, *How's Your News?* (2004), which had a brief run as a series on MTV as well. In that film, five outgoing disabled people travel the country conducting "man-on-the-street interviews" and offering simple wisdom on the meaning of life.

24. For a discussion of fatness as a disability issue, see Chan and Gillick (2009).

25. The film also includes a character who fakes a disability. More recently, Ben Stiller's *Tropic Thunder* (2008) brought forth criticism from disability activists for its repeated use of "retard" to describe Stiller's character (Adler 2008).

8

The Future of Disability

IN THIS CONCLUDING CHAPTER, WE EXAMINE A RANGE OF issues that inform prospects for the future of disability. We begin with a consideration of computer technology, which offers paradoxical possibilities for people with disabilities. We then turn to the specter of genetic selection and physician-assisted suicide, two problematic practices that reflect the societal view that a disabled life is not worth living. Next, we revisit the disability studies critique of the medical model and what this portends for the future of disability studies. In the course of discussing these issues, we also consider disparate disability policy agendas: the agenda of cure, celebration, care, and civil rights (Baker 2011), concluding with some observations about disability and international human rights.

The Paradox of Computer Technology

Few would deny that technology has brought forth an array of benefits for people with disabilities. One need only begin with the availability of corrective eyewear to acknowledge this truism. Indeed, as we noted in Chapter 1, nowadays people who wear eyeglasses or contacts do not even think of themselves as having impairments. For people with hearing impairments, hearing aids have become more or less commonplace as well. People who use wheelchairs—whether they are of the lightweight variety or power-operated—are much less restricted in their mobility than they were decades earlier. And of course the computer age has brought forth closed captioning and telecommunications devices for the hearing impaired, video enlargers and voice readers for the visually impaired, voice-activated technologies, synthesized speech devices for those unable to speak—the list goes on and on (Jaeger 2012; Lupton and Seymour 2000). The Internet, too, has created new online communities, enabling people with disabilities to communicate and network with other like-minded individuals (Seymour and Lupton 2004; see Box 2.1). Additionally, the availability of online education and online shopping, as well as new opportunities to work through telecommuting, make it easier to participate more fully in the life of society. Thus, by the turn of the twenty-first century, a Harris Poll found that adults with disabilities were even more likely than the general population to believe that the Internet improved the quality of their lives (48 vs. 27 percent), made them better informed about the world (52 vs. 39 percent), and helped them meet people with similar interests and experiences (42 vs. 30 percent) (Jaeger 2012).

At the same time, there are available technologies that are rejected by some elements of the disability community. In Chapter 2, for example, we noted the resistance to cochlear implants by proponents of Deaf culture. In this case, technology is perceived not as a benefit but as "an 'artificial' invader of the body" (Lupton and Seymour 2000:1852). For most disability advocates, however, the key issue is not the desirability of technology, but its accessibility and cost (Jaeger 2012).

In his examination of disability and the Internet, Paul Jaeger (2012) notes the existence of a **digital divide** between disabled and nondisabled people. The term "digital divide" was first popularized by a series of reports called *Falling Through the Cracks* that were commissioned by the US Department of Commerce between 1995 and 2000. Even as recently as 2008–2009, nearly 40 percent of US households still lacked Internet access, a figure that was 62 percent in rural communities, where access speeds can be extremely slow by contemporary standards. Moreover, the access rate for people with disabilities is only about half the rate of the general population (Dobransky and Hargittai 2006).

Internet users with disabilities also report incompatibility problems with the interface between computer software and websites and the assistive technologies they need to use them. This problem is exacerbated with smart phones and other mobile devices, which utilize small screens that people with visual impairments have difficulty seeing; and those with hearing impairments often face problems with "speech-to-text conversion, interoperability, and hearing aid compatibility" (Jaeger 2012:40; see also Baker and Moon 2008; Husson 2011). There is also considerable lag time between the launch of a new Web technology and the emergence of accessibility features that make it usable for people with disabilities, and even an updating of "some minor software program may negatively affect the functioning of the various accessibility programs and features" that disabled people rely upon (Jaeger 2012:35). At the same time, when assistive technology is available and works properly, it is an extra cost to disabled users that nondisabled users do not incur (Stienstra, Watzke, and Birch 2007).

Jaeger adds that developers of "information technology have relied heavily on the undue burden exemptions written . . . [into disability] laws to avoid making accessible versions of their products" (2012:64; see Chapter 3). In the federal district court case of ***National Federation of the Blind v. Target Corporation*** (2006), the court did rule that commercial websites that are closely integrated with a retail outlet's physical stores are covered by the Americans with Disabilities Act (ADA). In Target's case, the court found that the company's "online presence" was in fact closely integrated with its "physical presence," and therefore Target's website must be accessible (2012:65). At the same time, the court also ruled that "online-only" retailers like Amazon.com and Priceline.com are exempt from the accessibility mandate.[1]

Accessibility barriers also have significant impacts on the already disadvantaged educational and occupational opportunities for people with disabilities. Although online education has been a boon, a 2008 survey found that only 20 percent of institutions of higher education had a policy requiring accessible websites (Connell 2008). Furthermore, "the use of social media and interactive online spaces for education purposes are heavily limited by overall low levels of accessibility in social media and network services" (Jaeger 2012:90). Thus, one US Department of Education official has estimated that "only about 10 percent of online materials for higher education are accessible" to people with disabilities (Jaeger 2012:90; Parry 2010).

In the world of work, many job tasks that were once difficult or impossible for disabled people to perform can now be handled with the help of computer technology, and among those who are employed, about 90 percent use some type of assistive technology in their work (Dispenza 2002; Schartz, Schartz, and Blanck 2002). Telecommuting, on the other hand, may not be the panacea for people with disabilities that so many had hoped for. First, telecommuting is only an option for employees that have the appropriate technology, and courts have not found that "people with disabilities have a legal right to telecommute as a reasonable accommodation" (Jaeger 2012:86; Ludgate 1997; Tennant 2009). Second, it is likely that telecommuting, which isolates users from physical interaction with employers and coworkers, will limit career options and opportunities for career advancement (Baker, Moon, and Ward 2006; Bricout 2004; Light 2001).[2]

Jaeger notes that because of negative attitudes about and resistance to accessibility, many business and government organizations "have not educated their managers and staff about accessibility," and even when it is viewed as desirable, they lack the expertise to deliver accessible products (2012:73). He also cites a 2009 survey of Web developers (Loiacono, Romano, and McCoy 2009), which found that "86 percent of developers [did] not have adequate training in accessibility, 64 percent felt management was unaware of the importance of accessibility, and 48 percent believe[d] that development cycles are too short to incorporate any form of accessibility" (2012:73).[3]

Ultimately, we need to recognize there is an ethical-moral dimension to technology, as philosophers from Martin Heidegger (1954) to Jacques Ellul (1964) pointed out some time ago. As long as the dominant ethic that drives the technology industry is *innovation*—the production of an ever-expanding array of new products for consumption-hungry consumers (Morozov 2012)—rather than **universal design** —the production of products, buildings, and environments that are inclusive of and accessible to people of diverse backgrounds and abilities (Burgstahler and Cory 2008)—people with disabilities will inevitably have difficulty crossing the digital divide.[4] Robert Merton was arguably correct when he observed that ours "is a civilization committed to the quest for continually improved means to carelessly examined ends" (1967:vi). For people with disabilities, as is perhaps true for nondisabled people as well, technology can be a double-edged sword—a means of becoming both more integrated and more segregated in society.[5]

FURTHER EXPLORATION

Box 8.1 Universal Design
and the Teaching of Architecture

Following the passage of the ADA, the profession of architecture had an opportunity to revise its philosophy of design to make the built environment more accessible to people with disabilities. But in her study of post-ADA architecture schools, Carla Corroto (2012) found that the teaching of universal design remains marginalized and is perceived as antithetical to the more creative, artistic elements of design, which bring greater recognition and status to architects in the field. As one architect professor explained, the teaching of universal design principles "is horrible, really. I mean, nothing is more prescriptive than graphic standards. I didn't get into teaching architecture to teach [this]." Another professor said, the "ADA and issues of bodies experiencing architecture never gets talked about here. We are a design school, for christ sakes."

When universal design is taught in architecture schools, it is often segregated in a special course that is perceived as marginal to architectural training. As one student recalled, "You know, we had . . . what was her name? . . . [The ADA] was all she talked about. She wasn't a very good designer." Another professor said, "I am the faculty designated for universal design. You know, all things disability. . . . They bring me in for juries and expect me to only talk ADA. Well, I have more value to architecture than that, so I don't comply with their wishes." And another professor said, "Oh, yes, I talk to students about ADA shit when I can't think of anything else to say [laughs] and when a student is just really, you know, lame."

The Problem of Genetic Selection

In Chapter 2, we introduced the controversy associated with reproductive technology that can be used for the purpose of selective abortion of fetuses with prenatal diagnoses of disabilities. We also noted that this controversy reveals a divide between the feminist reproductive rights/choice movement and the disability rights movement. Whereas feminists want to preserve a woman's right to choose, disability advocates question the choice to abort an otherwise wanted fetus because of disability.

The general issue at stake here is one of genetic selection and involves both **genetic screening** and **genetic engineering**. The former entails prenatal testing, already a part of routine medical practice, to detect genetic disabilities that guide decisions about selective abortion; the latter entails technology, not yet widely available and affordable, that allows prospective parents to design their "perfect child," also known as "designer babies" (Glover 2006; Landsman 2009).

Ruth Hubbard (1990) has been concerned for some time that the thrust of these practices implies a eugenics mentality aimed at eliminating people with disabilities. But unlike Nazi Germany, which we discussed in Chapter 3, contemporary eugenics is not imposed by the government but enabled by those who choose abortion as a response to a known disability, a practice that may be encouraged and reinforced by the medical establishment (Hampton 2005; Landsman 2009). As D. A. Caeton observes, "Whereas infants once had to greet the world after gestation and birth before they could be classified as [normal or] aberrant, we now live in an era of preventative medicine, as it were" (2011:10). Marsha Saxton adds, "It is ironic that just when disabled citizens have achieved so much, the new reproductive and genetic technologies are promising to eliminate births of disabled children" (1998:375).

Under current abortion law, the question of the fetus's viability outside the mother's womb is key. It is at this point that the right of a fetus begins to assert itself in opposition to a woman's right to reproductive choice. Indeed, one of the key features of the landmark US Supreme Court decision of *Roe v. Wade* (1973) is its focus on the distinction between the first, second, and third trimesters of pregnancy. In that ruling, the Court said that a woman's right to choose during the first trimester is inviolable. The Court held that by the second trimester the state has an emerging interest in regulating the procedure. And by the third trimester, as the infant remains viable outside of the mother, an abortion is prohibited except when a continued pregnancy would threaten the health or life of the mother. The implication here is that as prenatal technology improves the survival rate of premature babies, *Roe v. Wade* may be on a collision course with itself, as the amount of time in which an abortion would be permitted decreases due to technological innovation.[6]

Be that as it may, D. A. Caeton has a more philosophical point to make regarding the question of viability. According to the choice/rights position:

> The rights of the woman carrying the fetus are assumed to take precedence over those of the fetus, because the fetus is presumed to be an unviable entity. It is incapable of survival without assistance and as such it possesses no discernible subjectivity. This discursive treatment of the fetus takes on a new dimension, however, when one considers disability. Are adults who require the assistance of machines also to be considered unviable? What really is the difference between such people and a second-term fetus? (2011:9)

Paul Longmore (2003) makes a similar point with regard to physician-assisted suicide, a matter we will take up shortly, arguing that it is the specter of "dependency" that most instills contempt and fear of people with disabilities. But Caeton asks, "Is independence—which serves as the basis for viability—really the most important metric of humanity? . . . [This] rhetoric of viability only remains unproblematic so long as disability is ignored" (2011:9).

Caeton (2011) notes that those who have the commendable goal of eradicating human suffering in the world, feminists included, often think that eradicating disability would reduce suffering. When they do so, they are aligning themselves with what Dana Lee Baker (2011) calls the **cure agenda**, which focuses on the elimination of social differences due to disability. Disability advocates bristle at the ways in which proponents of the cure agenda equate disability with suffering and disease and assume that eradicating disability differences is a moral preference. At its extreme, this voice has a prominent proponent in philosopher Peter Singer (1999), who holds an endowed professorship at Yale University. Singer has gone so far as to advocate infanticide of babies with disabilities, which he says, in the tradition of utilitarian philosophy, would reduce suffering and promote the greatest good for the greatest number of people (Longmore 2003).

Caeton argues that the central issue from a pro-disability perspective is accepting disability "as an alternative modality of being, one that is no less, nor no more, despicable than any other category of being" (2011:12). Or, to put it more positively, disability is a valued form of difference that can be celebrated for contributing positively to human innovation and diversity (see Box 1.3). Baker calls this the **celebration agenda**, which has two primary goals: the integration of disabled people into mainstream society and, in some cases, the "development of vibrant subcultures of individuals with particular functional differences" (2011:39). Caeton does not think that prohibitions on choice or the use of technologies will solve the problem of protecting "fetuses that exhibit traits of physical and cognitive alterity. . . . Instead, if we are to choose wisely when presented

---

FURTHER EXPLORATION

Box 8.2 Jerry Lewis vs. the Disability Rights Movement

In Chapter 1 we suggested that disability rights activists were not fond of Jerry Lewis's annual muscular dystrophy telethon, which features pitiable "poster children" who help raise money for a preventative cure but does little to improve the lives of those who are already disabled. In truth, the clash between the disability rights movement, some of whom include former poster children themselves, and Lewis goes farther than this.

Lewis's association with the Muscular Dystrophy Association (MDA) and its annual fundraising telethon spans more than five decades, from the 1960s through the 2000s (Haller 2010). Under his tutelage, the MDA even positioned itself as having a philosophy that was in contradistinction to the ADA. While dedicating himself to the agenda of preventing muscular dystrophy, Lewis became known for his disparaging comments about people with disabilities. During the 1973 telethon, for example, Lewis said, "God goofed, and it's up to us to correct His mistakes" (quoted in Haller 2010:141).

The protests against Lewis galvanized in the early 1990s after he called people with disabilities "half persons" in a *Parade* magazine article (Haller 2010:150). In the early 2000s, when Lewis was asked about the protests during a *CBS Sunday Morning* broadcast, he said, "Pity? You don't want to be pitied for being a cripple in a wheelchair? Stay in your house." Along the way, Lewis also used antigay slurs during the telethons, raising the ire of other groups. As fewer and fewer TV stations began carrying the telethon, and when they did, showing it late at night, Lewis became increasingly disgruntled, and the "more disability activists pushed against [him], the more he said outrageous things" (p. 151).

with choice, then we must continue to labor to make disability recognizable as a valid mode of being" (2011:12).

The Problem of Physician-Assisted Suicide

As we have suggested, the question of physician-assisted suicide raises similar issues as the question of genetic selection. In a celebrated case in Spain, Ramón Sampedro (1943–1998) became an admired figure of the **right-to-die movement**, which aims to legalize euthanasia.[7] A physically active person his whole life, Sampedro became a quadriplegic in a diving accident when he was twenty-five years old. Physically unable to take his life on his own, Sampedro fought for three decades in the Spanish courts to be granted the right to an assisted suicide, even going to the European Commission on Human Rights. He eventually devised a plan whereby he divided up small pieces of potassium cyanide for different helpers to feed him. No single dose was enough to kill him, so no one was held criminally liable for his death.

While the Sampedro case gained more notoriety in Europe, the United States was preoccupied with Dr. Jack Kevorkian (1928–2011), who became a peculiar folk hero of sorts, dubbed by the press and public, sometimes trivially, as "Dr. Death." Claiming he was all about reducing suffering, Kevorkian sought to assist those seeking his aid to terminate their lives. Kevorkian's argument was that he was helping individuals who were mentally competent to make their own medical decisions, but who were physically unable to carry out their wishes. After previously being acquitted of assisting in the deaths of two women, he was convicted in 1999 of second-degree homicide for the death by lethal injection of Thomas Youk, who was in the final stages of amyotrophic lateral sclerosis, or Lou Gehrig's disease. Following his conviction, Kevorkian served more than eight years in prison (Katsh and Rose 2002; Longmore 2003).

A notable US Supreme Court case in the area of physician-assisted suicide is ***Cruzan v. Director, Missouri Department of Health*** (1990). In that case, Nancy Beth Cruzan had sustained a severe and irreversible brain injury in an automobile accident. Characterized as being in a "persistent vegetative state," Cruzan "displayed no discernible cognitive functioning and was kept alive through the use of artificial hydration and feeding equipment" (Katsh and Rose 2002:38). Four years after the accident, Cruzan's parents began legal proceedings to withdraw the artificial means of life support.

The Cruzan case highlighted a distinction between **passive euthanasia** and **active euthanasia**. The former involves death that stems from a failure to act, such as a decision to not resuscitate an endangered patient, or from the removal of life-saving equipment that is keeping someone alive; the latter involves a positive act such as the administration of a lethal injection. In the case of passive euthanasia, the Court in the Cruzan case was concerned with whether there was "clear and convincing" evidence that a patient like Cruzan would have wanted to die, ruling that passive euthanasia was permitted if such evidence was available. Subsequently, Cruzan's parents asked for a court hearing to present additional evidence that they were acting on behalf of their daughter's wishes. A judge ruled that her feeding tube could be removed (Katsh and Rose 2002).

As such, the Cruzan case had little bearing on the question of active euthanasia, and it is here that the disability rights movement has most clashed with the right-to-die movement, as the former has staked out a position against physician-assisted suicide. The key to their argument is a critique of the decisionmaking context in which a disabled person might decide that he or she prefers to die. To begin with, as we noted in Chapter 4, medical professionals all too often assume that a disabled life is not worth living. In one study of emergency-care professionals, for example, 80 percent thought that a quadriplegic person could expect to have a poor quality of life (Gerhart et al. 1994). On the other hand, the study also found that more than 90 percent of quadriplegic people themselves said they had an average or above-average quality of life. A number of other studies, too, find that medical professionals significantly underestimate the quality of life of disabled people compared to the assessments of disabled people themselves (Gill 2000; Longmore 2003). Of particular concern is that "these inaccurate and pessimistic professional views . . . are implicitly conveyed to patients and their families" while they are in the midst of making difficult decisions about how to respond to a newly acquired disability (Gill 2000:530).

Proponents of the right-to-die movement often argue that their primary objective is to obtain a right to die for people with terminal illnesses. This is, for instance, the aim of Oregon's **Death with Dignity Act** of 1994, which was upheld in the US Supreme Court decision case of ***Gonzales v. Oregon*** (2006). Longmore notes that although the Oregon law limits the right to physician-assisted suicide to those who are "diagnosed as terminally ill with six months or less to live," such predictions are "notoriously inaccurate" (2003:189). He also notes that while the Oregon Medical Assistance Program approved physician-assisted suicide among the list of eligible "treatments," it simultaneously cut health-care services for the terminally ill, disabled, and elderly. Longmore argues that medical "choices" are not made in a vacuum, and in the absence of real options, "death by physician-assistance becomes not an act of personal autonomy, but an act of desperation" (p. 195).

To illustrate his point, Longmore (2003) cites two 1989 cases, one involving David Rivlin and the other Larry McAfee, both of whom were spinal-cord injured quadriplegics who relied on a ventilator to breathe. In Rivlin's case, he found the cost of paying for the assistance he needed for independent living prohibitive. Even though it would have cost the state of Michigan less money to leave Rivlin in his own apartment than it cost to put him in a nursing home, he was forced into an institutionalized existence. Rivlin came to the conclusion that "he would rather be dead," and he obtained "a court order authorizing a doctor to sedate him and disconnect his ventilator" to end his life (p. 182).

In McAfee's case, the state of Georgia offered him no financial "support for independent living [and] no Georgia nursing home would admit a ventilator user because the state paid so little" (Longmore 2003:182). He was eventually placed in an intensive-care hospital unit, even though he did not need such care. McAfee found this environment impossible to live in. Longmore describes the circumstances of the intensive-care unit: "The lights are always turned on. Medical personnel ceaselessly move about. Patients are assaulted by the constant noise of medical machines. Noise levels from the equipment and the conversation of staff continue day and night. . . . Patients are caught in the disorienting atmosphere of . . . emotional stress, . . . crisis and sensory overload" (p. 182). After eight months of living under these conditions, McAfee asked for "court authorization to have a doctor help him die" (p. 182). At the hearing, a professor of rehabilitative medicine and medical ethics at Emory University told the court, "We acknowledge an individual's right to autonomy, self-determination and liberty as part of our ethical vision in this country" (p. 182). The judge proceeded to grant McAfee's request and express admiration for his courage.

Disability activists in Georgia spoke out against everyone involved in the case, including the media, for asking the wrong questions. In a joint press release from four disability rights organizations, they expressed outrage that the state of Georgia had "for years left Larry McAfee without enough support for independent living and now steps in willingly to help with his suicide. . . . The state creates an unbearable quality of life and then steps in and says disabled people should be assisted to die because their quality of life is so poor" (quoted in Longmore 2003:184).

The McAfee case caught the attention of Dr. Russ Fine, director of the Injury Prevention Center at the University of Alabama at Birmingham, who introduced McAfee to representatives from the United Cerebral Palsy of Greater Birmingham, who helped him find work as a computer engineer and regain control of his life. Later, he would say that if more funding for independent living had been available, he would never have despaired to the point of seeking suicide. McAfee lived an independent life until he died of a stroke in 1998 (Applebome 1990; Longmore 2003).

Longmore notes that in states that provide more support for independent living, people like Rivlin and McAfee can "live in their own homes, raise families, go to school, and hold jobs" (2003:181). In neither of these cases were the desperate men even given psychological evaluation or counseling. The nondisabled people around them assumed that when a person with a severe disability says that he or she wants to die, they must be acting rationally. But Longmore thinks the public fails to acknowledge the untenable situation such individuals are put in, as if the impairment itself is the sole reason they seek relief through death.

Longmore also explains why disability rights advocates are distrustful of the judiciary. While many judicial decisions have found a "liberty interest" in upholding a person's right to terminate treatment and even receive physician-assisted suicide, no US court has ever found that "an American citizen has a general right to health care" (2003:194). In a 1996 right-to-die case, the US Ninth Circuit Court of Appeals even had the audacity to declare that "in a society in which the costs of protracted healthcare can be so exorbitant, we are reluctant to say that it is improper for competent, terminally ill adults to take the economic welfare of their families and loved ones into account" (cited in Longmore 2003:194). Yet the very same court went on to say that it did not have the authority to address the problem of access to health care. That, it said, was up to the legislature.

The pro-disability critique of physician-assisted suicide brings to light what Baker (2011) calls the **care agenda** component of the disability rights movement. In general, the care agenda involves the provision of services to people with disabilities who are unable to perform functional activities without assistance, including the services they need to live independently. In the absence of this care, as we have seen, people with disabilities may be more likely to give in to despair and shortsightedly decide that suicide is an option that is preferable to life.

Revisiting the Medical Model and Its Place in Disability Studies

In Chapter 2, we introduced the disability studies critique of the medical model, which identifies "disability" as essentially an *individual* matter rather than as a product of the *social* environment, the latter referred to as the social model. While being concerned with the etiology, diagnosis, prevention, and treatment of physical and cognitive impairments, the medical model is constituted by a set of disciplinary practices that aim to administer rehabilitative treatments to patients or clients. In doing so, medical professionals exert institutional authority over those who desire their services and expertise. As we have seen, when this authority is exercised vis-à-vis people with disabilities, a number of controversies emerge, not the least of which is disabled people's objection to being treated as "objects" rather than as "active participants" in the treatments they receive (Barnes, Mercer, and Shakespeare 1999:42; French and Swain 2001).[8]

In part, the authority of medical professionals lies in the inherent asymmetry of knowledge that exists between professionals and patients (Lupton 1997). But here the disability rights movement finds a potential ally in the **consumer health movement**, which tries to empower patients to take charge of their health and health-care needs by encouraging them to ask questions about doctors' recommendations, seek additional opinions, and make decisions for themselves.[9] The rise of the Internet, too, has given more impetus to this movement, offering consumers of medical services instant access to a wealth of information and putting them in touch with others who share their concerns, including issues pertaining to disability (Brown et al. 2004; Conrad and Stults 2010; Gabe and Calnan 2000; Henderson and Petersen 2002).

FURTHER EXPLORATION

Box 8.3 The Plight of Contemporary US War Veterans

Disabled war veterans have always played a central role in the history of disability in the United States (see Chapter 3), and one would expect US veterans of the Afghanistan and Iraq wars to do the same. By July 2012, according to Department of Defense (DoD) statistics, between Operation Enduring Freedom (Afghanistan), launched in October 2001, and Operation Iraqi Freedom, launched in March 2003, nearly 6,500 US soldiers had died, far more than the number who were killed in the September 11, 2001, terrorist attacks. Additionally, about 48,800 US troop members had been wounded in action, suffering from a range of injuries, including paralysis and severed arms and legs; organ, back, and joint damage; facial disfigurement; hearing and vision loss; brain injuries; and post-traumatic stress (PTS) (Iraq and Afghanistan Veterans of America 2012).

However, some critics have accused the DoD of "fudging" these numbers downward—by primarily counting acute injuries caused by enemy munitions that pierce or penetrate the body, and by undercounting injuries from accidents and "friendly fire," partial hearing and vision loss, milder brain injuries, and countless cases of PTS (Sandels 2010). Including these injuries in the estimates would raise the number of wounded substantially above 48,800, perhaps explaining why about 45 percent of post-9/11 veterans had filed disability-related claims with the Department of Veterans Affairs seeking compensation for their injuries, with nearly 830,000 cases still pending, as of May 2012 (La Ganga 2012; Marchione 2012).

These numbers aside, there is also the matter of the poor treatment of injured veterans in military medical facilities, a plight first brought to the attention of the US public in an exposé of Walter Reed Army Medical Center that was published in the *Washington Post* in 2007 (Priest and Hull 2007). Walter Reed, the army's flagship medical facility, was the site of substandard care. Mold, rot, and rodents plagued some of the patient facilities. Sometimes there was no heat or water. Hospital staff were disengaged and overworked, underserving their patients, losing paperwork, and taking forever to help with simple needs. Veterans with impaired memories from brain injuries sat for weeks without receiving treatment

continues

Box 8.3 continued

(see Box 6.3). Veterans who were dealing with psychological disorders of their own were put in charge of others who were at risk of suicide. And veterans were released from the hospital with less rehabilitation than veterans of prior wars (Donahue and Spiro 2007; Ephron and Childress 2007; Priest and Hull 2007).

The DoD swiftly responded by promising to remedy these problems, but Walter Reed was not an isolated case. In a subsequent investigation of its own, *Newsweek* magazine examined not just one facility but an entire range of services offered by the Department of Veterans Affairs (Ephron and Childress 2007). Their report painted "a grim portrait of an overloaded bureaucracy cluttered with red tape; veterans having to wait weeks or months for mental-health care and other appointments; families sliding into debt as VA case managers studied disability claims for many months, and the seriously wounded requiring help from outside experts just to understand the VA's arcane system of rights and benefits" (p. 31). The *Washington Post* expanded its investigation, too, finding conditions comparable to Walter Reed at other facilities around the country (Hull and Priest 2007). A veteran at a naval medical center in California reported that his outpatient barracks was swarming with fruit flies and overflowing with trash. Veterans at an army facility in Kentucky reported peeling paint, mold, and windows that would not open. At another army facility in California, veterans were forced to sign waivers indicating they understood that the outpatient housing they were given did not meet governmental standards.

Although consumerism can be empowering, in the United States its potential to deliver health-care services is compromised by the corporatization of health care, which treats health care as a commodity (partially subsidized by the government) that can be bought and sold in the marketplace. In a system like this, medical professionals are often put in the position of being "double agents," needing to attend to the interests of both their patients and their employers/reimbursers (Gray 1991; Waitzkin 2000).

Earlier we noted that adequate funding for people with disabilities who need access to health-care services is problematic (see Chapters 2 and 5). Funding is also problematic for those who might be the beneficiaries of social policies that reflect the agenda of *care*. And then there is the matter of the agenda of *cure*, which asserts its moral influence by purporting to reduce suffering, but which also raises issues regarding the existential and social status of people with disabilities, who don't want others to think, "Wouldn't they rather be 'normal'?" (Chapter 2). It is as if disabled people are always walking around with the constant awareness of an unasked question, as W. E. B. Du Bois (1903) famously observed of black people in America: "How does it feel to be a problem?" This concern informs the disability studies critique of ableism, which narrows the baseline of what is deemed to be a quality human being, defining the standards by which someone is considered to have a life worth living (Chapter 1). As Tobin Siebers (2008) reminds us, it is almost always true that disabled people have a better chance of enjoying a fulfilling life if they accept their disability as a positive aspect of their identity, one that provides them with a unique and at times contentious way of being embodied in the world. Moreover, it is this point that the *celebration* agenda takes further by appreciating disability as a valued form of social difference, akin to appreciating other forms of diversity such as those based on race, ethnicity, gender, and sexual orientation. This is the essence of the cultural model of disability, which views disability as a site of resistance to socially constructed conceptions of normality (Chapter 2). In this way, the celebration agenda asserts its affinity with a broader vision of **multiculturalism**, a movement of respect and appreciation of human difference as the essential feature of humanity (Alexander 2006; Berger 2012; Gilson and DePoy 2000).[10]

The celebration agenda, as Baker (2011) points out, tends to focus on disabled people who are relatively high functioning, whereas the care agenda tends to focus on those who need more assistance with daily living.[11] Whether viewed as complementary or competing orientations, the priorities of each raise different issues, issues that impact the field of disability studies itself, where medical-model–oriented professionals and students may clash with social-model–oriented professionals and students. Whereas the medical approach asserts that the "rehabilitation of deficient bodies" should have a prominent place in the field, the social model approach rejects the idea that "disability is a difference that exists only to be undone" (Snyder and Mitchell 2006:190, 192). From the latter point of view, the problem with the medical model is not that medical-rehabilitative interventions have no value for people with disabilities. Rather, it is to point out that this approach narrowly constitutes the subject matter of the field, which should more broadly illuminate the interface between embodied differences and the social environment, what Siebers (2008) calls the theory of complex embodiment (see Chapter 2).

FURTHER EXPLORATION

Box 8.4 Becoming Un-Wheeled

In Chapter 6, we discussed the process of becoming *en-wheeled,* that is, the process by which a person with a newly acquired spinal cord injury learns "to live through (the use of) a wheelchair in order to become newly abled" (Papadimitriou 2008a:695). But changes in medical insurance coverage now threaten to undermine disabled people's opportunity to become en-wheeled, leading to a process that might be characterized as becoming *un-wheeled.* To begin with, as Rory Cooper and Rosemarie Cooper (2012) point out, the average person with paraplegia spends considerably less time in medical rehabilitation than in the past. In the 1980s, for instance, a person with paraplegia would spend about six months in inpatient medical rehabilitation. Nowadays, that same person might be sent home in four weeks. Not only does this mean that a newly disabled person learns fewer life skills that would aid them in independent living, but also that they receive less training in performing wheelies, traversing curb cuts, conducting preventative maintenance on their wheelchairs, and loading their wheelchair into their vehicle. That person would also not likely have their own wheelchair at the time they are released from the hospital.

Additionally, changes in medical insurance coverage are making it more difficult for people with paraplegia to obtain a state-of-the-art lightweight wheelchair, such as those made out of titanium, that are customized to their particular needs. Even when one is fortunate enough to have a physical therapist or physician who is knowledgeable about wheelchair technology, and this is not always the case, getting funding for the best wheelchair can be challenging if not impossible. In this context, wheelchair manufacturers have been reducing the types of wheelchairs available in their product lines, leaving disabled consumers with fewer choices that would enhance their quality of life (Cooper and Cooper 2012).

Disability and Human Rights

In her study of disability policy agendas, Baker (2011) identifies the sometimes competing and sometimes overlapping agendas of cure, celebration, care, and civil rights. Among these four agendas, the **civil rights agenda** that culminated in the passage of the ADA in 1990 marked a seminal point in the history of disability in the United States.[12] As we have seen, however, the US Supreme Court has interpreted this law in varying ways that leave the future of disability rights in the United States very much in doubt (see Chapter 3). While there may be general agreement that people with disabilities have certain legally protected rights and should be protected from discrimination, the specific ways in which this sentiment is defined and enforced leaves much room for ambiguity as to what those rights actually entail.

Be that as it may, Baker also makes a distinction between civil rights and **human rights**, with the former being concerned with "responsibilities and privileges associated with legal status in a particular nation," and the latter being concerned with rights that transcend particular nations and involve "access to the resources, opportunities, and dignity that are fundamental to the human condition" (2011:28–29). As such, the concept of human rights is a transnational aspiration, an aspiration that was first articulated by an international body in the **Universal Declaration of Human Rights** (UDHR) that was passed by the UN in 1948, which asserted "the inherent dignity and . . . equal and inalienable rights of all members of the human family [as] the foundation of freedom, justice and peace in the world" (cited in Berger 2012:215). In the aftermath of the Nazi atrocities of World War II,[13] this included the right to be free from slavery, torture, and cruel, inhuman, or degrading punishment. It also included the right to equal protection under the law, freedom of religion and belief, employment under decent conditions and with fair remuneration, a standard of living adequate for health and wellbeing, and the right to a free education (at least during the fundamental years of childhood development). While the UDHR and subsequent human rights documents lacked the status of enforceable law, it was nonetheless "the first inclusive instrument for the normative regulation of human rights" throughout the globe (Savić 1999:4; see also Bickenbach 2001).[14]

In this context, the first UN statement of human rights that specifically addressed people with disabilities was the **Declaration on the Rights of Disabled Persons** in 1975 (Priestley 2001).[15] More recently, in 2006, the **Convention on the Rights of Persons with Disabilities** (CRPD) was noteworthy for adopting a social model discourse in "[r]ecognizing that disability is an evolving concept and that disability results from the interaction between persons with impairments and attitudinal and environmental barriers that hinder their full and effective participation in society on an equal basis with others" (cited in Harpur 2012:3). It also makes specific mention of a right to access buildings, schools, and public transportation; a right to live independently and be included in the community; a right to personal mobility, information access, and political participation; and a right to participate in the recreation, leisure, and cultural life of society.

Paul Harpur believes that the CRPD, as a moral document of international stature, should be seen as settling once and for all the right of people with disabilities to be fully included in the societies in which they live (2012:11).[16] It should also make clear that disability studies, as a field of scholarly inquiry, is linked to this moral aspiration and dedicated to the proposition that, in spite of our differences, or perhaps because of them, we are all equally valuable human beings. As Michael Ignatieff has insightfully observed, it is our differences, "both fated and created," that constitute "the very basis of the consciousness of our individuality, and this consciousness, based on difference, is a constitutive element of what it means to be a human being" (2001:28). Indeed, Ignatieff suggests, our humanity is "valuable to the degree that it allows us to elaborate the dignity and the honor that we give to our differences," and this reality of our differences is "our common inheritance, the shared integument that we might fight to defend whenever any of us" is harmed or diminished for manifesting it.

Summary

In this chapter, we concluded the book by examining a range of issues that inform prospects for the future of disability, and in doing so we considered four disability policy agendas: the agendas of cure, celebration, care, and civil rights. To begin with, we noted the paradoxical nature of computer technology, which has arguably enhanced the quality of life for people with disabilities, but which also raises problems of accessibility that have created a digital divide between disabled and nondisabled people. Whereas the ethic of innovation drives the technology industry, universal design remains an unrealized aspiration of our technological society.

Next we considered two problematic practices that, quite literally, threaten the future of people with disabilities: genetic selection and physician-assisted suicide. Genetic selection avails itself of reproductive technologies that allow for the prenatal detection of traits deemed undesirable and that warrant abortion. It also entails technology that allows for the creation of "designer babies" without disabilities. In either case, pro-disability advocates believe these practices reflect a eugenics vision of a future without people with disabilities, a narrowing of the human gene pool that would deprive humanity of a valued source of innovation and diversity. Physician-assisted suicide, too, reflects a societal view that a disabled life is not worth living. But pro-disability advocates think that most disabled people who contemplate suicide would choose otherwise if they could count on more support for independent living that would enhance their quality of life.

In this chapter, we also had an opportunity to revisit the disability studies critique of the medical model and its place in disability studies. On the one hand, we noted the critique of this model's view of disability as a deficient bodily existence. On the other hand, we noted disabled people's need for health-care and other care services that are often underfunded. In either case, we suggested, the field of disability studies must more broadly construe its subject matter as pertaining to the interface between embodied differences and the social environment.

Lastly, we distinguished between disability as a matter of civil rights and disability as a matter of human rights, with the former being concerned about rights within particular nations and the latter about rights that transcend particular nations. We also noted the status of disability in the human rights documents of the UN that have established an international norm and aspiration for full inclusion of people with disabilities in all societies in which they live. The vision here is for a multicultural world in which differences are not only tolerated but respected and appreciated for their capacity to enlarge and enrich humankind.

Notes

1. Target chose to settle with the disability rights group that had entered the class action lawsuit rather than appeal the decision (Jaeger 2012).

2. E-government is another area of society that raises accessibility issues. Much of the work of applying for government benefits, paying taxes, applying for government jobs, enrolling children in school, applying for permits, and so forth can now be done online—but not if these websites are inaccessible (Jaeger 2012).

3. Microsoft is the company that is given highest marks in adding accessibility features to their products (Jaeger 2012; Vandenbark 2010).

4. The concept of universal design, which emerged in the 1970s, is credited to architect Ronald L. Mace, who was a victim of polio (Woodward 2008). Jaeger (2012), however, makes a distinction between universal design, universal access, and universal usability.

5. Heidegger (1954) suggested that at its extremes technology presents itself as both a "saving power" and a "supreme danger."

6. *Roe v. Wade* was followed by other US Supreme Court cases on abortion, most notably cases that upheld the constitutionality of requirements for fetal viability testing, parental notification for minors, and waiting periods (*Webster v. Reproductive Health Services*, 1989; *Planned Parenthood v. Casey*, 1992).

7. Sampedro was the subject of a highly acclaimed feature film, *The Sea Inside*, starring Javier Bardem, in 2004.

8. Similar criticisms have been levied against the special education and social work professions (Hayashi 2005; see Chapter 4).

9. In the medical literature, "shared decisionmaking" refers to a model that encourages physicians to share the evidence base of medical knowledge and engage "patients in the process of deciding which treatments and tests are appropriate for them" (Kaplan, Ganiats, and Frosch 2004:30). It is akin to the notion of "patient-centered care," which focuses on the "whole person," not just the illness, and aims to foster patient-doctor relationships in which both parties "engage in two-way sharing of information; explore patients' values and preferences; help patients and their families make clinical decisions; facilitate access to appropriate care; and enable patients to follow through with often difficult behavioral changes needed to maintain and improve health" (Epstein et al. 2010:2).

10. Jeffrey Alexander (2006) contrasts assimilation with multiculturalism as modes of incorporation. In assimilation, minority groups are accepted by core majority groups as long as they act like the majority and do not threaten to change the essential qualities of the core. In multiculturalism, minority

groups are not only accepted but are also valued for their capacity to enlarge and transform the core.

11. Tom Shakespeare also makes a distinction between people with congenital impairments that are relatively stable and who "tend to be well-adjusted to their situation, partly because they have known no other state," and those who have a disability due to a degenerative illness that gets worse over time (2006:107).

12. For a discussion of future prospects for leadership in the US disability movement, see Foster-Fishman et al. (2007).

13. The UN was established in 1945, and in 1948 it also passed the Convention on the Prevention and Treatment of Genocide (Berger 2012).

14. For more philosophical discussions of the concept of rights in the context of disability issues, see Carey (2009), Nussbaum (2006), and Silvers, Wasserman, and Mahowald (1998).

15. In 1985 the UDHR was extended to include people with disabilities.

16. Albrecht (2010) suggests the experiences of disabled immigrants as an important topic for future disability research.

References

Abbott, David, Jenny Morris, and Linda Ward. 2001. "The Best Place to Be? Policy, Practice and the Experiences of Residential School Placements for Disabled Children." Joseph Rowntree Foundation, Oct. 10, available at http://www.jr.org.

Adelson, Betty M. 2005. *Dwarfism: Medical and Psychosocial Aspects of Profound Short Stature.* Baltimore: Johns Hopkins University Press.

Adler, Shawn. 2008. "'Tropic Thunder' Director/Star Ben Stiller Says Disability Advocates' Planned Boycott Is Unwarranted." *MTV.com*, available at http://mtv.com.

Albrecht, Gary L. 1992. *The Disability Business: Rehabilitation in America.* Thousand Oaks, CA: Sage.

———. 2010. "The Sociology of Disability: Historical Foundations and Future Directions." In *Handbook of Medical Sociology,* 6th ed., eds. Chloe E. Bird, Peter Conrad, Allen M. Fremont, and Stefan Timmermans. Nashville, TN: Vanderbilt University Press.

Albrecht, Gary L., and Michael Bury. 2001. "The Political Economy of the Disability Marketplace." In *Handbook of Disability Studies*, eds. Gary L. Albrecht, Katherine D. Seelman, and Michael Bury. Thousand Oaks, CA: Sage.

Albrecht, Gary L., Katherine D. Seelman, and Michael Bury (eds.). 2001. *Handbook of Disability Studies.* Thousand Oaks, CA: Sage.

Alcoff, Linda Martín, and Satya P. Mohanty. 2006. "Reconsidering Identity Politics: An Introduction." In *Identity Politics Reconsidered,* eds. Linda Martín Alcoff, Michael Hames-Garcia, Satya P. Mohanty, and Paula M. L. Moya. New York: Palgrave.

Alexander, Franz G., and Sheldon T. Selesnick. 1964. *The History of Psychiatry: An Evaluation of Psychiatric Thought and Practice from Prehistoric Times to the Present.* New York: Harper & Row.

Alexander, Jeffrey C. 2006. *The Civil Sphere.* New York: Oxford University Press.

Altman, Barbara M. 2001. "Disability Definitions, Models, Classification Schemes, and Applications." In *Handbook of Disability Studies*, eds. Gary L. Albrecht, Katherine D. Seelman, and Michael Bury. Thousand Oaks, CA: Sage.

Anders, Charlie Jane. 2009. "20 Science Fiction Characters Who Got Their Legs Back." *io9.com* (Dec. 23), available at http://www.io9.com.

Anderson, Kristen G. 1997. "Gender Bias and Special Education Referrals." *Annals of Dyslexia* 47: 151–162.

Antonetta, Susanne. 2005. *A Mind Apart: Travels in a Neurodiverse World.* London: Penguin.

Applebome, Peter. 1990. "An Angry Man Fights to Die, Then Tests Life." *New York Times* (Feb. 7), available at http://www.nytimes.com.

Arons, Bernard S. 2000. "Mental Health and Criminal Justice." Washington, DC: US Department of Health and Human Services, available at http://www.hhs.gov.

Aronson, Josh (director). 2001. *Sound and Fury*. PBS documentary.

Artiles, Alfredo, Robert Rueda, Jesús José Salazar, and Ignacio Higareda. 2005. "Within-Group Diversity in Minority Disproportionate Representation: English Language Learners in Urban School Districts." *Exceptional Children* 71: 283–300.

Asch, Adrienne. 2001. "Disability, Bioethics, and Human Rights." In *Handbook of Disability Studies*, eds. Gary L. Albrecht, Katherine D. Seelman, and Michael Bury. Thousand Oaks, CA: Sage.

Asch, Adrienne, and Gail Geller. 1996. "Feminism, Bioethics and Genetics." In *Feminism, Bioethics: Beyond Reproduction*, ed. Susan M. Wolf. Oxford, UK: Oxford University Press.

Ashton-Shaeffer, Candace, Heather J. Gibson, Cari E. Autry, and Carolyn S. Hanson. 2001. "Meaning of Sport to Adults with Physical Disabilities: A Disability Sport Camp Experience." *Sociology of Sport Journal* 18: 95–114.

Bagatell, Nancy. 2010. "From Cure to Community: Transforming Notions of Autism." *Ethos* 38: 33–55.

Bagenstos, Samuel R. 2009. *Law and the Contradictions of the Disability Rights Movement.* New Haven, CT: Yale University Press.

Baker, Dana Lee. 2011. *The Politics of Neurodiversity: Why Public Policy Matters.* Boulder, CO: Lynne Rienner.

Baker, Paul M. A., and Nathan W. Moon. 2008. "Wireless Technologies and Accessibility for People with Disabilities: Findings from a Policy Research Instrument." *Assistive Technology* 20: 149–156.

Baker, Paul M. A., Nathan W. Moon, and Andrew C. Ward. 2006. "Virtual Exclusion and Telework: Barriers and Opportunities of Technocentric Workplace Accommodation Policy." *Work* 27: 4212–4230.

Barbaresi, William, Slavica Katusic, Robert Colligan, Amy Weaver, and Steven Jacobsen. 2005. "The Incidence of Autism in Olmstead County, Minnesota, 1967–1997: Results from a Population Based Study." *Archives of Pediatric and Adolescent Medicine* 159: 37–44.

Barnes, Colin, and Geof Mercer. 2001. "Disability Culture: Assimilation or

Inclusion?" In *Handbook of Disability Studies*, eds. Gary L. Albrecht, Katherine D. Seelman, and Michael Bury. Thousand Oaks, CA: Sage.

Barnes, Colin, Geof Mercer, and Tom Shakespeare. 1999. *Exploring Disability: A Sociological Introduction*. Cambridge, UK: Polity Press.

Barnes, Colin, and Alison Sheldon. 2010. "Disability, Politics and Poverty in a Majority World Context." *Disability & Society* 25: 771–782.

Baron-Cohen, Simon. 2000. "Is Asperger's Syndrome/High Functioning Autism Necessarily a Disability?" *Developmental Pathology* 12: 480–500.

Barounis, Cynthia. 2008. "Cripping Heterosexuality, Queering Able-Bodiedness: *Murderball, Brokeback Mountain*, and the Contested Masculine Body." *Journal of Visual Culture* 8: 54–75.

Barr, Martin. [1904] 1913. *Mental Defectives: Their History, Treatment, and Training*. Philadelphia: Blakiston.

Barton, Len, and Felicity Armstrong. 2001. "Disability, Education, and Inclusion: Cross-Cultural Issues and Dilemmas." In *Handbook of Disability Studies*, eds. Gary L. Albrecht, Katherine D. Seelman, and Michael Bury. Thousand Oaks, CA: Sage.

Baynton, Douglas. [1992] 2010. "'A Silent Exile on This Earth': The Metaphorical Construction of Deafness in the Nineteenth Century." In *The Disability Studies Reader*, 3rd ed., ed. Lennard Davis. New York: Routledge.

Becker, Howard S. 1963. *Outsiders: Studies in the Sociology of Deviance*. New York: Free Press.

Benderly, Beryl Lieff. 1990. *Dancing Without Music: Deafness in America*. Washington, DC: Gallaudet University Press.

Berger, Ronald J. 2009a. "Adolescent Subcultures, Social Type Metaphors, and Group Delinquency: Continuity and Change." In *Juvenile Delinquency and Justice: Sociological Perspectives*, eds. Ronald J. Berger and Paul D. Gregory. Boulder, CO: Lynne Rienner.

———. 2009b. *Hoop Dreams on Wheels: Disability and the Competitive Wheelchair Athlete*. New York: Routledge.

———. 2009c. "Hoops and Wheels." *Context: Understanding People in Their Social Worlds* 8 (3): 40–45.

———. 2012. *The Holocaust, Religion, and the Politics of Collective Memory: Beyond Sociology*. New Brunswick, NJ: Transaction.

Berger, Ronald J., and Jon Feucht. 2011. "'Thank You for Your Words': Observations from a Disability Summer Camp." *Qualitative Inquiry* 18: 76–85.

Bérubé, Michael. 1996. *Life as We Know It: A Father, a Family, and an Exceptional Child*. New York: Vintage.

Bickenbach, Jerome E. 2001. "Disability Human Rights, Law, and Policy." In *Handbook of Disability Studies*, eds. Gary L. Albrecht, Katherine D. Seelman, and Michael Bury. Thousand Oaks, CA: Sage.

Bishop, Anne H., and John R. Scudder Jr. 1990. *The Practical, Moral, and Personal Sense of Nursing*. Albany, NY: State University of New York Press.

Bishop, Dorothy, Andrew Whitehouse, Helen Watt, and Elizabeth Line.

2008. "Autism and Diagnostic Substitution: Evidence from a Study of Adults with a History of Developmental Language Disorder." *Developmental Medicine and Child Neurology* 50: 341–345.

Blinde, Elaine M., Diane Taub, and Han Lingling. [1993] 2001. "Sport Participation and Women's Personal Empowerment: Experiences of the College Athlete." In *Contemporary Issues in Sociology of Sport*, eds. Andrew Yiannakis and Merril J. Melnick. Champaign, IL: Human Kinetics.

Blume, Harvey. 1997. "Connections: Autistics Are Communicating." *New York Times* (June 30), available at http://www.nytimes.com.

———. 1998. "Neurodiversity." *The Atlantic* (Sept. 30), available at http://www.theatlantic.com.

Boebinger, Carolyn. 2012. "Modern Evolution." *Sports 'N Spokes* (Mar.): 30–33.

Bogdan, Robert. 1988. *Freak Show: Presenting Human Oddities for Amusement and Profit*. Chicago: University of Chicago Press.

Bogdan, Robert, and Steven J. Taylor. 1989. "The Social Construction of Humanness: Relationships with Severely Disabled People." *Social Problems* 36: 135–158.

Bogle, Jane Elder, and Susan L. Shaul. 1981. "Body Image and the Woman with a Disability." In *Sexuality and Physical Disability: Personal Perspectives*, eds. David Bullard and Susan Knight. St. Louis: C. V. Mosby.

Braddock, David L., and Susan L. Parish. 2001. "An Institutional History of Disability." In *Handbook of Disability Studies*, eds. Gary L. Albrecht, Katherine D. Seelman, and Michael Bury. Thousand Oaks, CA: Sage.

Branfield, Fran. 1998. "What Are You Doing Here? 'Non-disabled' People and the Disability Movement." *Disability & Society* 13: 143–144.

Bricout, John C. 2004. "Using Telework to Enhance Return to Work Outcomes for Individuals with Spinal Cord Injuries." *Neuro-Rehabilitation* 19: 147–159.

Brittain, Ian. 2004. "Perceptions of Disability and Their Impact upon Involvement in Sport for People with Disabilities at All Levels." *Journal of Sport & Social Issues* 28: 429–452.

Bromberg, Walter. 1975. *From Shaman to Psychotherapist: A History of the Treatment of Mental Illness*. Chicago: Henry Regnery.

Brosnan, John. 1976. *The Horror People*. New York: St. Martin's Press.

Brown, Phil. 1995. "Naming and Framing: The Social Construction of Diagnosis and Illness." *Journal of Health and Social Behavior* 33: 267–281.

Brown, Phil, Stephen Zavestoski, Sabrina McCormick, Brian Mayer, Rachel Morello-Frosch, and Rebecca Gasior. 2004. "Embodied Health Movements: New Approaches to Social Movements in Health." *Sociology of Health & Illness* 26: 50–80.

Browner, Carole H., and Nancy Press. 1995. "The Normalization of Prenatal Diagnosis Screening." In *Conceiving the New World Order: The Global Politics of Reproduction*, eds. Faye D. Ginsburg and Rayna Rapp. Berkeley: University of California Press.

Burgstahler, Sheryl A., and Rebecca C. Cory (eds.). 2008. *Universal Design in Higher Education: From Principles to Practice.* Cambridge, MA: Harvard Education Press.

Burkett, Brendan, Mike McNamee, and Wolfgang Potthast. 2011. "Shifting Boundaries in Sports Technology and Disability: Equal Rights or Unfair Advantage in the Case of Oscar Pistorious?" *Disability & Society* 26: 643–654.

Bury, Michael. 2000. "On Chronic Illness and Disability." In *Handbook of Medical Sociology*, 5th ed., eds. Chloe E. Bird, Peter Conrad, and Allen M. Fremont. Upper Saddle River, NJ: Prentice-Hall.

Butler, Judith. 1999. *Gender Trouble: Feminism and the Subversion of Identity.* New York: Routledge.

Butterworth, John, and William E. Kiernan. 1996. "Access to Employment for All Individuals: Legislative Systems and Service Delivery Issues." In *People with Disabilities Who Challenge the System*, eds. Donna H. Lehr and Fredda Brown. Baltimore: Paul H. Brookes.

Byrom, Brad. 2001. "A Pupil and a Patient: Hospital-Schools in Progressive America." In *The New Disability History: American Perspectives*, eds. Paul K. Longmore and Lauri Umansky. New York: New York University Press.

Cabin, William. 2010. *Phantoms of Home Care: Alzheimer's Disease Patients as Victims of Medicare's Designed Neglect.* Saarbrücken, Germany: LAP LAMPERT Academic.

Caeton, D. A. 2011. "Choice of a Lifetime: Disability, Feminism, and Reproductive Rights." *Disability Studies Quarterly* 31 (1), available at http://dsq-sds.org.

Cahill, Spencer E., and Robin Eggleston. 1994. "Managing Emotions in Public: The Case of Wheelchair Users." *Social Psychology Quarterly* 57: 300–312.

———. 1995. "Reconsidering the Stigma of Physical Disability: Wheelchair Use and Public Kindness." *The Sociological Quarterly* 36: 681–698.

Calton, Cindee. 2010. "The Obscuring of Class in Memoirs of Parents and Children with Disabilities." *Disability & Society* 25: 849–860.

Camilleri, Joseph M. 1999. "Disability: A Personal Odyssey." *Disability & Society* 14: 845–853.

Campbell, Elizabeth, and Graham Jones. 2002. "Sources of Stress Experienced by Elite Male Wheelchair Basketball Players." *Adapted Physical Activity Quarterly* 19: 82–99.

Carey, Allison. 2009. *On the Margins of Citizenship: Intellectual Disability and Civil Rights in Twentieth-Century America.* Philadelphia: Temple University Press.

Carrier, James. 1986. *Learning Disability: Social Class and the Construction of Inequality in American Education.* New York: Greenwood Press.

Caton, Sue, and Carolyn Kagan. 2007. "Comparing Transition Expectations of Young People with Moderate Learning Disabilities with Other Vulnerable Youth and with Their Non-disabled Counterparts." *Disability & Society* 22: 473–488.

Centers for Disease Control and Prevention (CDCP). 2011. "Number of U.S. Adults Reporting a Disability Increasing," available at http://www .cdc.gov.

Chan, Nathan Kai-Cheong, and Allison C. Gillick. 2009. "Fatness as a Disability Issue: Questions of Personal and Group Identity." *Disability & Society* 24: 231–243.

Chapkis, Wendy. 1986. *Beauty Secrets: Women and the Politics of Appearance*. London: Women's Press.

Charlton, James I. 1998. *Nothing About Us Without Us: Disability Oppression and Empowerment*. Berkeley: University of California Press.

Cherney, James L. 2006. Review of *The Ringer*. *Disability Studies Quarterly* 26 (3), available at http://dsq-sds.org.

Cleigh, W. C. 2005. "Why We Protest." *Inside Higher Ed* (Feb. 24), available at http://www.insidehighered.com.

Coakley, Jay. 2004. *Sports in Society: Issues and Controversies*. Boston: McGraw-Hill.

Cohen, Leah Hager. 1994a. "The 'Inclusion' Debate: Schools for All, or Separate but Equal?" *Baltimore Sun* (Feb. 23): 11A.

———. 1994b. *Train Go Sorry: Inside a Deaf World*. New York: Vintage.

Colker, Ruth. 2005. *The Disability Pendulum: The First Decade of the Americans with Disabilities Act*. New York: New York University Press.

Collins, Carol. 1999. "Reproductive Technologies for Women with Physical Disabilities." *Sexuality & Disability* 17: 299–307.

Connell, Ruth S. 2008. "Survey of Web Developers in Academic Libraries." *Journal of Academic Librarianship* 34: 121–129.

Connor, David J., and Beth A. Ferri. 2007. "The Conflict Within: Resistance to Inclusion and Other Paradoxes in Special Education." *Disability & Society* 22: 63–77.

Connors, Clare, and Kirsten Stalker. 2007. "Children's Experiences of Disability: Pointers to a Social Model of Childhood Disability." *Disability & Society* 22: 19–33.

Conrad, Peter, and Cheryl Stults. 2010. "The Internet and the Illness Experience." In *Handbook of Medical Sociology*, 6th ed., eds. Chloe E. Bird, Peter Conrad, Allen M. Fremont, and Stefan Timmermans. Nashville, TN: Vanderbilt University Press.

Coo, Helen, Helene Ouellette-Kuntz, Jennifer Lloyd, Liza Kasmara, Jeanette Holden, and Suzanne Lewis. 2008. "Trends in Autism Prevalence: Diagnostic Substitution Revisited." *Journal of Autism and Developmental Disorders* 38: 1036–1046.

Cooley, Charles H. [1902] 1964. *Human Nature and Social Order*. New York: Scribner.

Cooper, Rory A., and Rosemarie Cooper. 2012. "Emerging Developments." *Sports 'N Spokes* (Mar.): 58–61.

Corroto, Carla. 2012. "The Architecture of Compliance: ADA and the Profession of Architecture." Paper presented at the International Congress of Qualitative Inquiry (May), Urbana-Champaign, IL.

Coutinho, Martha J., and Donald P. Oswald. 2005. "State Variation in Gender Disproportionality in Special Education Findings and Recommendations." *Remedial and Special Education* 26: 7–15.

Cowley, Geoffrey. 2003. "Girls, Boys, and Autism." *Newsweek* (Sept. 8): 42–50.

Crase, Nancy. 1982. "Rules and Regs: How Wheelchair Basketball Is Played." *Sports 'N Spokes* magazine reprint (May–June): 1–2.

Crow, Liz. 2000. "Helen Keller: Rethinking the Problematic Icon." *Disability & Society* 15: 845–859.

Cunningham, Ian C., Philip James, and Pauline Dibben. 2004. "Bridging the Gap Between Rhetoric and Reality: Line Managers and the Protection of Job Security for Ill Workers in the Modern Workplace." *British Journal of Management* 15: 274–290.

Danforth, Scot. 2009. *The Incomplete Child: An Intellectual History of Learning Disabilities*. New York: Peter Lang.

Darling, Rosalyn Benjamin. 1979. *Families Against Society: A Study of Reactions to Children with Birth Defects*. Beverly Hills, CA: Sage.

———. 1988. "Parental Entrepreneurship: A Consumerist Response to Professional Dominance." *Journal of Social Issues* 44: 141–158.

———. 2000. "Only for Individuals with Disabilities?" *Footnotes* (May/June): 6.

Darling, Rosalyn B., and D. Alex Heckert. 2010. "Orientations Toward Disability: Differences over the Lifecourse." *International Journal of Disability, Development and Education* 57: 131–143.

Davies, Megan, Allison Connolly, and John Horan (eds.). 2001. *State Injury Indicators Report*. Atlanta: Centers for Disease Control and Prevention, National Center for Injury Prevention and Control.

Davis, Fred. 1961. "Deviance Disavowal: The Management of Strained Interaction by the Visibly Handicapped." *Social Problems* 9: 120–132.

Davis, Lennard J. 1995. *Enforcing Normalcy: Disability, Deafness, and the Body*. New York: Verso.

———. 2001. "Identity Politics, Disability, and Culture." In *Handbook of Disability Studies*, eds. Gary L. Albrecht, Katherine D. Seelman, and Michael Bury. Thousand Oaks, CA: Sage.

———. 2002. *Bending Over Backwards: Disability, Dismodernism, and Other Difficult Positions*. New York: New York University Press.

———. 2005. "Why Disability Studies Matters." *Inside Higher Ed* (Feb. 21), available at http://www.insidehighered.com.

Deaf Linx. 2012. "Deaf Education Options Guide," available at http://www.deaflinx.com.

Deal, Mark. 2003. "Disabled People's Attitudes Toward Other Impairment Groups: A Hierarchy of Impairments." *Disability & Society* 18: 897–910.

DeJong, Gerben, and Ian Basnett. 2001. "Disability and Health Policy: The Role of Markets in the Delivery of Health Services." In *Handbook of Disability Studies,* eds. Gary L. Albrecht, Katherine D. Seelman, and Michael Bury. Thousand Oaks, CA: Sage.

de Mause, Lloyd. 1981. "The Fetal Origins of History." *Journal of the History of Ideas* 30: 413–422.

Denzin, Norman K. 1989. *Interpretive Biography*. Newbury Park, CA: Sage.

———. 1998. "The New Ethnography." *Journal of Contemporary Ethnography* 27: 405–415.

DePauw, Karen P. 1997. "The (In)Visibility of Disability: Cultural Contexts and 'Sporting Bodies.'" *Quest* 49: 416–430.

DePauw, Karen P., and Susan G. Gavron. 2005. *Disability and Sport*. 2nd ed. Champaign, IL: Human Kinetics.

Devlieger, Patrick, and Gary L. Albrecht. 2000. "The Concept and Experience of Disability on Chicago's Near West Side." *Journal of Disability Policy Studies* 11: 51–60.

Devlieger, Patrick, Gary L. Albrecht, and Miram Hertz. 2007. "The Production of Disability Culture Among Young African-American Men." *Social Science & Medicine* 64: 1948–1959.

Diamond, Milton. 1984. "Sexuality and the Handicapped." In *The Psychological and Social Impact of Physical Disability*, eds. Robert P. Marinelli and Arthur E. Dell Orto. New York: Springer.

Dillon, Erin. 2007. "Labeled: The Students Behind NCLB's 'Disabilities' Designation." *Education Sector* (July 12), available at http://www.eductionsector.org.

Dispenza, Mary L. 2002. "Overcoming the New Digital Divide: Technology Accommodations and the Undue Hardship Defense Under the Americans with Disabilities Act." *Syracuse Law Review* 52: 159–181.

Dobransky, Kerry, and Eszter Hargittai. 2006. "The Disability Divide in Internet Access and Use." *Information Communication and Society* 9: 313–334.

Donahue, Phil, and Ellen Spiro (producer/director). 2007. *Body of War*. Documentary film by docuramafilms.

Du Bois, W. E. B. [1903] 1996. *The Souls of Black Folk*. New York: Penguin.

Duckett, Paul S. 1998. "What Are You Doing Here? 'Non-Disabled' People and the Disability Movement: A Response to Fran Branfield." *Disability & Society* 13: 625–628.

Dyer, Bryce T. J., Siamak Noroozi, Sabi Redwood, and Philip Sewell. 2010. "The Design of Lower-Limb Prostheses: Fair Inclusion in Disability Sport." *Disability & Society* 25: 593–602.

Edwards, R. A. R. 2001. "'Speech Has an Extraordinary Humanizing Power': Horace Mann and the Problem of Nineteenth-Century American Deaf Education." In *The New Disability History: American Perspectives*, eds. Paul K. Longmore and Lauri Umansky. New York: New York University Press.

Eisenstadt, Stuart N. 1956. *From Generation to Generation: Age Groups and Social Structures*. New York: Free Press.

Elder, Glen H., Jr., Kirkpatrick Johnson, and Robert Crosnoe. 2004. "The Emergence and Development of Life Course Theory." In *Handbook of the Life Course*, eds. Jeylan T. Mortimer and Michael J. Shanahan. New York: Springer.

Ellul, Jacques. [1964] 1967. *The Technological Society*, trans. John Wilkinson. New York: Vintage.

Engel, David M., and Frank W. Munger. 2003. *Rights of Inclusion: Law and Identity in the Life Stories of Americans with Disabilities*. Chicago: University of Chicago Press.

England, Ralph W. 1967. "A Theory of Middle-Class Delinquency." In *Middle-Class Juvenile Delinquency*, ed. Edmund W. Vaz. New York: Harper & Row.

Ephron, Dan, and Sarah Childress. 2007. "Forgotten Heroes." *Newsweek* (Mar. 5): 29–37.

Epstein, Ronald M., Kevin Fiscella, Cara S. Lesser, and Kurt C. Stange. 2010. "Why the Nation Needs a Policy Push on Patient-Centered Health Care." *Health Affairs* 29: 1–7.

Fenton, Andrew, and Tim Krahn. 2007. "Autism, Neurodiversity, and Equality Beyond the 'Normal.'" *Journal of Ethics in Mental Health* 2: 1–6.

Fine, Michelle, and Adrienne Asch. 1988. "Disability Beyond Stigma: Social Interaction, Discrimination, and Activism." *Journal of Social Issues* 44: 3–21.

Fiske, Susan T., Amy J. C. Cuddy, Peter Glick, and Jun Xu. 2001. "A Model of (Often Mixed) Stereotype Content: Competence and Warmth Respectively Follow from Perceived Status and Competition." *Journal of Personality and Social Psychology* 82: 878–902.

Flad, Jennifer, Ronald J. Berger, and Jon Feucht. 2011. "Can You Hear Me Now? Augmentative Communication, Methodological Empowerment, and the Life Story of Jon Feucht." *Disability Studies Quarterly* 31 (4), available at http://dsq-sds.org.

Fleischer, Doris Zames, and Frieda Zames. 2001. *The Disability Rights Movement: From Charity to Confrontation*. Philadelphia: Temple University Press.

Foster-Fishman, Pennie, Tiffeny Jimenez, Maria Valenti, and Tash Kelley. 2007. "Building the Next Generation of Leaders in the Disabilities Movement." *Disability & Society* 22: 341–356.

Foucault, Michel. 1979. *Discipline and Punish: The Birth of the Prison*. New York: Vintage.

Frank, Gelya. 1988. "Beyond Stigma: Visibility and Self-Empowerment of Persons with Congenital Limb Deficiencies." *Journal of Social Issues* 44: 95–115.

———. 2000. *Venus on Wheels: Two Decades of Dialogue on Disability, Biography, and Being Female in America*. Berkeley: University of California Press.

Franks, Beth. 2001. "Gutting the Golden Goose: Disability in Grimms' Fairy Tales." In *Embodied Rhetorics: Disability in Language and Culture*, eds. James C. Wilson and Cynthia Lewiecki-Wilson. Carbondale: Southern Illinois University Press.

French, Sally, and John Swain. 2001. "The Relationship Between Disabled People and Health and Welfare Professionals." In *Handbook of Disability Studies,* eds. Gary L. Albrecht, Katherine D. Seelman, and Michael Bury. Thousand Oaks, CA: Sage.

Fries, Kenny (ed.). 1997. *Staring Back: The Disability Experience from the Inside Out.* New York: Plume.

Fujiura, Glenn T., Kiyoshi Yamaki, and Susan Czechowicz. 1998. "Disability Among Ethnic and Racial Minorities in the United States." *Journal of Disability Policy Studies* 9: 111–130.

Gabe, Jonathan, and Michael Calnan. 2000. "Health Care and Consumption." In *Health Medicine and Society: Key Theories, Future Agendas*, eds. Simon J. Williams, Jonathan Gabe, and Michael Clanan. New York: Routledge.

Galvin, Ruth. 2003. "The Paradox of Disability Culture: The Need to Combine Versus the Imperative to Let Go." *Disability & Society* 18: 675–690.

Garland, Rosemarie. 1995. *The Eye of the Beholder: Deformity and Disability in the Graeco-Roman World.* Ithaca, NY: Cornell University Press.

Garth, Belinda, and Rosalie Aroni. 2003. "'I Value What You Have to Say': Seeking the Perspective of Children with a Disability, Not Just Their Parents." *Disability & Society* 18: 561–576.

Gerhart, Kenneth A., Jane Kozoil-McLain, Steven R. Lowenstein, and Gale G. Whiteneck. 1994. "Quality of Life Following Spinal Cord Injury: Knowledge and Attitudes of Emergency Care Providers." *Annals of Emergency Medicine* 23: 807–812.

Gerschick, Thomas J. 2000. "Toward a Theory of Disability and Gender." *Signs: Journal of Women in Culture and Society* 25: 1263–1268.

Gerschick, Thomas J., and Adam S. Miller. 1995. "Coming to Terms: Masculinity and Physical Disability." In *Men's Health and Illness: Gender, Power and the Body*, eds. Donald F. Sabo and David Frederick Gordon. Thousand Oaks, CA: Sage.

Gibson, Pamela Reed, and Amanda Lindberg. 2007. "Work Accommodation for People with Multiple Chemical Sensitivity." *Disability & Society* 22: 717–732.

Gill, Carol J. 1994. "Questioning Continuum." In *The Ragged Edge: The Disability Experience from the Pages of the First Fifteen Years of the Disability Rag*, ed. Barrett Shaw. Louisville, KY: Advocado Press.

———. 2000. "Health Professionals, Disability, and Assisted Suicide: An Examination of Relevant Empirical Evidence and Reply to Batavia." *Psychology, Public Policy, and Law* 6: 526–545.

———. 2001. "Divided Understandings: The Social Experience of Disability." In *Handbook of Disability Studies*, eds. Gary L. Albrecht, Katherine D. Seelman, and Michael Bury. Thousand Oaks, CA: Sage.

Gilman, Sander L. 1985. *Difference and Pathology: Stereotypes of Sexuality, Race, and Madness.* Ithaca, NY: Cornell University Press.

Gilson, Stephen French, and Elizabeth DePoy. 2000. "Multiculturalism and Disability: A Critical Perspective." *Disability & Society* 15: 207–217.

Glenn, Evelyn N. 2010. *Forced to Care: Coercion and Caregiving.* Cambridge, MA: Harvard University Press.

Glidden, Laraine Masters. 2006. "Adoption and Foster Care." In *Encyclopedia of Disability*, vol. 1, ed. Gary L. Albrecht. Thousand Oaks, CA: Sage.

Glover, Jonathan. 2006. *Choosing Children: Genes, Disability, and Design.* Oxford: Clarendon Press.

Goffman, Erving. 1959. *The Presentation of Self in Everyday Life.* New York: Doubleday.

———. 1963. *Stigma: Notes on the Management of Spoiled Identity.* Englewood Cliffs, NJ: Prentice-Hall.

Goodall, Jane. 1971. *In the Shadow of Man.* New York: Dell.

Gordon, Beth Omansky, and Karen E. Rosenblum. 2001. "Bringing Disability into the Sociological Frame: A Comparison of Disability with Race, Sex, and Sexual Orientation Statuses." *Disability & Society* 16: 5–19.

Grabham, Emily, Davina Coop, Jane Krishnadas, and Didi Herman. 2009. *Intersectionality and Beyond: Law, Power and the Politics of Location.* New York: Routledge.

Grandin, Temple. 2006. *Thinking in Pictures: My Life with Autism*, expanded ed. New York: Vintage.

Graungaard, Anette Hauskov, John Sahl Andersen, and Lisolette Skov. 2011. "When Resources Get Sparse: A Longitudinal, Qualitative Study of Emotions, Coping and Resource-Creation When Parenting a Young Child with Severe Disabilities." *Health* 15: 115–136.

Gray, Bradford H. 1991. *The Profit Motive and Patient Care.* Cambridge, MA: Harvard University Press.

Grealy, Lucy. 1997. "Pony Party." In *Staring Back: The Disability Experience from the Inside Out*, ed. Kenny Fries. New York: Plume.

Green, Sara E., Julia Barnhill, Sherri Green, Diana Torres Hawken, Loretta Sue Humphrey, and Scott Sanderson. 2011. "Creating a Village to Raise a Child: Constructing Community in Families of Children with Disabilities." In *Disability and Community*, eds. Allison C. Carey and Richard K. Scotch. Bringley, UK: Emerald.

Greenwood, Michael C., David A. Dzewaltowski, and Ron French. 1990. "Self-Efficacy and Psychological Well-Being of Wheelchair Tennis Participants and Wheelchair Nontennis Participants." *Adapted Physical Activity Quarterly* 7: 12–21.

Groce, Nora E. 1985. *Everyone Here Speaks Sign Language: Hereditary Deafness in Martha's Vineyard.* Cambridge, MA: Harvard University Press.

Groch, Sharon. 2001. "Free Spaces: Creating Oppositional Consciousness in the Disability Rights Movement." In *Oppositional Consciousness: The Subjective Roots of Protest*, eds. Jane J. Mansbridge and Aldon Morris. Chicago: University of Chicago Press.

Grönvik, Lars. 2009. "Defining Disability: Effects of Disability Concepts on Research Outcomes." *International Journal of Social Research Methodology* 12: 1–18.

Grossman, Francis. 1972. *Brothers and Sisters of Retarded Children.* New York: Syracuse University Press.

Guthrie, Sharon R., and Shirley Castelnuovo. 2001. "Disability Management Among Women with Physical Impairments: The Contribution of Physical Activity." *Sociology of Sport Journal* 18: 5–20.

Hahn, Harland. 1984. "Sports and the Political Movement of Disabled Persons: Examining Nondisabled Social Values." *Arena Review* 8: 1–15.

———. 1988. "The Politics of Physical Difference: Disability and Discrimination." *Journal of Social Issues* 44: 39–47.

Haller, Beth A. 2010. *Representing Disability in an Ableist World.* Louisville, KY: Advocado Press.

Hampton, Simon Jonathan. 2005. "Family Eugenics." *Disability & Society* 20: 553–561.

Hardin, Marie Meyers, and Brent Hardin. 2004. "The 'Supercrip' in Sport Media: Wheelchair Athletes Discuss Hegemony's Disabled Hero." *Sociology of Sport Online* 7 (1), available at http://www.physed.otago.ac.nz/sosol.

Harpur, Paul. 2012. "Embracing the New Disability Rights Paradigm: The Importance of the Convention on the Rights of Persons with Disabilities." *Disability & Society* 27: 1–14.

Hayashi, Reiko. 2005. "The Environment of Disability Today: A Nursing Home Is Not a Home." In *Ending Disability Discrimination: Strategies for Social Workers*, eds. Gary E. May and Martha B. Raske. Boston: Pearson Education.

Hearn, Kirsten. 1991. "Disabled Lesbians and Gays Are Here to Stay." In *High Risk Lives: Gay and Lesbian Politics After the Clause*, eds. Tara Kaufman and Paul Lincoln. London: Prism Press.

Hedderly, Tammy, Gillian Baird, and Helen McConachie. 2003. "Parental Reaction to Disability." *Current Pediatrics* 13: 30–35.

Hedrick, Brad. 2000. "Olympic Inequities." *Sports 'N Spokes* (Nov.): 74.

Hehir, Thomas. 2002. "Eliminating Ableism in Education." *Harvard Educational Review* 72: 1–32.

Heidegger, Martin. [1954] 1994. "The Question Concerning Technology." In *Basic Writings*, ed. David Krell. New York: HarperCollins.

Heller, Tamar, and Beth Marks. 2006. "Aging." In *Encyclopedia of Disability*, vol. 1, ed. Gary L. Albrecht. Thousand Oaks, CA: Sage.

Henderson, Sara, and Alan R. Petersen. 2002. *Consuming Health: Commodification of Health Care.* New York: Routledge.

Herman, Nancy J. 1993. "Return to Sender: Reintegrative Stigma-Management Strategies of Ex-Psychiatric Patients." *Journal of Contemporary Ethnography* 22: 295–330.

Hermann, Dorothy. 1998. *Helen Keller: A Life.* Chicago: University of Chicago Press.

Hernandez, Brigida. 2005. "A Voice in the Chorus: Perspectives of Young Men of Color on Their Disabilities, Identities, and Peer-Mentors." *Disability & Society* 20: 117–133.

Heward, William L. 2008. *Exceptional Child: An Introduction to Special Education.* Upper Saddle River, NJ: Prentice-Hall.

Hickel, K. Walter. 2001. "Medicine, Bureaucracy, and Social Welfare: The Politics of Disability Compensation for American Veterans of World War I." In *The New Disability History: American Perspectives*, eds. Paul K. Longmore and Lauri Umansky. New York: New York University Press.

Hockenberry, John. 1995. *Moving Violations: War Zones, Wheelchairs, and Declarations of Independence*. New York: Hyperion.

Hogan, Dennis. 2012. *Family Consequences of Children's Disabilities*. New York: Russell Sage Foundation.

Holland, Daniel. 2006. "Franklin D. Roosevelt's Shangri-La: Foreshadowing the Independent Living Movement in Warm Springs, Georgia, 1926–1945." *Disability & Society* 21: 513–535.

Holstein, Martha M. 1997. "Alzheimer's Disease and Senile Dementia, 1885–1920: An Interpretive History of Disease Negotiation." *Journal of Aging Studies* 11: 1–13.

Hubbard, Ruth. 1990. *The Politics of Women's Biology*. New Brunswick, NJ: Rutgers University Press.

Hughes, Bill, and Kevin Paterson. 1997. "The Social Model of Disability and the Disappearing Body: Towards a Sociology of Impairment." *Disability & Society* 12: 325–340.

Hughes, Everett Cherrington. 1945. "Dilemmas and Contradictions of Status." *American Journal of Sociology* 50: 353–359.

Hull, Anne, and Dana Priest. 2007. "It's Just Not Walter Reed." *Washington Post* (Mar. 5), available at http://www.washingtonpost.com.

Husson, Thomas. 2011. "Why the 'Web versus Application' Debate Is Irrelevant." *Forrester Blogs* (May 3), available at http://blogs.forrester .com.

Ignatieff, Michael. 2001. "Lemkin's Words." *The New Republic* (Feb. 26): 25–28.

Ingstad, Benedicte, and Susan Reynolds Whyte (eds.). 1995. *Disability and Culture*. Berkeley: University of California Press.

Iraq and Afghanistan Veterans of America. 2012. "Honor the Fallen" (July 2), available at http://iava.org.

Jacobs, James B., and Kimberly Potter. 1998. *Hate Crimes: Criminal Law and Identity Politics*. New York: Oxford University Press.

Jaeger, Paul T. 2012. *Disability and the Internet: Confronting a Digital Divide*. Boulder, CO: Lynne Rienner.

Jaggar, Alison M. 1983. *Feminist Politics and Human Nature*. Totowa, NJ: Rowman and Allanheld.

Johnson, Greg. 2011. "Rehabilitating Soldiers After the War." *Penn Current* (Dec. 15), available at http://www.upenn.edu.

Jones, Edgar, Nicola T. Fear, and Simon Wessely. 2007. "Shell Shock and Mild Traumatic Brain Injury in People with Moderate or Severe Traumatic Brain Injury." *Journal of Neuroscience Nursing* 37: 42–50.

Jones, Gwen A. 1997. "Advancement Opportunity Issues for Persons with Disabilities." *Human Resource Management Review* 7: 55–76.

Jönson, Hakan, and Annika Taghizadeh Larsson. 2009. "The Exclusion of Older People in Disability Activism and Policies—A Case of Inadvertent Ageism?" *Journal of Aging Studies* 23: 69–77.

Jost, B. C., and G. T. Grossberg. 1995. "The Natural History of Alzheimer's Disease: A Brain Bank Study." *Journal of the American Geriatric Society* 43: 1248–1255.

Juette, Melvin, and Ronald J. Berger. 2008. *Wheelchair Warrior: Gangs, Disability, and Basketball.* Philadelphia: Temple University Press.

Kahuna, Jeffrey S., Eva Kahuna, and Loren D. Lovegreen. 2011. "The Graying of Disability: People and Policies in the 21st Century." Unpublished manuscript.

Kalb, Claudia. 2005. "When Does Autism Start?" *Newsweek* (Feb. 28): 45–53.

Kanner, Leo. 1943. "Autistic Disturbances of Affective Contact." *The Nervous Child* 2: 217–250.

———. 1964. *A History of the Care and Study of the Mentally Retarded.* Springfield, IL: Charles C. Thomas.

Kaplan, Robert M., Theodore G. Ganiats, and Dominick L. Frosch. 2004. "Diagnostic and Treatment Decisions in US Healthcare." *Journal of Health Psychology* 9: 29–40.

Karner, Tracy Xavia. 1998. "Professional Caring: Homecare Workers as Fictive Kin." *Journal of Aging Studies* 12: 69–82.

Katsh, M. Ethan, and William Rose (eds.). 2002. *Taking Sides: Clashing Views on Controversial Legal Issues*, 10th ed. Guilford, CT: McGraw-Hill/Dushkin.

Kaufman, Miriam, Cory Silverberg, and Fran Odette. 2003. *The Ultimate Guide to Sex and Disability.* San Francisco: Cleis Press.

Kemp, Gina, Melinda Smith, and Jeanne Segal. 2012. "Leaving Disabilities in Children: Types of Learning Disorders and Their Signs," available at http://helpguide.org.

King, Marissa D., and Peter S. Bearman. 2009. "Diagnostic Change and the Increased Prevalence of Autism." *International Journal of Epidemiology* 38: 1124–1134.

———. 2011. "Socioeconomic Status and the Increased Prevalence of Autism in California." *American Sociological Review* 76: 320–346.

Kirk, Mike (director/producer). 2002. *Misunderstood Minds.* PBS documentary.

Kirkby, Robert J. 1995. "Wheelchair Netball: Motives and Attitudes of Competitors with and Without Disabilities." *Australian Psychologist* 30: 109–112.

Kirtley, Donald. 1975. *The Psychology of Blindness.* Chicago: Nelson-Hall.

Kitchin, Rob. 2000. "The Researched Opinions on Research: Disabled People and Disability Research." *Disability & Society* 15: 25–47.

Kittay, Eva Feder, and Ellen K. Feder (eds). 2002. *The Subject of Care: Feminist Perspectives on Dependency.* Lanham, MD: Rowman & Littlefield.

Kleege, Georgina. 1999. *Sight Unseen.* New Haven, CT: Yale University Press.

Kohrman, Arthur F., and Claire H. Kohrman. 2006. "Health Care Systems." In *Encyclopedia of Disability*, vol. 2, ed. Gary L. Albrecht. Thousand Oaks, CA: Sage.

Kondracke, Morton. 2001. *Saving Milly: Love, Politics, and Parkinson's Disease.* New York: Ballantine Books.

Kraus, Jess F., and Lawrence D. Chu. 2005. "Epidemiology." In *Textbook of Traumatic Brain Injury,* eds. Jonathan M. Silver, Thomas W. McAllister, and Stuart D. Yudofsky. Washington, DC: American Psychiatric Publishing.

Kriegel, Leonard. 1987. "The Cripple in Literature." In *Images of the Disabled, Disabling Images,* eds. Alan Gartner and Tom Joe. New York: Praeger.

Krupa, Terry. 2006. "Sheltered Employment." In *Encyclopedia of Disability,* vol. 4, ed. Gary L. Albrecht. Thousand Oaks, CA: Sage.

Kübler-Ross, Elisabeth. 1967. *On Death and Dying.* New York: Scribner.

Kuttai, Heather. 2010. *Maternity Rolls: Pregnancy, Childbirth and Disability.* Halifax, Nova Scotia: Fernwood.

Kuusisto, Stephen. 1998. *Planet of the Blind: A Memoir.* New York: Delta.

Labanowich, Stan. 1987. "The Physically Disabled in Sports." *Sports 'N Spokes* magazine reprint (Mar.–Apr.): 1–6.

———. 1988. "Wheelchair Basketball Classification: National and International Perspectives." *Palaestra: The Forum of Sport, Physical Education and Recreation for the Disabled* (Spring): 14–15, 38–40, 54.

La Ganga, Maria L. 2012. "Angry Vets Demand End to Backlog of Disability Claims." *Los Angeles Times,* May 22, available at http://articles.latimes.com.

Lamb, H. Richard, and Leona L. Bachrach. 2001. "Some Perspectives on Deinstitutionalization." *Psychiatric Services* 52: 1039–1045.

Lamb, Michael E., and Donald J. Meyer. 1991. "Fathers of Children with Special Needs." In *The Family with a Handicapped Child,* ed. Milton Seligman. Boston: Allyn & Bacon.

LaMere, Thomas John, and Stan Labanowich. 1984. "The History of Sport Wheelchairs—Part I: The Development of the Basketball Wheelchair." *Sports 'N Spokes* magazine reprint (Mar.–Apr.): 1–4.

Landsman, Gail Heidi. 2009. *Reconstructing Motherhood and Disability in the Age of "Perfect" Babies.* New York: Routledge.

Lane, Harlan. 1995. "Construction of Deafness." *Disability & Society* 10: 171–189.

Langan, Mary. 2011. "Parental Voices and Controversies in Autism." *Disability & Society* 26: 192–205.

Langlois, Jean A., Wesley Rutland-Brown, and Karen E. Thomas. 2004. *Traumatic Brain Injury in the United States: Emergency Department Visits, Hospitalizations, and Deaths.* Atlanta: Centers for Disease Control and Prevention, National Center for Injury Prevention and Control.

Lareau, Annette, and Erin McNamara Horvat. 1999. "Moments of Social Inclusion and Exclusion: Race, Class, and Cultural Capital in Family-School Relationships." *Sociology of Education* 72: 37–53.

Leamer, Laurence. 1994. *The Kennedy Women: The Saga of an American Family.* New York: Villard.

LeBesco, Kathleen. 2004. "There's Something About Disabled People: The Contradictions of Freakery in the Films of the Farrelly Brothers." *Disability Studies Quarterly* 24 (4), available at http://dsq-sds.org.

Leiter, Valerie. 2004. "Parental Activism, Professional Dominance, and Early Childhood Disability." *Disability Studies Quarterly* 24 (2), available at http://dsq-sds.org.

———. 2007. "'Nobody's Just Normal, You Know': The Social Creation of Developmental Disability." *Social Science & Medicine* 65: 1630–1641.

———. 2011. "Bowling Together: Foundations of Community Among Youth with Disabilities." In *Disability and Community*, eds. Allison C. Carey and Richard K. Scotch. Bingley, UK: Emerald.

———. 2012. *Their Time Has Come: Youth with Disabilities Entering Adulthood*. New Brunswick, NJ: Rutgers University Press.

Lenney, Michael, and Howard Sercombe. 2002. "'Did You See That Guy in the Wheelchair Down in the Pub?' Interactions Across Difference in a Public Place." *Disability & Society* 17: 5–18.

Lerner, Gerda. 1997. *Why History Matters: Life and Thought*. New York: Oxford University Press.

Light, Jennifer S. 2001. "Separate but Equal? Reasonable Accommodation in the Information Age." *Journal of the American Planning Association* 67: 263–278.

Linker, Beth. 2011. *War's Waste: Rehabilitation in World War I America*. Chicago: University of Chicago Press.

Linton, Simi. 1998. *Claiming Disability: Knowledge and Identity*. New York: New York University Press.

Lipsky, Dorothy Kezner, and Alan Gartner. 1997. *Inclusion and School Reform: Transforming America's Classroom*. Baltimore: Paul H. Brookes.

Lipson, Juliene G., and Judith G. Rogers. 2000. "Pregnancy, Birth, and Disability: Women's Health Care Experiences." *Health Care for Women International* 21: 11–26.

Litvak, Simi, and Alexandra Enders. 2001. "Support Systems: The Interface Between Individuals and Environments." In *Handbook of Disability Studies*, eds. Gary L. Albrecht, Katherine D. Seelman, and Michael Bury. Thousand Oaks, CA: Sage.

Llewellyn, A., and K. Hogan. 2000. "The Use and Abuse of Models of Disability." *Disability & Society* 15: 157–165.

Loiacono, Eleanor T., Nicholas C. Romano Jr., and Scot McCoy. 2009. "The State of Corporate Website Accessibility." *Communications of the Association for Information Systems* 52: 128–132.

Long, Lawrence Carter. 2012. "Disability on Screen: Mr. Magoo to Josh Blue, Who's Laughing Now." *Disaboom*, available at http://www.disaboom.com.

Longmore, Paul K. 2003. *Why I Burned My Books and Other Essays on Disability*. Philadelphia: Temple University Press.

Lorenz, J. M., D. E. Wooliever, J. R. Jetton, and N. Paneth. 1998. "A Quantitative Review of Mortality and Developmental Disability in Extremely Premature Newborns." *Archives of Pediatric and Adolescent Medicine* 152: 425–435.

Lorenz, Laura S. 2010. *Brain Injury Survivors: Narratives of Rehabilitation and Healing.* Boulder, CO: Lynne Rienner.

Ludgate, Kristen M. 1997. "Telecommuting and the Americans with Disabilities Act: Is Working from Home a Reasonable Accommodation?" *Minnesota Law Review* 81: 1309.

Lupton, Deborah. 1997. "Consumerism, Reflexivity and the Medical Encounter." *Social Science & Medicine* 45: 373–381.

Lupton, Deborah, and Wendy Seymour. 2000. "Technology, Selfhood and Physical Disability." *Social Science & Medicine* 50: 1851–1862.

Mairs, Nancy. 1996. *Waist-High in the World: A Life Among the Nondisabled.* Boston: Beacon Press.

Makas, Elaine. 1988. "Positive Attitudes Toward Disabled People: Disabled and Nondisabled Persons' Perspectives." *Journal of Social Issues* 44: 49–62.

Mallett, Christopher A. 2013. *Linking Disorders to Delinquency: Treating High-Risk Youth in the Juvenile Justice System.* Boulder, CO: FirstForum Press.

Mandell, David S., and Raymond F. Palmer. 2005. "Differences Among States in the Identification of Autism Spectrum Disorder." *Archives of Pediatric and Adolescent Medicine* 159: 266–269.

Mansbridge, Jane J., and Aldon Morris (eds.). 2001. *Oppositional Consciousness: The Subjective Roots of Protest.* Chicago: University of Chicago Press.

Marchione, Marilyn. 2012. "AP IMPACT: Almost Half of New Vets Seek Disability." *Salon.com* (May 27), available at http://www.salon.com.

Marshak, Laura E., Milton Seligman, and Fran Prezant. 1999. *Disability and the Family Life Cycle.* New York: Basic Books.

McCarthy, Jenny. 2007. *Louder Than Words: A Mother's Journey into Healing Autism.* New York: Dutton.

McDermott, Jeanne. 2000. *Babyface: A Story of Heart and Bones.* New York: Penguin.

McDonald, Katherine. 2006. "Community Living and Group Homes." In *Encyclopedia of Disability*, vol. 1, ed. Gary L. Albrecht. Thousand Oaks, CA: Sage.

McRuer, Robert. 2006. *Crip Theory: Cultural Signs of Queerness and Disability.* New York: New York University Press.

———. [2002] 2010. "Compulsory Able-Bodiedness and Queer/Disabled Existence." In *The Disability Studies Reader*, 3rd ed., ed. Lennard Davis. New York: Routledge.

Mead, George Herbert. [1934] 1962. *Mind, Self and Society: From the Standpoint of a Social Behaviorist.* Chicago: University of Chicago Press.

Medland, Joan, and Caroline Ellis-Hill. 2008. "Why Do Able-Bodied People Take Part in Wheelchair Sports?" *Disability & Society* 23: 107–116.

Meekosha, Helen. 2004. "Drifting Down the Gulf Stream: Navigating the Cultures of Disability Studies." *Disability & Society* 19: 721–733.

Merleau-Ponty, Maurice. 1962. *Phenomenology of Perception.* London: Routledge & Kegan Paul.

Merton, Robert K. 1967. "Foreword" to Jacques Ellul, *The Technological Society.* New York: Vintage.

Meyer, Donald J. (ed.). 1995. *Uncommon Fathers: Reflections on Raising a Child with a Disability.* Bethesda, MD: Woodbine House.

Meyer, Maonna Harrington (ed.). 2000. *Care Work: Gender, Class, and the Welfare State.* New York: Routledge.

Meyer, Michelle, Michelle Donelly, and Patricia Weerakoon. 2007. "'They're Taking the Place of My Hands': Perspectives of People Using Personal Care." *Disability & Society* 22: 595–608.

Mezey, Susan Gluck. 2005. *Disabling Interpretations: The Americans with Disabilities Act in Federal Court.* Pittsburgh: University of Pittsburgh Press.

Michalko, Rob. 1998. *Mystery of the Eye and the Shadow of Blindness.* Toronto: University of Toronto Press.

Miller, Nancy B., and Catherine C. Sammons. 1999. *Everybody's Different: Understanding and Changing Our Reactions to Disabilities.* Baltimore: Paul H. Brookes.

Mills, C. Wright. 1959. *The Sociological Imagination.* New York: Oxford University Press.

Milner, Murray, Jr. 2004. *Freaks, Geeks, and Cool Kids: American Teenagers, Schools, and the Culture of Consumption.* New York: Routledge.

Money, John. 1989. "Paleodigms and Paleodigmatics: A New Theoretical Construct Applicable to Munchausen's Syndrome by Proxy, Child-Abuse Dwarfism, Paraphilias, Anorexia Nervosa and Other Syndromes." *American Journal of Psychotherapy* 43: 15–24.

Moore, Timothy. 2009. "How Many Disabled Americans Are There?" *Ezine Articles* (June), available at http://ezinearticles.com.

Moreno, Jonathan D. 1999. *Undue Risk: Secret State Experiments on Humans.* New York: Freeman.

Morozov, Evgeny. 2012. "Form and Fortune: Steve Jobs' Pursuit of Perfection—and the Consequences." *The New Republic* (Mar. 15): 18–27.

Morris, Jenny. 1991. *Pride Against Prejudice: Transforming Attitudes to Disability.* Philadelphia: New Society.

———. 1993. *Independent Lives: Community Care and Disabled People.* London: Macmillan.

Morris, Kimberly A., and Richard J. Morris. 2006. "Disability and Juvenile Delinquency: Issues and Trends." *Disability & Society* 21: 613–627.

Murphy, Robert. 1987. *The Body Silent.* New York: Henry Holt.

Murphy, Robert, Jessica Scheer, Yoland Murphy, and Robert Mack. 1988. "Physical Disability and Social Liminality: A Study in the Rituals of Adversity." *Social Science & Medicine* 26: 235–242.

Naraine, Mala D., and Peter H. Lindsay. 2011. "Social Inclusion of Employees Who Are Blind or Low Vision." *Disability & Society* 26: 389–403.

Nasar, Sylvia. 1998. *A Beautiful Mind: The Life of Mathematical Genius and Nobel Laureate John Nash.* New York: Touchstone.

Naseef, Robert A. 2001. *Special Children, Challenged Parents: The Struggles and Rewards of Raising a Child with a Disability*. Baltimore: Paul H. Brookes.

National Center for Education Statistics. 2009. "Digest of Education Statistics, 2008," available at http://nces.ed.gov.

———. 2011. "Fast Facts: How Many Students with Disabilities Receive Services," available at http://nces.ed.gov.

National Center for Injury Prevention and Control. 2005. "Heads Up: Concussion in High School Sports." Centers for Disease Control and Prevention. Atlanta, GA.

National Institute of Aging. 2011. "Alzheimer's Disease Fact Sheet," available at http://www.nia.nih.gov.

National Institute of Mental Health (NIMH). 1993. *Learning Disabilities*. Washington, DC: US Government Printing Office.

———. 2012. "Schizophrenia," available at http://www.nimh.nih.gov.

National Organization on Disability/Harris Poll. 2004. "The NOD/Harris 2004 Survey of Americans with Disabilities." New York: Harris Interactive.

National Wheelchair Basketball Association (NWBA). 2012. "History of Wheelchair Basketball," available at http://www.nwba.org.

Neff, Patricia E. 2010. "Fathering an ADHD Child: An Examination of Paternal Well-Being and Social Support." *Sociological Inquiry* 80: 531–553.

Neuman, W. Lawrence. 2011. *Social Research Methods: Qualitative and Quantitative Approaches*. Boston: Allyn & Bacon.

New York Times. 1992. "Update: 'Baby Jane Doe' Turns 9 This Year" (May 17), available at http://www.nytimes.com.

Nicolaisen, Ida. 1995. "Persons and Nonpersons: Disability and Personhood Among the Punan Bun of Central Borneo." In *Disability and Culture*, eds. Benedicte Ingstad and Susan Reynolds Whyte. Berkeley: University of California Press.

Nielsen, Kim E. 2004. *The Radical Lives of Helen Keller*. New York: New York University Press.

Nixon II, Howard L. 2002. "Sport and Disability." In *Handbook of Sports Studies.*, eds. Jay Coakley and Eric Dunning. Thousand Oaks, CA: Sage.

Norden, Martin F. 1994. *The Cinema of Isolation: A History of Physical Disability in the Movies*. New Brunswick, NJ: Rutgers University Press.

Nowell, Nefertiti L. 2006. "Oppression." In *Encyclopedia of Disability*, vol. 3, ed. Gary L. Albrecht. Thousand Oaks, CA: Sage.

Nussbaum, Martha C. 2006. *Frontiers of Justice: Disability, Nationality, and Species Membership*. Cambridge, MA: Belknap Press.

Oakley, Ann. 1972. *Sex, Gender, and Society*. London: Temple Smith.

O'Connor, Tom. 2002. "Disability and David Lynch's 'Disabled' Body of Work." *Disability Studies Quarterly* 22 (1), available at http://dsq-sds.org.

Offit, Paul A. 2008. *Autism's False Prophets: Bad Science, Risky Medicine, and the Search for a Cure*. New York: Columbia University Press.

Oliver, Michael. 1990. *The Politics of Disablement*. New York: Macmillan.

———. 1997. "Emancipatory Research: Realistic Goal or Impossible Dream?" In *Doing Disability Research*, eds. Colin Barnes and Geof Mercer. Leeds, UK: Disability Press.

———. 2004. "The Social Model in Action: If I Had a Hammer." In *Implementing the Social Model of Disability: Theory and Research*, eds. Colin Barnes and Geof Mercer. Leeds, UK: Disability Press.

Omansky, Beth. 2011. *Borderlands of Blindness*. Boulder, CO: Lynne Rienner.

O'Neil, Sara. 2008. "The Meaning of Autism: Beyond Disorder." *Disability & Society* 23: 787–799.

Ong-Dean, Colin. 2006. "High Roads and Low Roads: Learning Disabilities in California, 1976–1998." *Sociological Perspectives* 49: 91–113.

———. 2009. *Distinguishing Disability: Parents, Privilege, and Special Education*. Chicago: University of Chicago Press.

Ostrander, R. Noam. 2008. "When Identities Collide: Masculinity, Disability, and Race." *Disability & Society* 23: 585–597.

Ownsworth, T. L., and T. P. S. Oei. 1998. "Depression After Traumatic Brain Injury: Conceptualization and Treatment Considerations." *Brain Injury* 12: 735–752.

Palmer, Raymond F., Stephen Blanchard, Carlos R. Jean, and David S. Mandell. 2005. "School District Resources and Identification of Children with Autistic Disorder." *American Journal of Public Health* 95: 125–130.

Papadimitriou, Christina. 2001. "From Dis-ability to Difference: Conceptual and Methodological Issues in the Study of Physical Disability." In *Handbook of Phenomenology and Medicine*, ed. S. Kay Toombs. Dordrecht, Netherlands: Kluwer Academic.

———. 2008a. "Becoming En-wheeled: The Situated Accomplishment of Re-embodiment as a Wheelchair User After Spinal Cord Injury." *Disability & Society* 23: 691–704.

———. 2008b. "The 'I' of the Beholder: Phenomenological Seeing in Disability Research." *Sport, Ethics, and Philosophy* 2: 216–233.

———. 2008c. "'It Was Hard but You Did It': The Co-Production of 'Work' in a Clinical Setting Among Spinal Cord Injured Adults and Their Physical Therapists." *Disability and Rehabilitation* 30: 365–374.

Papadimitriou, Christina, and David A. Stone. 2011. "Addressing Existential Disruption in Traumatic Spinal Cord Injury: A New Approach to Human Temporality in Inpatient Rehabilitation." *Disability and Rehabilitation* 33: 2121–2133.

Park, Jennifer M., Dennis P. Hogan, and Frances K. Goldscheider. 2003. "Child Disability and Mothers' Tubal Ligation." *Perspectives on Sexual and Reproductive Health* 35: 138–143.

Parrish, Tom. 2002. "Racial Disparities in the Identification, Funding, and Provision of Special Education." In *Racial Inequality in Special Education*, eds. Daniel J. Losen and Gary Orfield. Cambridge, MA: Harvard Education Press.

Parry, Marc. 2010. "Colleges Lock Out Blind Students." *Chronicle of Higher Education* (Dec. 12), available at http://www.chronicle.com.

Parsons, Talcott. 1951. *The Social System*. Glencoe, IL: Free Press.

Peters, Jeremy W. 2005. "In Wisconsin, Fallout Grows over Decision on Pageant." *New York Times* (Apr. 6), available at http://www.nytimes.com.

Petersen, Amy J. 2011. "Research with Individuals Labeled 'Other': Reflections on the Research Process." *Disability & Society* 26: 293–305.

Peterson, Michael, Laurie Beth Clark, and Lisa Nakamura. 2010. "'I See You?' Gender and Disability in *Avatar*." *Flow TV* (Feb. 5), available at http://www.flowtv.org.

Pincus, Fred. 2011. *Understanding Diversity: An Introduction to Class, Race, Gender, Sexual Orientation and Disability*, 2nd ed. Boulder, CO: Lynne Rienner.

Pope, Andrew M., and Alvin R. Tarlov (eds.). 1991. *Disability in America: Toward a National Agenda for Prevention*. Washington, DC: National Academy Press.

Potok, Andrew. 2002. *A Matter of Dignity: Changing the World of the Disabled*. New York: Bantam.

Powell, William E. 2005. "Becoming Quasimodo: The Shaping of a Life." In *Storytelling Sociology: Narrative as Social Inquiry*, eds. Ronald J. Berger and Richard Quinney. Boulder, CO: Lynne Rienner.

Priest, Dana, and Anne Hull. 2007. "Soldiers Face Neglect, Frustration at Army's Top Medical Facility." *Washington Post* (Feb. 18), available at http://www.washingtonpost.com.

Priestley, Mark (ed.). 2001. *Disability and the Life Course: A Global Perspective*. Cambridge, UK: Cambridge University Press.

Prilleltensky, Ora. 2003. "A Ramp to Motherhood: The Experiences of Mothers with Physical Disabilities." *Sexuality and Disability* 21: 21–47.

———. 2004. "My Child Is Not My Carer: Mothers with Physical Disabilities and the Well-Being of Children." *Disability & Society* 19: 209–223.

Rainey, Sarah Smith. 2011. *Love, Sex, and Disability: The Pleasures of Care*. Boulder, CO: Lynne Rienner.

Randolph, Diane Smith, and Elena M. Andresen. 2004. "Disability, Gender, and Unemployment Relationships in the United States from the Behavioral Risk Factor Surveillance System." *Disability & Society* 19: 403–414.

Rapp, Emily. 2007. *Poster Child: A Memoir*. New York: Bloomsbury.

Reid, D. Kim, Edy Hammond Stoughton, and Robin M. Smith. 2006. "The Humorous Construction of Disability: 'Stand-Up' Comedians in the United States." *Disability Studies Quarterly* 21 (6), available at http://dsq-sds.org.

Reinharz, Shulamit. 1992. *Feminist Methods in Social Research*. New York: Oxford University Press.

Rich, Adrienne. 1983. "Compulsory Heterosexuality and Lesbian Existence."

In *Powers of Desire: The Politics of Sexuality*, eds. Ann Snitow, Christine Stansell, and Sharon Thompson. New York: Monthly Review Press.

Ridolfo, Heather, and Brian W. Ward. 2013. *Mobility Impairment and the Construction of Identity*. Boulder, CO: FirstForum Press.

Rocque, Bill. 2010. "Mediating Self-hood: Exploring the Construction and Maintenance of Identity by Mothers of Children Labeled with Autism Spectrum Disorder." *Disability & Society* 25: 485–497.

Rosenhan, D. L. 1973. "Being Sane in Insane Places." *Science* 179: 250–258.

Rosenthal, Richard. 1978. *The Hearing Loss Handbook*. New York: Shocken.

Roswal, Glenn M., and Mariusz Damentko. 2006. "A Review of Completed Research in Sports for Individuals with Intellectual Disability." *Research Yearbook 2006* 12: 181–183.

Rothman, David J. 1990. *The Discovery of the Asylum: Social Order and Disorder in the New Republic*, rev. ed. Boston: Little, Brown.

Rothman, David J., and Sheila M. Rothman. 1984. *The Willowbrook Wars*. New York: Harper & Row.

Rubenstein, Richard L., and John K. Roth. 1987. *Approaches to Auschwitz: The Holocaust and Its Legacy*. Atlanta: John Knox Press.

Ryan, Sara, and Katherine Runswick-Cole. 2008. "Repositioning Mothers: Mothers, Disabled Children, and Disability Studies." *Disability & Society* 23: 199–210.

Samuel, Preethy S., Karen L. Hobden, and Barbara W. LeRoy. 2011. "Families of Children with Autism and Developmental Disabilities: A Description of Their Community Interaction." In *Disability and Community*, eds. Allison C. Carey and Richard K. Scotch. Bingley, UK: Emerald.

Sandels, Alexandra. 2010. "Iraq, Afghanistan: American Casualties Total 500,000, Counting Injury and Disease, Writer Claims." *Los Angeles Times* (June 4), available at http://latimesblogs.latimes.com.

Sanford, Matthew. 2006. *Waking: A Memoir of Trauma and Transcendence*. New York: Rodale.

Sapey, Bob, John Stewart, and Gelnis Donaldson. 2005. "Increases in Wheelchair Use and Perceptions of Disablement." *Disability & Society* 20: 489–505.

Savić, Obrad (ed.) 1999. *The Politics of Human Rights*. London: Verso.

Saxton, Marsha. 1998. "Disability Rights and Selective Abortion." In *Abortion Wars: A Half-Century of Struggle, 1950–2000*, ed. Ricki Solinger. Berkeley: University of California Press.

Schairer, Cynthia. 2011. "Communities of Prosthesis Users and Possibilities for Personal Information." In *Disability and Community*, eds. Allison C. Carey and Richard K. Scotch. Bingley, UK: Emerald.

Schartz, Kevin M., Helen A. Schartz, and Peter Blanck. 2002. "Employment for Persons with Disabilities in Information Technology Jobs: Literature Review for 'IT Works.'" *Behavioral Sciences and the Law* 20: 637–657.

Scheer, Jessica, and Nora Groce. 1988. "Impairment as a Human Constant:

Cross-Cultural and Historical Perspectives on Variation." *Journal of Social Issues* 44: 23–37.

Schriner, Kay. 2001. "A Disability Studies Perspective on Employment Issues and Policies for Disabled People: An International View." In *Handbook of Disability Studies*, eds. Gary L. Albrecht, Katherine D. Seelman, and Michael Bury. Thousand Oaks, CA: Sage.

Schwalbe, Michael, and Douglas Mason-Schrock. 1996. "Identity Work as Group Process." *Advances in Group Process* 13: 113–147.

Schwartz, Gary, and Don Merten. 1967. "The Language of Adolescence: An Anthropological Approach to the Youth Culture." *American Journal of Sociology* 72: 453–468.

Schweik, Susan M. 2009. *The Ugly Laws: Disability in Public*. New York: New York University Press.

Scotch, Richard K. 2001a. "American Disability Policy in the Twentieth Century." In *The New Disability History: American Perspectives*, eds. Paul K. Longmore and Lauri Umansky. New York: New York University Press.

———. 2001b. *From Good Will to Civil Rights: Transforming Federal Disability Policy*. Philadelphia: Temple University Press.

Scotch, Richard K., and Kay Schriner. 1997. "Disability as Human Variation: Implications for Policy." *The Annals of the American Academy of Political and Social Science* 549: 148–160.

Scott, Robert A. 1969. *The Making of Blind Men*. New York: Russell Sage.

Scull, Andrew. 1991. "Psychiatry and Social Control in the Nineteenth and Twentieth Centuries." *History of Psychiatry* 2: 149–169.

Sedgwick, Eve Kosofsky. 1990. *Epistemology of the Closet*. Berkeley: University of California Press.

Seymour, Wendy, and Deborah Lupton. 2004. "Holding the Line Online: Exploring Wired Relationships for People with Disabilities." *Disability & Society* 19: 291–305.

Shakespeare, Tom. 2006. *Disability Rights and Wrongs*. London: Routledge.

———. 2010. "The Social Model of Disability." In *The Disability Studies Reader*, 3rd ed., ed. Lennard Davis. New York: Routledge.

Shakespeare, Tom, Kath Gillespie-Sells, and Dominic Davies. 1996. *The Sexual Politics of Disability: Untold Desires*. London: Cassell.

Shakespeare, Tom, and Nicholas Watson. 2001. "The Social Model: An Outdated Ideology?" In *Research in Social Science and Disability*, vol. 2, eds. Barbara Altman and Sharon Barnartt. Bingley, UK: Emerald.

Shannon, Jeff. 2005. "Timmy of 'South Park' Challenges Viewers' Attitudes About People with Disabilities." *Seattle Times* (Nov. 28), available at http://seattletimes.nwsource.com.

Shapiro, Joseph P. 1993. *No Pity: People with Disabilities Forging a New Civil Rights Movement*. New York: Times Books.

Shattuck, Paul. 2006. "Contribution of Diagnostic Substitution to the Growing Administrative Prevalence of Autism." *Pediatrics* 117: 1028–1037.

Sherry, Mark. 2004. "Overlaps and Contradictions Between Queer Theory and Disability Studies." *Disability & Society* 19: 769–783.

————. 2006. *If I Only Had a Brain: Deconstructing Brain Injury*. New York: Routledge.

————. 2010. *Disability Hate Crimes: Does Anyone Really Hate Disabled People?* Burlington, VT: Ashgate.

Shifrer, Dara, Chandra Muller, and Rebecca Callahan. 2010. "Disproportionality: A Sociological Perspective of the Identification by Schools of Students with Learning Disabilities." In *Disability as a Fluid State*, ed. Sharon N. Barnartt. Bingley, UK: Emerald.

Shilling, Chris. 2003. *The Body and Social Theory*. Thousand Oaks, CA: Sage.

Shogan, Debra A. 1999. *The Making of High-Performance Athletes: Discipline, Diversity, and Ethics*. Toronto: University of Toronto Press.

Shohat, Ella (ed.). 1998. *Talking Visions: Multicultural Feminism in a Transnational Age*. New York: New Museum of Contemporary Art.

Shonkoff, Jack P., and Deborah A. Phillips. 2000. *From Neurons to Neighborhoods: The Science of Early Childhood Development*. Washington, DC: National Research Council and Institute of Medicine, National Academics.

Siebers, Tobin. 2006. "Disability Studies and the Future of Identity Politics." In *Identity Politics Reconsidered*, eds. Linda Martín Alcoff, Michael Hames-Garcia, Satya P. Mohanty, and Paula M. L. Moya. New York: Palgrave.

————. 2008. *Disability Theory*. Ann Arbor: University of Michigan Press.

Siegal, Bryna. 1996. *The World of the Autistic Child*. New York: Oxford University Press.

Silberman, Steve. 2001 "The Geek Syndrome." *Wired* (Dec.), available at http://www.wired.com.

Silvers, Anita, David Wasserman, and Mary B. Mahowald. 1998. *Disability, Difference, Discrimination: Perspectives on Justice in Bioethics and Public Policy*. Lanham, MD: Rowman & Littlefield.

Singer, Judy. 1999. "Why Can't You Be Normal for Once in Your Life?" In *Disability Discourse*, ed. Mairian Corker. Berkshire, UK: Open University Press.

Singer, Peter. 1999. *Practical Ethics*, 2nd ed. Cambridge, MA: Cambridge University Press.

Singh, Vanessa, and Anita Ghai. 2009. "Notions of Self: Lived Realities of Children with Disabilities." *Disability & Society* 24: 129–145.

Smedley, Brian D., Adrienne Y. Stith, and Alan R. Nelson. 2003. *Unequal Treatment: Confronting Racial and Ethnic Disparities in Health Care*. Washington, DC: National Academy Press.

Smith, Ralph W., David R. Austin, Dan W. Kennedy, Youngkhill Lee, and Peggy Hutchison. 2005. *Inclusive and Special Recreation: Opportunities for Persons with Disabilities*, 5th ed. New York: McGraw-Hill.

Snider, Eric D. 2005. Review of *The Ringer* (Dec. 23), available at http://www.ericsnider.com.

Snyder, Sharon L. 2006. "Disability Studies." In *Encyclopedia of Disability*, vol. 1, ed. Gary L. Albrecht. Thousand Oaks, CA: Sage.

Snyder, Sharon L., and David T. Mitchell. 2006. *Cultural Locations of Disability.* Chicago: University of Chicago Press.

Sobsey, Dick. 1994. *Violence and Abuse in the Lives of People with Disabilities: The End of Silent Acceptance?* Baltimore: Paul H. Brookes.

Sobsey, Dick, Wade Randall, and Rauno K. Parrila. 1997. "Gender Differences in Abuse of Children with and Without Disabilities." *Child Abuse and Neglect* 21: 707–720.

Special Education Elementary Longitudinal Study. 2005. "SEELS Info and Reports: Wave 1 Wave 2 Overview," available at http://www.seels.net.

Stainton, Tim. 2008. "Reason, Grace and Charity: Augustine and the Impact of Church Doctrine on the Construction of Intellectual Disability." *Disability & Society* 23: 485–496.

Stevens, Geoff Ruggeri. 2002. "Employers' Perceptions and Practices in the Employability of Disabled People: A Survey of Companies in Southeast UK." *Disability & Society* 17: 779–796.

Stienstra, Deborah S., James Watzke, and Gary E. Birch. 2007. "A Three-Way Dance: The Global Public Good and Accessibility in Information Technologies." *Information Society* 23: 149–158.

Stodden, R. A., and P. W. Dowrick. 2000. "Postsecondary Education and Employment of Adults with Disabilities." *American Rehabilitation* 25: 19–23.

Stone, Collins. 1848. "The Religious State and Instruction of the Deaf and Dumb." *American Annals of the Deaf* 1 (Apr.).

Straus, Joseph N. 2010. "Autism as Culture." In *The Disability Studies Reader*, 3rd ed., ed. Lennard Davis. New York: Routledge.

Sullivan, P. M., and J. F. Knutson. 2000. "Maltreatment and Disabilities: A Population-Based Epidemiological Study." *Child Abuse and Neglect* 24: 1257–1273.

Switzer, Jacqueline Vaughn. 2003. *Disabled Rights: American Disability Policy and the Fight for Equality.* Washington, DC: Georgetown University Press.

Switzky, H. N., M. Dudzinski, R. Van Acker, and J. Gambro. 1988. "Historical Foundations of Out-of-Home Residential Alternative for Mentally Retarded Persons." In *Integration of Developmentally Disabled Individuals into the Community,* eds. Laird W. Heal, Janell I. Haney, and Angela R. Novak Amado. Baltimore: Brookes.

Talle, Aud. 1995. "A Child Is a Child: Disability and Equality Among the Kenya Maasai." In *Disability and Culture*, eds. Benedicte Ingstad and Susan Reynolds Whyte. Berkeley: University of California Press.

Taub, Diane E., Elaine M. Blinde, and Kimberly R. Greer. 1999. "Stigma Management Through Participation in Sport and Physical Activity: Experiences of Male College Students with Physical Disabilities." *Human Relations* 52: 1469–1484.

ten Have, Henk A. M. J., and Ruth B. Purtilo. 2004. "Introduction: Historical Overview of a Global Problem." In *Ethical Foundations of*

Palliative Care for Alzheimer's Disease, eds. Ruth B. Purtilo and Henk A. M. J. ten Have. Baltimore: Johns Hopkins University Press.

Tennant, Jennifer. 2009. "The Reasonableness of Working from Home in the Digital Age." *Review of Disability Studies* 5: 10–20.

Thiara, Ravi K., Gill Hague, and Audrey Mullender. 2011. "Losing on Both Counts: Disabled Women and Domestic Violence." *Disability & Society* 26: 757–771.

Thomas, Carol. 2004. "How Is Disability Understood? An Examination of Sociological Approaches." *Disability & Society* 19: 569–583.

Thomson, Rosemarie Garland. 1997. *Extraordinary Bodies: Figuring Physical Disability in American Culture and Literature*. New York: Columbia University Press.

———. [2002] 2010. "Integrating Disability, Transforming Feminist Theory." In *The Disability Studies Reader*, 3rd ed., ed. Lennard Davis. New York: Routledge.

Tollifson, Joan. 1997. "Imperfection Is a Beautiful Thing: On Disability and Meditation." In *Staring Back: The Disability Experience from the Inside Out*, ed. Kenny Fries. New York: Plume.

Torrey, E. Fuller. 1997. *Out of the Shadows: Confronting America's Mental Health Crisis*. New York: John Wiley.

Tucker, Bonnie Poitras. 1998. "Deaf Culture, Cochlear Implants, and Elective Disability." *Hastings Center Report* 28: 6–14.

Turner, Bryan S. 2001. "Disability and the Sociology of the Body." In *Handbook of Disability Studies*, eds. Gary L. Albrecht, Katherine D. Seelman, and Michael Bury. Thousand Oaks, CA: Sage.

US Department of Health and Human Services (USDHHS). 2008. *Disability and Health in the United States, 2001–2005*. Washington, DC.

Vandenbark, R. Todd. 2010. "Tending a Wild Garden: Library Web Design for Persons with Disabilities." *Information Technology and Libraries* 29: 23–29.

Vernon, Ayesha. 1999. "The Dialectics of Multiple Identities and the Disabled People's Movement." *Disability & Society* 14: 385–398.

Virginia Department of Education. 2012. "Emotional Disability," available at http://www.doe.virginia.gov.

Waitzkin, Howard. 2000. "Changing Patient-Physician Relationships in the Changing Health-Policy Environment." In *Handbook of Medical Sociology*, 5th ed., eds. Chloe E. Bird, Peter Conrad, and Allen M. Fremont. Upper Saddle River, NJ: Prentice Hall.

Waldrop, Judith, and Sharon Stern. 2003. "Disability Status: 2000." Washington, DC: US Census Bureau.

Wang, Qi. 2005. "Disability and American Families: 2000." Washington, DC: US Census Bureau.

Warner, Michael. 1999. *The Trouble with Normal: Sex, Politics, and the Ethics of Queer Life*. New York: Free Press.

Watson, Nick. 2002. "Well, I Know This Is Going to Sound Very Strange to You, but I Don't See Myself as a Disabled Person: Identity and Disability." *Disability & Society* 17: 509–527.

Wedgwood, Nikki. 2011. "A Person with Abilities: The Transition to Adulthood of a Young Woman with a Severe Physical Impairment." *Young* 19: 433–452.

Wendell, Susan. 1996. *The Rejected Body: Feminist Philosophical Reflections on Disability.* New York: Routledge.

Whittington-Walsh, Fiona. 2002. "From Freaks to Savants: Disability and Hegemony from *The Hunchback of Notre Dame* (1939) to *Sling Blade* (1997)." *Disability & Society* 17: 695–707.

Whyte, Susan Reynolds, and Benedicte Ingstad. 1995. "Disability and Culture: An Overview." In *Disability and Culture*, eds. Benedicte Ingstad and Susan Reynolds Whyte. Berkeley: University of California Press.

Wilde, Alison. 2010. "Alison Wilde Reviews *Avatar*—The Most Expensive Film Yet Made." *Disability Arts* (Jan. 14), available at http://www.disabilityarts.org.

Williams, Donna. 1992. *Nobody Nowhere: The Extraordinary Autobiography of an Autistic.* New York: Times Books.

Williams, Gareth. 2001. "Theorizing Disability." In *Handbook of Disability Studies,* eds. Gary L. Albrecht, Katherine D. Seelman, and Michael Bury. Thousand Oaks, CA: Sage.

Wilson-Kovacs, Dana, Michelle K. Ryan, S. Alexander Haslam, and Anna Rabinovich. 2008. "Just Because You Can Get a Wheelchair in the Building Doesn't Necessarily Mean That You Can Still Participate." *Disability & Society* 23: 705–717.

Wilton, Robert D. 2008. "Workers with Disabilities and the Challenges of Emotional Labour." *Disability & Society* 23: 361–373.

Winzer, Margret A. 1997. "Disability and Society Before the Eighteenth Century." In *The Disability Studies Reader*, ed. Lennard Davis. New York: Routledge.

———. 2000. "The Inclusion Movement: Review and Reflections on Reform in Special Education." In *Special Education in the 21st Century: Issues of Inclusion and Reform*, eds. Margret A. Winzer and Kaz Mazurek. Washington, DC: Gallaudet University Press.

Winzer, Margret A., and Kaz Mazurek (eds.). 2000. *Special Education in the 21st Century: Issues of Inclusion and Reform.* Washington, DC: Gallaudet University Press.

Womble, Laura. 2012. "Contagious Classic." *Sports 'N Spokes* (Mar.): 14–19.

Woodward, Stephanie. 2008. "Ronald Mace and His Impact on Universal Design." *Center for Disability Rights, Inc.* (Dec. 17), available at http://www.cdrnys.org.

World Health Organization. 2011. *World Report on Disability and Rehabilitation.* Geneva, Switzerland, and Washington, DC: World Health Organization and World Bank.

Wright, Beatrice. 1960. *Physical Disability: A Psychosocial Approach.* New York: Harper & Row.

Wright, David. 2004. "Mongols in Our Midst: John Landon Down and the

Ethnic Classification of Idiocy, 1854–1924." In *Mental Retardation in America: A Historical Reader*, eds. Steven Noll and James W. Trent Jr. New York: New York University Press.

Ytterhus, Borgunn, Christian Wendelborg, and Hege Lundeby. 2008. "Managing Turning Points and Transitions in Childhood and Parenthood—Insight from Families with Disabled Children in Norway." *Disability & Society* 23: 625–636.

Zarb, Gerry. 1992. "On the Road to Damascus: First Steps Towards Changing the Relations of Research Production." *Disability, Handicap, and Society* 7: 125–138.

Zhang, L., B. Masel, R. S. Scheibel, C. H. Christiansen, N. Huddleston, and K. J. Ottenbacher. 2001. "Virtual Reality in the Assessment of Selective Cognitive Function After Brain Injury." *American Journal of Physical Medicine and Rehabilitation* 80: 597–604.

Zitzelsberger, Hilde. 2005. "(In)visibility: Accounts of Embodiment of Women with Physical Disabilities and Differences." *Disability & Society* 20: 389–403.

Zola, Irving. 1982. *Missing Pieces: A Chronicle of Living with a Disability.* Philadelphia: Temple University Press.

———. 1984. "Communication Barriers Between 'the Able-Bodied' and 'the Handicapped.'" In *The Psychological and Social Impact of Physical Disability*, eds. Robert P. Marinelli and Arthur E. Dell Orto. New York: Springer.

———. 1991. "Bringing Our Bodies and Ourselves Back In: Reflections on the Past, Present and Future of Medical Sociology." *Journal of Health and Social Behavior* 32: 1–16.

Zucchino, David. 2012. "They Butchered Me Like a Hog." *Wisconsin State Journal* (Jan. 29): B1.

Zuckoff, Mitchell. 2002. *Choosing Naia: A Family's Journey.* Boston: Beacon Press.

Index

Ableism, 14–15, 109
Abortion, 38, 82, 214–215
Accessibility barriers: in the
community, 67, 98–99, 151, 153,
157–159; computer technology
and, 210–212; in education, 17,
97, 99, 122, 125, 211; in homes,
96, 98, 131, 156–157; in the
workplace, 129. *See also*
Americans with Disabilities Act;
Architecture; Rehabilitation Act
of 1973
Adelson, Betty, 82
Adolescence: the life course and,
113; peer relationships during,
113–117, 119–120, 123. *See also*
Education
Adoption, 99
Adulthood, transition to, 123, 125.
See also Education;
Employment/work
AIDS, 11
Albrecht, Gary, 34–36, 121
Alcoff, Linda Martín, 33
Alzheimer, Alois, 141–142
Alzheimer's disease, 141–142
American Asylum for the Death and
Dumb, 56
American Sign Language, 56–57,
154. *See also* Sign language
Americans with Disabilities Act, 2,

72–73, 129–130, 211, 213, 226;
appellate court cases and, 73;
political history of, 18, 69–72; US
Supreme Court cases and, 73–76,
78 (n17)
Americans with Disabilities
Amendments Act, 78 (n17)
Amputees, 62, 64, 94–95, 222. *See
also* Prostheses
Amyotrophic lateral sclerosis, 217
Anthropological research. *See*
Preliterate societies
Apert, Eugene, 85
Apert syndrome, 85
Architecture: teaching of, 213;
universal design and, 213, 229
(n4)
Armstrong, Felicity, 106
Asch, Adrienne, 80
Asperger, Hans, 10
Asperger's syndrome, 10–11, 20
Attention deficit hyperactivity, 20,
92–93
Augustine, 53, 77 (n4)
Autism, 10–11, 20–21, 23 (n9), 85,
93, 102; Autism Spectrum
Disorder, 10; culture, 32;
diagnostic substitution effect and,
91; high functioning vs. low
functioning, 20; Internet and, 32;
prevalence of, 91. *See also*

259

About the Book

RONALD BERGER PROVIDES STUDENTS WITH A COMPREHEN-
sive, accessible introduction to the key themes and controversies in
disability studies. This innovative textbook:

- provides historical context, from ancient times to the present
- traces disability's impact throughout the life course
- gives prominence to the voices of people with disabilities
- explores popular culture's role in distorting ideas about disability
- addresses emerging ethical issues, such as the implications of
  genetic selection

Illustrating the profound consequences of differing conceptions of
physical, sensory, and cognitive impairments, Berger provides a solid
foundation for making sense of disability as a social phenomenon.

RONALD J. BERGER is professor of sociology at the University of
Wisconsin–Whitewater. He is coauthor of *Wheelchair Warrior: Gangs,
Disability, and Basketball* (with Melvin Juette) and *Hoop Dreams on
Wheels: Disability and the Competitive Wheelchair Athlete*.